Cognitive Behavior Therapy with Gifted Adults

I0025388

This book presents a cognitive behavior approach to therapy with gifted adults, providing insight into and offering practical tools for diagnosing and working with the often unseen and unrecognized problems of these clients.

The book starts with a systematic outline of practical screening for giftedness and diagnosis of specific personality traits, discussing the common traits of giftedness along with the visible and invisible strengths and downsides of the diagnosis. It then offers a practical cognitive behavioral model for working with clients to understand and improve self-image, high sensitivity, creative stagnation, and interactional problems. Readers will learn how to create a case conceptualization, functional analysis, and treatment plan, as well as how to adapt goals and techniques for and with one's client. Specific attention is given to potential pitfalls and dysfunctions in the therapeutic relationship, and tools are provided to help the therapist specifically analyze and manage these. Practical case studies illustrate the methodology and provide further clarity for the reader.

The book will help any psychotherapist and mental-health-care professional to better support, work with, and help gifted adults in their professional practice.

Adriaan Sprey is a clinical psychologist/psychotherapist and in his private practice for education he gives supervision, psychotherapy, diagnostics/personality analysis, and post-academic training and education on psychodiagnostics and psychotherapy (www.adriaansprey.nl).

Cognitive Behavior Therapy with Gifted Adults

A Guide to Personality, Diagnostics, and the Therapeutic Relationship

Adriaan Sprey

Routledge
Taylor & Francis Group

LONDON AND NEW YORK

Designed cover image: © Lubomir Ferko

First published 2026
by Routledge
4 Park Square, Milton Park, Abingdon, Oxon OX14 4RN

and by Routledge
605 Third Avenue, New York, NY 10158

Routledge is an imprint of the Taylor & Francis Group, an informa business

© 2026 Adriaan Sprey

The right of Adriaan Sprey to be identified as author of this work
has been asserted in accordance with sections 77 and 78 of the
Copyright, Designs and Patents Act 1988.

All rights reserved. No part of this book may be reprinted
or reproduced or utilised in any form or by any electronic,
mechanical, or other means, now known or hereafter invented,
including photocopying and recording, or in any information
storage or retrieval system, without permission in writing from the
publishers.

Trademark notice: Product or corporate names may be trademarks
or registered trademarks, and are used only for identification and
explanation without intent to infringe.

British Library Cataloguing-in-Publication Data
A catalogue record for this book is available from the British
Library

ISBN: 978-1-032-72972-5 (hbk)
ISBN: 978-1-032-70755-6 (pbk)
ISBN: 978-1-003-42328-7 (ebk)

DOI: 10.4324/9781003423287

Typeset in Times New Roman
by Apex CoVantage, LLC

Contents

Acknowledgments

The glass object on the cover by artist Lubomir Ferko depicts a pyramid, one of the oldest timeless symbols of man's creative power. Giftedness, like this pyramid, has two sides that need to be balanced: advantages and disadvantages. Cognitive behavioral therapy (CBT), with its focus on personality development, can help.

Many people and my family have been sympathetic. I owe special thanks to some of them. I thank Lubomir Ferko for his art object and Nicky Dijkstra, with her vast clinical experience and deep interest in giftedness, for her perceptive reflections and comments on the content and language of the text in progress. Jan Bernard gave his accurate and experienced vision of the mental-health system, and Theo Verhoeven provided a beautiful case illustration of schema therapy.

Grace McDonnell as publisher: our communication was pleasant and creative.

Molly Isaacs and Edward Amend gave me good feedback on the definition of giftedness and permission to use the Webb et al. definition.

Rachel Heap translated the manuscript as a native speaker and as a psychologist: it was a happy coincidence that I had met her before in my teaching.

Carin Voskamp was once again a perfect secretary. She edited the version with great competence and persistent, personal involvement.

I have learned a lot from my clients and from the colleagues in my training, and I have learned a lot from my clients and colleagues.

Without the fantastic support of my wife, Ingrid, who contributed a great deal in terms of language, casuistry, content, and design, this book would not have been published. I therefore dedicate it to her.

Adriaan Sprey, summer 2024
The Netherlands/France

Introduction

Summary

Giftedness is far more common in clients than they and their therapists realize, because it is often difficult to distinguish from personality traits. Screening for the fact that the client is (or may be) gifted provides a different, often surprising, view of his or her functioning (including past functioning).

Through psychoeducation about the ten general characteristics of giftedness, the therapist can create awareness of the client's personal balance of advantages and disadvantages.

This book provides practical tools for understanding and improving self-image, hypersensitivity, and interactional problems.

Differential diagnoses, such as narcissistic personality disorder, are also provided.

Further diagnostics of symptoms and personality give the client a broader view of their own person (case conceptualization).

Rather than eliciting neutral or accepting reactions, gifted people often evoke resistance and/or admiration. Mental-health therapists also struggle with feelings of ambivalence toward their gifted clients. They are interesting, creative, and critical clients, but they also often cause the therapist to feel insecure, irritated, discouraged, or strongly involved.

The therapist should be aware of this through self-analysis and through a functional analysis of the therapeutic relationship.

Introduction

'Don't raise your head above the ground' is an old Dutch saying. Being excellent is considered a positive quality, but the word *excellent* comes from the Latin word *egregarius*, which means 'to stand out from the herd', which, from an evolutionary point of view is surely a dangerous aberration.

Giftedness is far more common in clients than they and their therapists realize, partly because it is often difficult to distinguish from personality traits and is therefore often overlooked due to a lack of knowledge.

DOI: 10.4324/9781003423287-1

Rather than eliciting neutral or accepting responses, gifted people often evoke resistance and/or admiration. Mental-health therapists also struggle with feelings of ambivalence towards their gifted clients. They are interesting, creative, and critical clients, but they also often cause the therapist to feel uncertain or irritated or, on the other hand, strong feelings of involvement.

Is giftedness not just an elitist problem? Is it a narcissistic explanation of social failure and as such a desirable diagnosis? Giftedness is not even included in the DSM–5. What is clinically and scientifically known about adult giftedness? It is certainly a subject that is rarely taught in university.

In diagnostics and cognitive behavior therapy, giftedness in adults is not considered to be a mental disorder, but rather a distinct form of information processing which is unique, fast, and complex. It is, however, much more than just a high IQ and includes a cluster of interrelated personality traits.

The interplay between personality traits and giftedness in adults is both complex and interesting. Personality traits influence giftedness and giftedness influences the development of the personality. For both therapist and client the combination of giftedness and personality makes both diagnostics and cognitive behavior therapy especially complicated. There is a lot of progress to be made here!

The gifted person is more likely than others to end up in an isolated position, which more often than not negatively affects how they view themselves and others. There is also a greater chance of abnormal or unbalanced development, interaction problems, and creative stagnation. In addition, the personality trait of high sensitivity is present in over 80% of cases of giftedness, as well as an intense inner world of experience and overexcitability. In mental health care, the gifted client often presents with complaints of anxiety, trauma, depression, burnout, ADHD, ASS, etc. This leads to an above average number of requests for assessment and cognitive behavior therapy within the mental-health system. Clients are then treated after being diagnosed also with a specific symptom disorder or personality disorder.

How to use cognitive behavior therapy with gifted adults

Screening for the fact that the client is (or may be) gifted provides a different, often surprising, view of his functioning (including past functioning) and leads often to greater self-acceptance and well-being.

Psychoeducation about the general characteristics of giftedness and awareness of the client's personal advantages and disadvantages gives the client more insight and hope for therapeutic change.

Further diagnostics of symptoms and personality give the client a broader overview of the totality of his own case (case conceptualization) and possible and desired entry points for therapy.

The central role that personality traits play in the individual coloring of giftedness makes cognitive behavior therapy particularly appropriate for changing core cognitions, such as view of self, view of others, and core behaviors (learned in the gifted person's individual learning history).

This practical guide integrates dimensional personality assessment with the functional analysis and cognitive behavior therapy for giftedness combined with specific personality traits. The case conceptualization provides the link between diagnosis and cognitive behavior therapy. Systematic steps are presented for the practical screening for giftedness and the diagnosis of specific personality traits. The book also offers practical tools for understanding and improving complaints such as view of self, high sensitivity, creative stagnation, and interactional problems. It also explains how to create a case conceptualization, a functional analysis, and a treatment plan as well as how to adapt goals and techniques. Attention is given to analyzing and managing the pitfalls and dysfunctions in the therapeutic relationship. Differential diagnosis is also discussed in detail: when are narcissism, perfectionism, avoidance of emotion, autonomy, etc. healthy and when are they pathological? Practical case studies provide illustrations throughout the book

The structure of the book is as follows.

Chapter 1 begins with a broad and multidimensional definition of personality traits in giftedness. This provides the basis for screening and a clear conceptualization of giftedness.

Chapter 2 presents a practical definition that enables clear screening of giftedness. The misdiagnosis and dual diagnosis of symptom-based disorders and personality traits or disorders are discussed. The theories of Millon, Beck, Young, and Cloninger, interaction-based diagnosis, the alternative DSM-5 dimensional personality model, and the five-factor model are reviewed and applied to giftedness combined with personality. When is narcissism or perfectionism or autonomy in giftedness pathological and when is it healthy? This can be determined using the Mental Health Index. A separate section is also devoted to the usually co-occurring personality trait of high sensitivity or overexcitability.

Chapter 3 explores the therapeutic process and presents a guide to creating a case conceptualization for giftedness which provides the core behavior of giftedness with its own place along with the core behavior of the specific personality. It also discusses a functional analysis of core behaviors, core cognitions, and core emotions for giftedness.

Chapter 4 addresses the implementation and evaluation of the treatment of giftedness through cognitive behavioral techniques. This cognitive behavior therapy is based on a concrete treatment plan which includes goals and appropriate cognitive behavioral techniques. The treatment plan is derived from the case conceptualization and includes the functional analyses of symptom behaviors and core behaviors of giftedness and of specific personality traits.

Chapter 5 deals with the functional analysis of the therapeutic relationship and the therapist's self-analysis of his or her own cognitions, feelings, and pitfalls, having first made an interactional diagnosis of both the general core behavior of giftedness and specific personality traits. Specific interactions and interactional dysfunctions per group of personality traits are manifested in the therapeutic relationship. The therapist can analyze and correct his or her own inappropriate responses and particular behaviors that influence the client's symptom-related behaviors, dual core behaviors of giftedness (general and specific), and practice behaviors (their typical approach to practicing new behaviors). The interaction of these factors is represented in a pentagon.

This book would not be complete without a survey of the diagnosis, the treatment, and the therapeutic relationship of narcissistic personality traits or personality disorder in Chapter 6.

Giftedness and narcissistic traits overlap in their view of self as being superior and unique. Therefore, the risk of a misdiagnosis is considerable. Too many gifted clients are misdiagnosed as having narcissistic personality disorders. The countertransference makes this problem even more complex. The therapist reacts in an insecure or irritated manner when the narcissistic client seems to devalue him. Moreover, there is the problem of distinguishing between pathological and healthy narcissism.

Much attention is also given to the disturbances and pitfalls in the therapeutic relationship and how to concretely self-analyze and deal with them.

NOTE: The names of the clients in the cases are fictitious. Specific names that seem to be identities of actual persons are purely coincidental.

Common personality traits in giftedness

Summary

Chapter 1 begins by presenting the general and multidimensional definitions of personality traits in giftedness. This is the foundation for the screening and for a clear conceptualization of giftedness. We then explore the prevalence of giftedness and high sensitivity in the general population. Of those who are gifted, the vast majority (87%) are also highly sensitive (Van Hoof, 2016). It is estimated that between 10% and 12% of the clients undergoing assessment or treatment in the mental-health system in the Netherlands are gifted, almost three times as many as in the general population (4%).

1.1 Definitions and prevalence of giftedness

1.1.1 Definitions

Many definitions of giftedness can be found in the literature, with many similarities and some differences in emphasis. Several definitions will be considered.

Renzulli (1978) defines giftedness as the coming together in a 'triangulation point' of high talent, creativity, and a high level of motivation leading to exceptional performance in academic or creative areas. A drawback of this definition is that it is limited to activities that have already been achieved and to results, while many gifted people suffer from creative stagnation which leads to their potential not being realized in achievements.

According to Webb et al. (2016), a gifted person has, in addition to a high intelligence (IQ > 130), the following six characteristics (or, together with high intelligence, seven characteristics):

1 intensity, sensitivity, overexcitability
2 different ways (linear and nonlinear) of thinking and learning
3 idealism
4 asynchronous development (motor, social, and intelligence)
5 intense, broad, and/or unusual interest patterns
6 creativity

DOI: 10.4324/9781003423287-2

For a detailed description of the characteristics, see Webb et al. (2016) (Chapter 1, reprinted with permission).

Kuipers' definition refers to additional intelligence and emphasizes, among other characteristics, the need for autonomy (Kuipers & Van Kempen, 2007).

The Delphi model of giftedness is based on expert opinions of coaches and therapists and provides a positive and nonperformance-oriented definition of gift-edness. The definition is high sensitivity, intensity, complexity, high intelligence, and autonomous behavior (Kooijman-Van Thiel, 2008).

Giftedness is often associated with perfectionism (Rogers & Silverman, 1997).

There is considerable agreement between the various definitions, with the expected differences in emphasis. The definition provided by Webb is the most comprehensive and detailed (Webb et al., 2016).

Giftedness is multidimensional and encompasses a range of personality traits and is therefore much broader than just intelligence or IQ in the narrowest sense.

In former definitions of giftedness, there is a *contradiction between potential talent* ('it's in there') *and talent that has been realized through achievement* ('it has come out through special achievement'). Potential achievements are often not realized because of psychological (see Section 2.3 symptom disorders) or physical complaints and/or personality problems (see Section 2.4 personality traits and disorders). A person can become better able to realize his or her talent through proper diagnosis and treatment with cognitive behavioral therapy.

In practice these one-sided definitions were not sufficient, and so the definition of giftedness from the National Association for Gifted Children (Webb et al., 2016) became exceptional behavior or talent in one or more of the following five areas:

1   intelligence (extremely good in learning, IQ above 4% of the population)
2   academic learning (extremely good in learning, IQ above 4% of the population)
3   creativity (recognized as competent and belonging to the best 10% of their reference group)
4   arts (recognized as competent and belonging to the best 10% of their reference group)
5   leadership (recognized as competent and belonging to the best 10% of their reference group)

Giftedness does not necessarily manifest itself in multiple areas and almost never in all five. One domain is sufficient to speak of giftedness (Webb et al., 2016).

In this book, we rely on the definition and seven characteristics of Webb et al. (2016), which includes most of the characteristics. Kuipers and Van Kempen (2007) give particular emphasis to autonomy, an important and specific personality characteristic that explicitly complements Webb's definition (see Section 2.1). In this book, we distinguish between autonomous thinking and autonomous action. The last characteristic is perfectionism (Rogers & Silverman, 1997).

Table 1.1 Percentages for the presence (+) or absence (−) of giftedness and high sensitivity in the total population

		Giftedness		
		+	−	
High Sensitivity	+	3.5%	16.5%	**20%**
	−	0.5%	79.5%	**80%**
		4%	**96%**	**100%**

1.1.2   Prevalence of giftedness

High intelligence is found in 3% to 5% of the population (Webb et al., 2016). This is defined as an IQ above 130. Exceptionally high intelligence is much rarer, occurring in one to two children in a thousand (Webb et al., 2016). This is when the IQ is above 155.

High sensitivity occurs in 20% of the population (Aron, 1996; Van Hoof, 2016).

Of those who are gifted, the vast majority (87%) are also highly sensitive (Van Hoof, 2016).

In Table 1.1 provides a summary of the different percentages.

1.2   Giftedness in mental health care

It is estimated that between 10% and 12% of the clients undergoing assessment or treatment in the mental-health system in the Netherlands are gifted, almost three times as many as in the general population (4%).

On the other hand, the benefits and necessity of providing special attention for clients with low intelligence are in line with 'common sense' because their needs are more quickly recognized by people around them with medium or high IQs and by health care providers. In fact, the balance of advantages and disadvantages for people with a low IQ will usually be negative, resulting from a generally lower adaptive capacity. How differently the client with high(er) intelligence is viewed. It is hard to understand how someone who has the luxury of so much inherited talent still fails at work and in relationships, or suffers from burnout, depression, addiction, or a personality disorder. This is also true for an empathetic and scientifically trained mental-health therapist. This leads to ambivalent thoughts and feelings and cognitive dissonance. Do these problems lie with the giftedness, the symptom disorder, or the personality trait or disorder? The gifted client, who in over 80% of cases is also highly sensitive, is aware of the therapist's conflict.

The therapist – and therefore also the client – has to come to terms with the current mental-health zeitgeist. What has changed? Due to the financial influence of the health insurance companies, short-term, protocol-based therapies have become the first treatment choice. This also fits in with the somatic disease model. The client is insured for mental disorders and sometimes receives medication and a few minutes of examination and psychological treatment, for example, for moderate depression. This is the purpose of the 'big handbook', the DSM-5, which lists the criteria for all 'recognized' mental disorders. The DSM classification system has many advantages, such as, clear and global criteria that enable better professional communication and scientific research. But it also has its drawbacks. The dominance of the DSM-5 classification ('is this moderate depression'?) means that the intake psychologist or psychiatrist has to sort clients into so-called disorder-specific care pathways and teams. Which team should this client go to – the anxiety and trauma, mood, psychosis, or personality disorder team? This is also where the focus of the protocol manifests itself. A 'diagnosis' has been made, that is, a client has been given a classification of their symptoms, and treatment is given according to a protocol for the established category of disorder. The specific protocol often works, but within the specialist mental health care we estimate that one-third of the protocols do not work in practice. The same applies to general practice medicine, where a third of the protocols do not work, but are deviated from in a well-founded way, leading to a treatment specifically adapted to the individual client. In the mental-health sector, treatments are also more likely to be transdiagnostic, for example, a negative view of self is treated across all types of diagnoses. Therapies are also more likely to be individualized; they take into account personality traits that may cause clients not to do the exercises in the protocol, or to do them differently. Mental-health therapists learn both the rules (the protocols) and the exceptions (De Groot, 1996). Furthermore, the dominant model is one that is 'pathology-focused'; a pathology or disorder is expected and is therefore sought after. Psychodiagnostics, that is, the testing of hypotheses by means of tests, is expensive and time-consuming and can only be used by the health insurance company to support quick classification and placement for treatment. This is counterproductive and may be at the expense of obtaining a full picture and other differential diagnoses, and of recommending and carrying out a more extensive personality assessment, which sometimes only happens after a year of unsuccessful intensive treatment. The excessive focus on classification therefore does have its drawbacks.

In this context, the idiosyncratic, critical, and autonomous gifted client meets the reductionist, classifying expert of the mental-health services. The personality traits of the gifted person and the diagnosis, which is not included in the DSM-5 and is therefore unknown, complicate the diagnostic process and the determination of an appropriate cognitive behavioral therapy. Both client and professional easily become demoralized. This is unfortunate for both as it distracts from the therapist–client interaction and is also often harmful for the client. Just as in his childhood, the client feels not understood; he is once again a painful exception for whom the professional cannot provide a clear framework and effective therapy. On a meta-level, this is a consequence of the zeitgeist, the compulsion to classify, leading to misdiagnosis and focusing on treating as quickly as possible, preferably by protocol. '*You don't see it until you know it*'. This gifted text should hang in every consulting room as a plea for proper, individualized, and thorough psychodiagnostics in complex cases. In addition to the therapeutic gains (demonstrated by

Layard & Clark, 2014), there are also diagnostic gains to be made. For society, inadequate diagnostics is costly in the long run due to ineffective treatment as a result of misdiagnosis.

In terms of content and emotion, the diagnostician and mental-health therapist are faced with a tricky problem with giftedness and high sensitivity, namely, their own feelings and cognitions about both. One trainee said that, in her academic environment and team, she would certainly not tell people that she herself was gifted and highly sensitive, nor would she say that she thought a client she was discussing was. Mockery and derision would be her lot, and she would go down in the academic hierarchy within her team. Colleagues would immediately see her as new age, alternative, and unscientific. In short, this colleague chose avoidance and her team chose to fight.

A second colleague was herself traumatized by being bullied as a sick, gifted child. She tried to compensate for this trauma as an adult. In every intelligent adult she saw a gifted person who had not been properly diagnosed and therefore not properly treated. At the same time, she was vicariously outraged by this, and in her team her work was based on the 'myth of uniformity', which led to the creation of a one-sided and therefore incorrect conceptualization of the case. She became one of the self-proclaimed psychotherapists as gifted, which irritated colleagues and pushed clients too much into the victim role.

A third colleague with dominant traits who was, to his annoyance, not gifted himself, struggled with super-intelligent clients who outwitted him and quickly became a narcissistic competitor. He was used to being the informal leader of the team, and his long training and experience as a psychotherapist made him feel like the most competent and all-knowing diagnostician and therapist on the team. His teammates were reluctant to stand up to him and went along with his illusion. Only the stubborn, autonomous gifted clients took the under–against and above–against position and made life difficult for him with their resistance, criticism, and devalu-ation, which he began to fight excessively. In his eyes, giftedness became a nar-cissistic personality disorder. A student who had diagnosed himself as gifted was dismissed as an inflated narcissist who, as a layman, had given himself a socially desirable and vain diagnosis.

For many colleagues in the mental-health field, *high sensitivity* is a term from the alternative medicine and coaching worlds and is seen as unscientific. This reac-tion plays a part in the problems of registering conditions such as burnout, chronic fatigue, and ADHD. Recent scientific research in Brussels (Van Hoof, 2016) found that high sensitivity is related to the deep processing of stimuli factors (see Sec-tion 2.10). However, many colleagues seem to be unaware of this, and it is a rare topic in professional training, so that experiences of high sensitivity are interpreted quite differently, leading the therapist to focus on and treat other personality traits and characteristics of the client. As a result, at best (with luck), the client learns to deal with some of the environmental factors that are distressing. In fact, the thera-pist who is unfamiliar with high sensitivity often tends to overburden the client in terms of exposure to stimuli.

Reference list

Aron, E. N. (1996). *The highly sensitive person – how to thrive when the world overwhelms you*. Carol Publishing Group.

De Groot, A. D. (1996). *Methodology: Foundations of interference and research in the behavioral sciences*. Mouton.

Kooijman-Van Thiel, M. B. G. M. (Ed.). (2008). *Hoogbegaafd, dat zie je zo!* Oya-Productions.

Kuipers, W., & Van Kempen, A. (2007). *Verleid jezelf tot excellentie!* Lecturium.

Layard, R., & Clark, D. (2014). *Thrive: The power of evidence-based psychological therapies*. Penguin.

Renzulli, J. S. (1978). What makes giftedness? Reexamining a definition. *Phi Delta Kappan, 60*(3), 180–184, 261.

Rogers, K. B., & Silverman, L. K. (1997). *Personal, medical, social and psychological factors in 160 + IQ children*. National Association for Gifted Children 44th Annual Convention.

Van Hoof, E. (2016). *Hoogsensitief*. LannooCampus.

Webb, J. T., Amend, E. R., Beljan, P., Webb, N. E., Kuzujanakis, M., Olenchak, F. R., & Goerss, J. (2016). *Misdiagnosis and dual diagnoses of gifted children and adults: ADHD, Bipolar, OCD, Asperger's, depression, and other disorders* (2nd ed.). Great Potential Press.

Chapter 2

Diagnostics for giftedness in relation to personality and symptoms

Summary

The aim of Chapter 2 is to provide practical guidance in screening in order to improve diagnosis and in particular to provide clarification in dual diagnosis of giftedness in relation to the individual's symptoms and personality. To this end, several theories are used, including those of Millon, Beck, Young, and Cloninger, as well as interaction-focused diagnostics.

A separate section focuses on the personality trait of high sensitivity, which commonly co-occurs with giftedness. The new dimensional model of personality disorders for pathological traits in the DSM-5 and the Five-Factor Model for general, 'normal' traits are both discussed in detail.

The Mental Health Index (i.e., limitations in personality functioning – APA, 2013) is also discussed as a tool to determine the functionality of the personality in four domains: identity, self-direction, empathy, and intimacy.

2.1 Screening for giftedness

When screening for giftedness in clinical practice, we consider a number of characteristics – the seven personality characteristics (1–7) of giftedness as defined by Webb et al. (2016).

Characteristic 1b – exceptionally competent and belonging to the best 10% of their reference group in creativity, arts, or leadership – was derived from the new definition of the National Association for Gifted Children (Webb et al., 2016).

These are added with the need for autonomy (Kuipers & Van Kempen, 2007), which this book has divided into autonomous thinking and autonomous acting (characteristics 8–9), and finally perfectionism, characteristic 10 (Rogers & Silverman, 1997).

The clinical approach on which this book is founded defines giftedness as the presence of at least six of these ten characteristics, whereby one has high intelligence or exceptional competence.

DOI: 10.4324/9781003423287-3

2.1.1 Screening definition

1a Most gifted persons are either highly intelligent or
1b exceptionally competent and belonging to the best 10% of their reference group in creativity, arts or leadership;
2 High sensitivity, an intense emotional world or easily over-stimulated;
3 Fast, complex, diverse and divergent thinking;
4 Idealistic and with a strong sense of right and wrong;
5 Asynchronous personal development (motor, social and intellectual development);
6 Curious, with an intense, wide-ranging and/or unusual pattern of interests;
7 Fast and creative in coming up with solutions;
8 Autonomous thinking;
9 Autonomous acting;
10 Perfectionistic.

This definition for screening is derived from Webb et al. (2016) for characteristics 1 through 7 (reproduced with permission).

2.1.2 Screening process

The characteristics are scored from 0 (I don't recognize myself in this at all) to 10 (I recognize myself completely), based on self-assessment, the assessment of another person, and the therapist's assessment (see Appendix B). The client is asked to write down the advantages and disadvantages for themselves of these character-istics. The correlation between the assessments is examined and corrected for any over- or underestimation by the client.

2.1.3 Processing the screening

Six or more characteristics with a score of 7.5 or higher indicate giftedness. If there is uncertainty or the client has little capacity for self-reflection, additional informa-tion can be provided by a 'healthy' objective person from the client's immediate environment as well as clinical observation and assessment. If necessary, tests can be used.

2.1.4 Clinical assessment of giftedness

The clinician assesses whether the general core behavior of the individual meets characteristic 7 – fast and creative in coming up with solutions – and whether that happens frequently and has been present throughout the individual's life from child-hood (is trans-temporal) and occurs across a range of different situations that are interesting to the individual (is trans-situational). Finally, the core behavior must fit in the functional analysis of the core behavior of giftedness (see Section 3.3)

It is important in the assessment of creativity to consider periods of creative stagnation, when the individual lacks their creative outlet and struggles and is often either depressed, overwhelmed by too many demands, or overworked. Conversely, the periods of creativity ('flow') are empowering and can be enjoyed by the individual.

The therapist's assessment of giftedness

High frequency of core behavior of being fast and creative in finding solutions   +
Trans-temporal – present from early childhood   +
Trans-situational – in engaging situations   +
Core behavior fits into the functional analysis of giftedness   +

2.1.5 Self-diagnosis of giftedness

A reasonably objective self-diagnosis is very difficult for clients; they often do not see themselves as gifted and compare themselves negatively with other people, such as classmates, fellow students, siblings, family members, people in their reference group and in the media who are exceptional, stand out, and are already known to be gifted.

Conversely, rather than underestimating themselves, the opposite is also possible: the client might really want to be labeled as gifted, but does not meet the criteria. The client overestimates themselves and is looking for compensation for negative experiences in the past (for example, failures and negative assessments at school, study, or within the family), which the diagnosis of 'actually I am and have always been gifted' would provide.

It is therefore important for the client to consider the (expected) advantages and disadvantages of a possible diagnosis of giftedness (the functional analysis, see Section 3.3) and to compare these with positive and negative examples in their immediate and wider environment, for example, in the media and in society. Who would you like to be like, and who definitely not? Included in this should be, in addition to the level of intelligence, the view of self, view of others, personality traits, and background (see Chapter 3). The IQ is actually the least interesting factor. A wide-ranging, comprehensive screening and personality analysis by a specialist psychologist is recommended and usually necessary.

The screening list in Table 2.1 was completed by a 30-year-old woman who kept encountering the same interaction problems at work. A therapist friend of the woman suggested that she complete the giftedness list and think about the pros and cons of a possible diagnosis of giftedness. The responses are illustrative of the responses of many gifted people. In the table, SA stands for self-assessment and OA other assessment, in this case by the therapist.

Table 2.1 Balance of advantages/disadvantages of ten characteristics of giftedness

giftedness characteristic	strength 0–10 self-assessment/ assessment by other	advantages	disadvantages
highly intelligent or exceptionally competent	5/9	• can cope with many different tasks • successful and interesting work	• must be involved in everything • threatening to colleagues
• highly sensible • highly sensitive • overexcitability (OE)	9/8	• observant • intense enjoyment of art and travel	• exhausting • needs time to recover
• quick thinking • complex thinking • divergent	8/10	• can come up with original solutions • can draw consequences and act on them	• cannot stop thinking • I'm always 'on'
idealistic and with a strong sense of justice	6/8	honesty	disappointed by the behavior of others and find it hard to let go
asynchronous development (learning history) motor, social, intellectual	3/5	flexibility	• restlessness • social exception
curious with an intense, broad or unusual pattern of interest	9/8	• enthusiasm • broad general development	• little focus • stress of choice • fragmentation
quick and creative in finding solutions	9/10	happy when successful	• it never ends • always wanting to come up with new solutions
autonomous thinking	8/9	• intellectual confidence • sailing by your own compass	• being an outsider • loneliness
acting autonomously	8/9	self-confidence	• social conflicts • fear of asking for help
perfectionistic	5/9	delivering quality	• it is never good enough • loss of time • less job satisfaction

This screening definition is based on Webb et al. (2016) for characteristics 1 through 7, reproduced with permission.

2.1.6   Processing

In our example, the client herself recognized seven of the ten characteristics, although not the high intelligence required for a diagnosis. In this situation a test could be used to assess intelligence. The therapist recognized all ten characteristics. In general, testing should always be done with a critical eye for possible underachievement. Based on the information given, it appears probable that the woman is gifted. The therapist's clinical assessment also included a consideration of the general criteria associated with giftedness (see box).

The therapist's assessment of giftedness

High frequency of core behavior of being fast and creative in finding solutions   +
Trans-temporal – present from early childhood   +
Trans-situational – in engaging situations   +
Core behavior fits into the functional analysis of giftedness   +

2.2   General diagnostic strategy for complaints, underlying problems, and personality

The word *diagnostics* comes from the Greek word *dia-gnosis,* which means 'to see through' or 'to judge accurately'. Even though a psychologist cannot see through a client – which is what clients are sometimes afraid of – their task is to clarify and order a great amount of information. What themes run through the client's story? What is leading to what in the present and from the past? Are the connections that are found coincidental correlations or causally linked? These questions are relevant at many different levels: when considering the symptoms, other problems both in the past and the present as well as the personality. A client often considers their personality to be a given, just like their body. The client suffers subjectively from negative feelings and the negative consequences of their behavior, as do those around them. In many cases, however, the client is not aware of the negative consequences of their behavior, which may only occur in the long term. A client with a narcissistic personality disorder usually feels good about themselves and is proud of themselves, but might notice that the people around them react more and more negatively towards them. Another form of suffering is failing to realize your personal potential. It may be possible that the client can become aware of this, in the same way that an undiagnosed illness can only be treated once the client is aware of the illness and the possibility of a cure.

The diagnostic process (Hofstee, 1990) starts with a question from the client and the people around them: 'What is the cause of the symptoms and problems and can something be done about it?' Discussions with both the client and people around them help to make the question clearer and more concrete, as well as broader by including background and personality, which may lead to a reformulation. The client becomes aware of the previously unclear problems caused by behavior that they have always taken for granted, as well as the unseen benefits. The clinician develops an hypothesis regarding the diagnosis of the symptoms, the relations between the problems and the possibility of a personality disorder. This hypothesis is tested using various theoretical models and different instruments, including observation during the appointment, an interview with the client and their environment, self-registration assignments by the client, and psychological tests. The hypothesis is then either confirmed or rejected. If rejected, the diagnostic process begins again until a probable answer to the initial question is found from which treatment goals can be clarified and a treatment plan formulated. How can this client be helped to attain the changes necessary to reach their treatment goals and what does the client need in order to learn to prevent a relapse in the future?

This chapter reviews a number of theories and testing instruments to create a clear, practical diagnostic process for personality disorders.

2.2.1   From client to diagnosis: from single to complex

Clients have varying degrees of awareness of themselves, their symptoms, and their personality. A client may come for cognitive behavioral therapy assessment with clear, specific symptoms and may already have a clear idea of a diagnosis. For another, the complaints might be multiple, complex, and diffuse, across different areas of psychopathology, such as a combination of a mood disorder, anxiety disorder, psychotic disorder, somatoform disorder, eating disorder, addiction, and/or an interpersonal disorder. Sometimes it is the client who experiences the most problems as a result of the symptoms (subjective suffering) and sometimes it is their environment. It is also possible that the client's psychosocial functioning is affected without the client experiencing too much distress.

The clinician starts by assessing, clarifying, and analyzing (the function of) the symptoms and complaints as well as the personality or personality disorder. This chapter lays out how the clinician in practice can come to a diagnosis (general diagnostic assessment strategy).

2.2.2   Three relevant dimensions of testing

The diagnostic assessment strategy involves the clinician assessing along three dimensions. Here we use case studies and examples to illustrate this strategy specifically for giftedness.

Firstly, complaints or symptoms can be placed on a continuum from single to diffuse and complex.

Case Study – Peter Sharp

Peter is gifted and afraid of injections, after having fainted several times after receiving one. He suffers from a single phobia, fear of injections. The researcher is unable to identify other symptoms. Peter is an example of a client with one, straightforward symptom.

Case study – Vera Broodening

Vera worries about everything. She is gifted and can think very fast. She worries about her health, about money, about her performance at work, about the future for her children, and about whether they will have an accident. She experiences continuous tension and is unable to stop worrying. She meets the criteria for a generalized anxiety disorder. In addition, Vera has suffered from mild depression for several years and meets the criteria of the DSM-5 for a persistent depressive disorder or dysthymia (a mild but long-lasting depression). She goes to her family doctor for recurrent migraines. CBT testing at a mental-health-care institution draws the conclusion that Vera has diverse, complex symptoms with the possibility of an underlying personality disorder.

It is generally the case that a client's symptoms vary in number, severity, and frequency and possibly according to the situation. A binge-eating episode as part of bulimia can occur several times a month or a few times a day, can last a varying length of time, and may or may not lead to purging. The situations in which a binge-eating episode occurs also vary; for example, a client might only binge at home or at work (usually in seclusion). Anxiety might be restricted to one clear situation, as in Peter's phobia for injections, or it might be so diffuse that numerous situations, thoughts, and fantasies trigger the anxiety, as in Vera's continual ruminating.

Secondly, the diagnostician looks for the problems underlying the symptoms, which can also vary in complexity. This is a search for the root causes of the symptoms, the underlying problems in the client's background. For example, there might be one root cause underlying an anxiety or depressive disorder such as a one-off panic attack, a recent loss, or a current overload. It becomes more complex when, for example, long-term traumatic experiences underlie the symptoms, as might be the case for clients who lived as children in the Second World War in a concentration camp or when there is an unresolved complex trauma.

It can be helpful here to distinguish between *late problems, middle problems,* and *early problems* (Hermans et al., 2018). *Late problems* refer to a person's symptoms and complaints. Difficulties in current daily life are called *middle problems,* and those in the past, *early problems.* Examples of early problems (past determinants) are an under- or overdeveloped ability to express anger; traumatic experiences such as physical abuse, incest, and sexual abuse; parental divorce or alcohol abuse; neglect or spoiling in childhood. These early experiences are stored in emotional memory and lead to the development of a particular view of self, others, and the world (Section 2.6). Middle problems (intermediate factors) are situations where the client now or in the last year has experienced stress, for example, frequent arguments or lack of communication in the relationship, a separation or divorce, recent traumas, conflict at work, being overwhelmed or overworked, lack of social support, and no leisure or enjoyable activities in the free time. Middle problems occur in the area of current relationships, work, and free time.

The diagnostician divides the underlying problems into current and past problems and single and complex. These categories do not directly map onto each other. Single background problems are often also current problems, for example, feeling overwhelmed at work. Past underlying problems can also be single, for example, a traumatic experience in childhood such as the death of a parent. Another example of a single past background problem is a simple form of *under-learning* resulting from emotional neglect or social isolation in childhood. A client with a dependent personality disorder might have been raised in a very protected environment within the family and never learned to be independent. Past background problems are often diverse and complex, but current problems may also be multiple and can occur in diverse areas of life simultaneously, such as work, social relations, free time, and relationship with a partner.

Thirdly, the diagnostician assesses the personality traits and the possibility of a personality disorder. For example, someone who is very cooperative may show dependent traits in certain situations. This person could be dependent in their relationship and with certain friends, although maybe not in all social situations, such as at work or in their free time. If this dependency becomes more pronounced this person will adapt and become dependent on everyone and in every situation (trans-situational). This person has then developed a dependent personality disorder (APA, 2013).

The diagnostician aims to come to one of the following conclusions:

- There is no personality disorder.
- There are some traits of a personality disorder.
- There are some traits of several personality disorders (a 'mixed situation').
- There is one specific personality disorder.
- There are several personality disorders present concurrently.

Millon (Section 2.4.1) conceives personality traits and personality disorders as a continuum; healthy traits become increasingly one-sided and more extreme, occur in more situations (trans-situational), and increasingly determine behavior (Millon & Everly, 1985). These personality traits then become pathological, and when there are enough pathological traits present (usually at least four or five criteria), a personality disorder can be diagnosed. Employing these three dimensions in the assessment creates a general diagnostic assessment strategy. See Figure 2.1.

2.2.3   Bilateral personality testing in giftedness

The complementary influence of personality traits and giftedness in adults is complex and fascinating. Personality traits have an impact on giftedness and, at the same time, giftedness colors and influences the development of the

problem behavior
symptoms

COMPLAINTS

single   multiple

	single		multiple	
single	1			1
	A	2	B	2
BACKGROUND PROBLEMS (past and present)		n/a		3
	1			1
multiple	C	2	D	2
	3			3

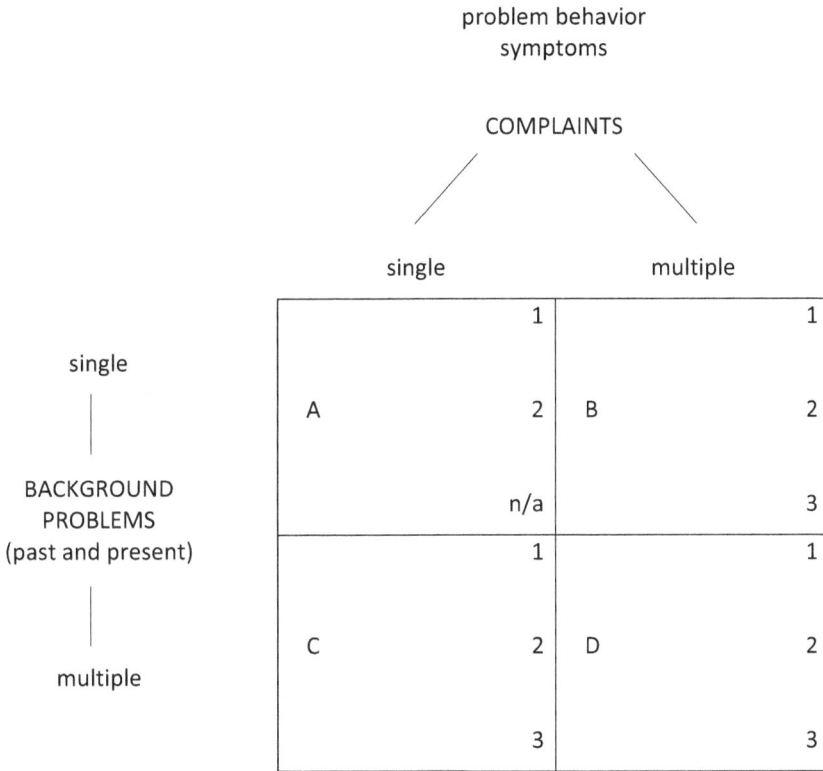

1.   No personality disorder
2.   Personality traits
3.   Personality disorder(s)

Figure 2.1 General diagnostic assessment strategy

personality. A gifted person is more quickly put in the position of being exceptional, which affects their view of themselves and of others, often negatively.
There is also a greater possibility of the person's general development being
skewed and one-sided, of interactional problems with others, and of creative
stagnation. Giftedness is also associated with the personality trait of high sensitivity (in more than 80% of cases), over-excitability (OE), and experiencing the
world very intensely.

   In the *screening* for giftedness, we assess whether six or more of the ten general
personality characteristics (see Section 2.1) are present. If necessary, we also test
for IQ, high sensitivity, etc.

   In addition we assess the client's specific personality traits and temperament.
For giftedness there is therefore a dual personality test necessary, the general

assessment of giftedness and the specific assessment of personality traits. In that assessment we make use of diverse theories, instruments, and approaches:

- the DSM-5 and personality disorders for the assessment of mental well-being and the presence of pathological traits
- the Five-Factor Model for general personality traits
- Beck's Cognitive Model for determining the view of self and view of others
- Young's Schema Model to determining the underlying schemas
- an interactional diagnosis to assess attachment and interaction positions in giftedness
- Cloninger's temperament model
- the increased chance of the presence of high sensitivity in giftedness (Aron, 1996; Van Hoof, 2016)
- specific (psychological) tests and measurement tools

We integrate all of these approaches in a case conceptualization, which also includes the development or learning history (see Section 3.2).

2.3   Misdiagnosis and functional analytical diagnosis for symptom disorders

The DSM-5 (APA, 2013) is a guide with criteria for the classification of all mental-health disorders. Full definitions can be found in the DSM-5 (APA, 2013). Here I discuss some common symptom disorders seen in gifted adults in mental-health settings.

We will look at the symptom behavior and its function. An example of a functional analysis of symptom behavior for anxiety, depression, and burnout follows.

ANXIETY DISORDERS

The characteristic symptom behavior of anxiety disorders is anxious avoidance. The function of the avoidance behavior is to reduce anxiety. Figure 2.2 shows an example of a functional analysis of social phobia.

DEPRESSIVE MOOD DISORDERS

The characteristic symptom behavior of depressive mood disorders is depressive withdrawal. The function of withdrawal is to reduce depression, failure, and stress. Figure 2.3 shows an example of a functional analysis of a depressive disorder.

Other symptom behaviors are:

AD(H)D

AD(H)D begins before the age of 12 and is characterized by high distractibility with or without hyperactivity. AD(H)D is often confused with giftedness (Webb et al., 2016), which can lead to misdiagnosis.

TRIGGERING EVENT
(CS/sd)
(impending) negative
evaluation

thoughts (COV)
I am not good enough, I am
strange, ridiculous

behavior (CAR)
avoiding social situations

feeling (CER)
shame
fear

consequences (C)
advantages
+C+ support, understanding
-C- fear and shame ▼
0C- no rejection

disadvantages
-C+ self-confidence ▼
+C- social isolation ▲
0C+ no intimacy

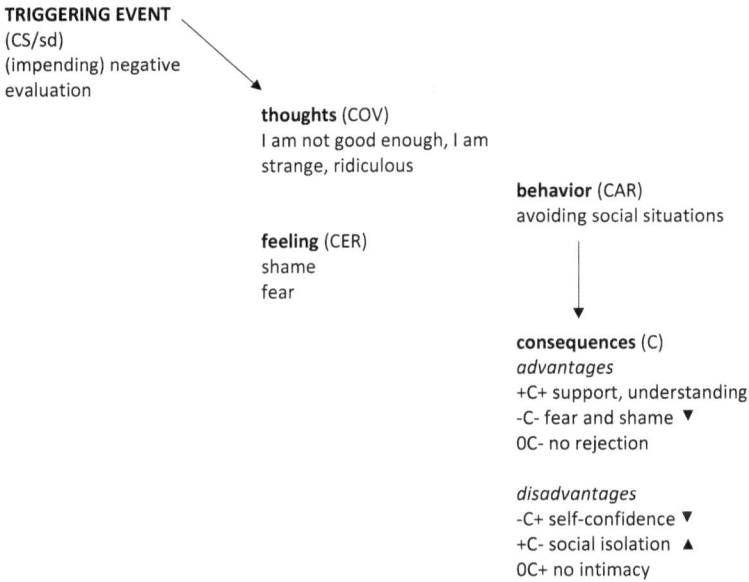

Figure 2.2 Functional analysis of social phobia

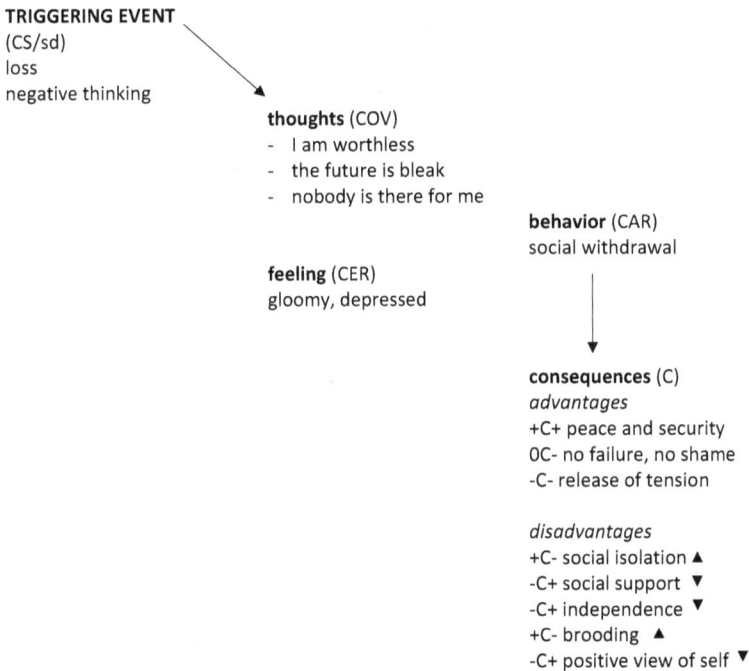

TRIGGERING EVENT
(CS/sd)
loss
negative thinking

thoughts (COV)
- I am worthless
- the future is bleak
- nobody is there for me

behavior (CAR)
social withdrawal

feeling (CER)
gloomy, depressed

consequences (C)
advantages
+C+ peace and security
0C- no failure, no shame
-C- release of tension

disadvantages
+C- social isolation ▲
-C+ social support ▼
-C+ independence ▼
+C- brooding ▲
-C+ positive view of self ▼

Figure 2.3 Functional analysis of depressive disorder

AUTISM SPECTRUM DISORDERS

Autism spectrum disorders (ASD) begin in infancy or early childhood and include life-long severe problems in social situations, which are sometimes masked. For highly intelligent people, the first problems often do not appear until high school. This is particularly true for females (due to social adjustment and perfectionism). Autism can also go hand in hand with special talents (Spek, 2019) and giftedness (Webb et al., 2016).

BURNOUT

Burnout is considered a work-related disorder with emotional exhaustion, absenteeism, and feeling unable to do what would normally be expected (Hoogendijk & De Rek, 2017). Work stress progresses through strain to burnout. Burnout is not included in the DSM-5, but is often associated with anxiety and depression or obsessive-compulsive disorder. For a functional analysis of burnout, see Figure 2.4. Giftedness together with high sensitivity increases the risk of burnout (Van Hoof, 2016).

TRIGGERING EVENT
(CS/sd)
prolonged stress
no social support
at work

thoughts (COV)
- I can't take it anymore
- I feel empty, exhausted, and discouraged
- I have no support

behavior (CAR)
stimulus and stress-reducing behavior

feeling (CER)
exhaustion
chronic stress

consequences (C)
advantages
-C- exhaustion ▼
-C- stress avoidance ▲

disadvantages
-C+ competence ▼
-C+ self-confidence ▼
+C- depersonalization ▲
+C- discouragement ▲

Figure 2.4 Functional analysis of burnout

Giftedness is neither a symptom disorder nor a personality disorder, but it can go hand in hand with them (dual diagnosis) and has the following functional analysis. See Figure 2.5 and see also Section 3.3.

TRIGGERING EVENT
(CS/sd)
complex and
engaging situation

thinking process
fast, complex, highly
associative, divergent,
creative, and autonomous

behavior (CAR)
thinking up quick and creative
solutions

thoughts (COV)
- I am autonomous, quick-thinking,
  and creative
- I am different from others
- I am curious and have many
  and intense interests
- I am responsible
- I need to be competent
- everything has to be
  perfect and fair
- I want to make things (the
  world) better
- I want to be fair and just (or
  am disillusioned)
- I am clever but lack social,
  sporting, or artistic skills
- different rules apply to me
- others are different,
  smarter or less smart,
  jealous or admiring, more
  social or sporty
- it is not possible for me to
  just be normal and
  participate
- I am an exception and I am
  not one of them
- others exclude me
- others don't like me
- others find me strange

consequences (C)
advantages
+C+ pride, self-esteem
+C+ appreciation,
       acceptance, admiration
       from others
+C+ satisfaction, flow, kick
+C+ creativity
-C- dullness diminishes

disadvantages
-C+ less sense of belonging
-C+ others drop out
+C- negative reactions
       from others, insecurity,
       jealousy, irritation
0C+ no resistance
+C- social isolation
+C- lack of understanding
+C- haste, impatience
+C- stress, tiredness
+C- frustration,
       dissatisfaction

emotional process
intense, usually overexcitable,
and highly sensitive

feeling (CER)
driven, intense excitement,
stress, fear of failure

Figure 2.5 Functional analysis (general) of giftedness

When the functional analysis of symptom behavior and/or core behavior overlaps, misdiagnosis is more likely. Webb et al. (2016), in their very practical book *Misdiagnosis of the Gifted*, provide a clinical guide to the entire DSM-5 with corresponding or conflicting features to arrive at a correct differential diagnosis of giftedness or symptom disorder.

The following criteria can be used to distinguish symptom behavior from core behavior in giftedness and core behavior in personality disorders (APA, 2013).

Symptom disorder

Varying Frequency Symptomatic behavior	often
Trans-temporal	no
Exception: trans-temporal before age 12 in ADHD	yes
Exception: trans-temporal manifestation from early childhood in ASD	yes
Trans-situational	no
Symptom behavior fits in the functional analysis of a specific symptom disorder	yes

Giftedness

High frequency of core behavior of creative and quick solution finding	yes
Trans-temporal from early childhood	yes
Trans-situational only in interesting situations	yes
Core behavior fits in the functional analysis of general giftedness	yes

Personality disorder

High frequency core behavior of personality disorder	yes
Trans-temporal from early adulthood	yes
Trans-situational	yes
Core behavior fits in the functional analysis of a specific personality disorder	yes

2.4 DSM-5, personality traits, and personality disorders

2.4.1 Millon and the diagnosis of the personality or personality disorder

Millon defines personality as a pattern of deeply rooted cognitive, affective, and *overt* behavioral traits that are broadly manifested and persist over long periods of time (Millon & Everly, 1985). Personality develops from a complex interplay between biological disposition (also called temperament) and learning experiences (social learning). Learning through experience occurs in the context of how the individual deals with the demands of the environment and the relationship they have with themselves. Millon is the creator of the DSM personality model.

People like different forms of validation: attention or isolation, power or reassurance, admiration or recognition for an achievement. Millon was not so much concerned with the content of the affirmation as he was with *how* people get affirmations and *where* they find it. He posits that individuals look for affirmations in two ways (how), namely, actively and passively (Millon & Everly, 1985). These two patterns of behavior are also referred to as instrumental. An active or proactive pattern of behavior means that the individual energetically seeks active control over their environment and is goal-oriented, forward-looking, vigilant, ambitious, and persistent. A person with a passive or reactive style waits to receive validation from the environment; the energy is much lower than in the energetic and active styles. Validation can be sought and found in four distinct sources, namely, within oneself (independent), in someone else (dependent), in oneself and in someone else (ambivalent), or neither in oneself nor in someone else (detached).

Millon favors 'syndrome continuity', the idea that there is not a qualitative but a quantitative difference between a normal and a disturbed personality. For example, the personality trait 'fun, energetic, and sociable' could develop into an histrionic personality disorder. Being cooperative and agreeable could develop into a dependent personality disorder, where the core behavior is adaptation. An avoidant personality disorder is an extreme form of normal inhibition. In other words, when the normal personality develops in a distorted and extreme way, it can gradually develop into a personality disorder without there being a clear moment of crossing a line.

People's reactions can also be seen as a continuum. For example, an accommodating person behaves in a dependent way in some situations, for example, in social and romantic relationships, but be independent at work. This person has dependent traits. A person who reacts in a dependent way in all situations (trans-situational) and has reacted this way in past situations as well as in the present (trans-temporal) has a dependent personality disorder. So, in the case of a dependent personality disorder, the accommodating reaction can be seen both in the present and in the past, and in all kinds of different situations.

A person's behavior may become increasingly one-sided and severe, occurring in some, several, or even almost all situations. This forms a continuum from situation-specific to trans-situational. The diagnostician must assess each situation for its degree of specificity (one moment) or generality across many situations (trans-situational) and over time (trans-temporal). There are many gradations between these two extremes.

As an example, we will discuss a client who, during his consultation, appears to have a narcissistic personality disorder. He behaves narcissistically during the consultation, exalting himself and devaluing the mental-health-care worker. But the question is how general or specific is this behavior? Is it just a narcissistic moment that only occurs during the consultation and sometimes in 'real' life? Does the narcissistic behavior occur in a significant relationship (a schema response), does it occur regularly with authority figures and in his contact with his parents, both in the past and now? Or is it a narcissistic stress response that occurs only in times of stress and when there is a symptomatic disorder, such as an anxiety disorder or depressive or bipolar mood disorder (also called a 'state', so not trans-temporal)? Or are there some clinically significant narcissistic traits, but fewer than the five required for the classification of a narcissistic personality disorder? Or are more than five traits present and therefore also a narcissistic personality disorder (APA, 2013)? All of these questions are summarized in the Application of Syndrome Continuity framework. See box.

Application of syndrome continuity

- narcissistic moments
- narcissistic behavior in a significant relationship (schema response)
- narcissistic stress response to anxiety, aggression, or depression (state)
- narcissistic traits < 5 criteria (> 60% = 3 or 4) (trait)
- narcissistic personality disorder ≥ 5 criteria (APA, 2013)

The clinician assesses the extent to which the client's reactions are frequent, trans-situational, and trans-temporal in situations inside and outside therapy. This is the condensed working definition of a personality disorder: frequent (and typical) core behaviors, trans-situational, and trans-temporal.

2.4.2   The DSM-5 categorical model and classification of the 12 groups of personality traits

In the field of psychopathology, the DSM-5 (APA, 2013) can be seen as the main 'guidebook', providing observable terms to describe psychopathology. For each personality disorder, specific criteria have been formulated, of which a minimum number must be met for a personality disorder to be diagnosed. For example, the avoidant personality disorder (APA, 2013) is characterized by a pervasive pattern of social inhibition, feelings of inadequacy, and hypersensitivity to negative judgment. This pattern begins in early adulthood and occurs in a variety of situations, as evidenced by, among other things, the criterion of avoiding occupational activities involving significant interpersonal contact because of fear of criticism, disapproval, or rejection, and the criterion of being unwilling to get involved with people unless he or she is sure to be liked.

Definitions of all of the personality disorders can be found in the DSM-5 (APA, 2013).

There are three groups or clusters of personality disorders – the A, B, and C clusters – and each group has certain characteristics in common. Each specific personality disorder also has its own specific impression. The researcher begins building an hypothesis based on the most striking impression made by the client. The client stands out because he always reacts in the same way. The way of responding is a broader concept than observable behavior; the characteristic emotions and thoughts are also an important part of the most striking impression. This pattern leads the diagnostician to suspect a specific personality disorder. Of course, this is only an initial hypothesis that will need to be tested later by a variety of other means. For example, when the most striking impression is suspiciousness, the diagnostician can think of a paranoid personality disorder. Or in case of a most striking impression of attention-seeking and excessively emotional behavior, a histrionic personality disorder can be suspected (APA, 2013).

The salient impression of the various personality disorders can be found in the DSM-5 manual (APA, 2013).

In this way the diagnosis of general giftedness from the screening (see Section 1.2) is supplemented by the classification of specific personality traits (see the DSM-5 manual; APA, 2013) or a personality disorder.

According to both Millon (see Section 2.4.1) and Beck (see Section 2.6), there is continuity rather than a hard boundary between personality traits and a personality disorder, with the disorder being characterized by unidimensionality. A histrionic personality disorder, according to Millon, is an overly sociable personality (the habitual personality trait) that is unidimensional. Almost all people, including gifted people, have some traits from these 12 groups; some have more and exhibit a unilateral core behavior with high frequency and are then considered to have a personality disorder in addition to giftedness. Assessing the 'general' personality traits of the Five-Factor Model (see Section 2.5.2) is also important. Starting with a clinical typology based on the 12 groups of traits is considered the most practical approach and leads to a quick typology. A gifted person with compulsive traits is called a 'compulsive gifted person', a gifted person with narcissistic traits is called a 'narcissistic gifted person', and so on.

This characterization is based on the most striking impression and the core behavior (see main strategy in Table 2.5, see Section 2.6). We speak of a personality disorder only when this characterization is well established. The client is entitled to this caution in diagnosis. If there is doubt, a cautious approach is recommended, stating the personality traits present without ascribing a personality disorder.

2.4.3 The relationship between classification and dimensional diagnosis

Classification involves assigning an individual client to a general category, for example, avoidant personality disorder. If the client meets four criteria, he "has" an avoidant personality disorder; if he meets three criteria, he does not have an avoidant personality disorder, but he does have avoidant traits.

A dimensional diagnosis aims to describe the individual pattern and severity of both the level of limitation of personality functioning and the pathological personality traits. An example is the narcissistic personality, where a person has moderate limitation in self-esteem and self-direction, and severe limitation in empathy and intimacy. These are the four areas in which limitations in personality functioning occur and are discussed further in Section 2.4.5. As a pattern of pathological personality traits, a narcissistic personality disorder has the traits of grandiosity and attention-seeking. On the test of pathological traits, the PID-5 (Personality Inventory for the DSM-5, Krueger et al., 2012), scores can be very high, high (above 1.5), moderate, or low. The PID-5 is designed as a test of the 25 pathological traits where each can be scored as very high, high (above 1.5), moderate, or low. There is a short version of 25 items for quick assessment of the five domains and also a long version of 220 items for self-report and 218 items for informant rating. It is free of charge for clinicians and researchers.

2.4.4   The innovative dimensional DSM-5 model and personality diagnostics

Following the mandatory classification, the dimensional model of the DSM-5 offers enriching and innovative possibilities for diagnostics.

According to the dimensional model of the DSM-5 (APA, Volume III, 2013), a personality disorder involves both at least moderate limitations in personality functioning in two (or more) of four areas (identity, self-direction, empathy, and intimacy) and at least one pathological personality trait.

Both the impairments in personality functioning and the pathological traits are rigid, trans-situational, and trans-temporal.

For the full criteria, see the DSM-5 (APA, 2013).

The DSM-5 distinguishes two groups of personality disorders, which must meet these general criteria: the prototypical and the trait-specific. The prototypical personality disorders are the schizotypal, antisocial, borderline, narcissistic, avoidant, and obsessive-compulsive personality disorders. The prototypical group has distinctive patterns of both limitations in personality functioning and pathological traits for the specific personality disorder. For all definitions, see (APA, 2013).

The trait-specific personality disorders are the paranoid, schizoid, histrionic, dependent, passive-aggressive, and depressive personality disorders, and the individualized mixtures. The trait-specific personality disorders are more individually determined. They have an individual pattern on the dimensions of both impairments in personality functioning and pathological traits.

2.4.5   Severity of impairments in personality functioning: the 'Mental Health Index'

The clinician assesses the client in four areas: (1) identity, (2) self-direction (disorders of the self), (3) empathy, and (4) intimacy (disorders of interpersonal functioning). Thus, for example, a stable sense of self with adequate self-esteem is an element of the area *identity*; the pursuit of coherent and meaningful short- and long-term goals is an element of *self-direction*; and understanding and appreciating the experiences and motives of others are elements of the area *empathy*. A deep and enduring positive connection with others is, for example, an element of *intimacy*. For the full definitions see APA (2013).

Clinical assessment

The DSM-5 (APA, 2013) begins with the clinical assessment of general criterion A, personality dysfunction. An initial global clinical assessment is based in part on the client's current functioning and learning history.

The clinician gives the client a plus, minus, or average global score in four areas. These four areas are (1) identity, (2) self-direction, (3) empathy, and (4) intimacy. We will now apply this to a case study.

Case study John Lear

John Lear is a handsome 35-year-old man who runs his own business as a tax and insurance consultant. He has an academic background and is intelligent, although at first glance he appears avoidant and dependent. He is being treated by an experienced therapist for recurrent depression. He also suffers from panic attacks and burnout. He has previously been treated by a psychiatrist with whom he made some progress. He comes from a small village where people are very close to each other. He often longs for this. Everyone knows and understands each other or gossips about each other. He has two sisters who raised him as their youngest brother. There was a lot of stress in the family because of his parents' relationship problems. His father also almost went bankrupt and subsequently fell into depression with burnout. John feels a closer relation to his mother's family and has a distant relationship with his father. Later in the therapy he has doubts about his parentage. He does not dare to discuss this with his mother and sisters. In therapy he also deals with this in an avoidant way. His identity is not solid or clear and his view of self is very negative. His first depression came when his dominant wife, a psychologist, cheated on him with a family friend and ran away. He struggled to continue to be a father to his two young children and quickly became attached to a new girlfriend, a woman with whom he worked. Together they formed a blended family of five children in which he found it difficult to assert himself and express his own wishes. In recent years he has suffered regular panic attacks, recurrent depression, and burnout at work.

On the Mental Health Index, he was moderately impaired in his identity, did not have a clear sense of who he was, and his self-esteem was unjustifiably low. He had studied and set up his own business with some success, but had difficulty being assertive and setting boundaries. As well as avoiding negative feelings and conflict in his working relationships, his dependency traits made it difficult for him to run his agency properly. Criminals took advantage of his friendly, accommodating nature in tax matters. As a highly gifted person, he could think autonomously but did not act autonomously. He thought quickly on many levels at once, which his colleagues often found difficult to follow. This resulted in him doing tasks himself quickly. The stress and exhaustion of all these factors led to burnout and depression.

In addition to symptoms of anxiety and depression, he did not feel angry easily, generally felt numb emotionally, was limited in his ability to distinguish a wide range of emotions and in feeling and expressing them appropriately. He could not name any short- or long-term goals. This reinforced his depression and his passive, dependent, and avoidant way of relating to others. There were also moderate limitations in his norms and values as he was quick to adapt to demanding, sometimes criminal clients. Self-reflection was also moderately limited; he did not think critically, easily, and effectively about himself. Empathy, on the other hand, was good; he came across as friendly and people liked him, even if they sometimes took advantage of his kindness. He was very understanding and appreciative of others and their experiences, could tolerate others thinking differently and having different points of view and understood the impact of his behavior on others. Empathy was a strength. Intimacy, on the other hand, was moderately limited. He had difficulty forming deep and lasting friendships and partner relationships. He had a desire for intimacy but limited capacity, and his behavior was conflict-avoidant and adaptive, and therefore insufficiently reciprocal in intimate relationships. He was, however, very respectful.

The global assessment of personality functioning for an avoidant personality disorder in the case of John Lear can be found in Table 2.2, including the clinical ratings on the Mental Health Index (impairments in personality functioning).

Table 2.2 Application of elements of personality functioning of John Lear (APA, 2013)

Identity, including a stable sense of self with appropriate self-esteem	3
Self-direction, including the pursuit of coherent and meaningful short- and long-term goals	3
Empathy, including understanding and appreciation of others' experiences and motives	1
Intimacy, including deep and lasting positive attachment to others	2

For the full definitions see APA 2013.

Positive scores in three or four areas of personality functioning indicate a low likelihood of a personality disorder and an increased likelihood of the presence of personality traits, in John's case, avoidant traits. These are important in therapy, but not sufficiently maladaptive to be considered a personality disorder. Two or more negative scores in the four areas indicate the likelihood of a personality disorder (APA, 2013). In John's case, only *empathy* is average, and the other three areas are negative. The next step in our clinical assessment is to examine the severity of the limitations in personality functioning in the underlying three aspects of the four domains. The clinician uses a five-point scale for the severity of the limitations in each of the four areas, from 0 (none), 1 (mild), 2 (moderate), 3 (severe) to 4 (extreme).

In summary, the clinician arrives at the following clinical judgment for this gifted person with avoidant personality disorder: a mental health score of 3–3–1–2. A test or structured interview such as the STiP–5.1 (Hutsebaut et al., 2015) has at this point not been administered for testing purposes but could be used when there are doubts about the diagnosis or other specific elements.

Self-assessment with tests focusing on identity, self-direction, empathy, and intimacy

The client can be assessed using the Rosenberg Self Esteem Scale (RSES) for self-esteem and the Empathy Quotient (EQ) (Baron-Cohen & Wheelwright, 2004) for empathy. The Relationship Questionnaire (RQ) (Bartholomew & Horowitz, 1991) can be used to assess four attachment styles. If necessary, an alternative judgment can be sought from an objective third party with adequate observational skills and good emotional intelligence.

A brief self-report version of 12 items, the LPFS-BF 2.0 (Hutsebaut et al., 2016), assesses identity, self-direction, empathy, and intimacy.

Structured interview focusing on identity, self-management, empathy, and intimacy

The clinician used the STiP–5.1 (Hutsebaut et al., 2015), which includes a five-point scale of severity of limitation in each of the four domains from 0 (none), 1 (mild), 2 (moderate), 3 (severe) to 4 (extreme).

A	DSM-5 DIMENSIONAL MODEL (APA 2013)				
	Are there impairments in personality functioning? Is there a personality disorder?				
		None ◄─────────────────► Severe impairment			
		none	mild	moderate	severe	extreme
	SELF				
1	identity	0	1	2y	3x	4
2	self-direction	0	1y	2	3x	4
	INTERPERSONAL				
3	empathy	0	1xy	2	3	4
4	intimacy	0	1y	2x	3	4
	≥ 2 out of 4	Score ≥ 2			
	Conclusion: moderate or more (namely: severe) impairments in 2 or more of the 4 domains indicates a diagnosis of a personality disorder				

Figure 2.6 DSM-5 impairments in personality functioning in client x with avoidant personality disorder and client y with avoidant traits and a negative view of self

Figure 2.6 shows the individual patterns of impairment in personality functioning in client x with an avoidant personality disorder and client y with only avoidant traits and a negative view of self. The difference in severity between the patterns of client x and client y is significant in terms of the severity of dysfunction (scores of 3–3–1–2 and 2–1–1–1 in the four domains, respectively).

2.4.6 Five domains and 25 pathological personality traits

Criterion B determines which specific personality disorder is present, provided that criterion A and the other general criteria (B to G) are met. At least one pathological trait must be identified from a 'collection' of 25. These 25 pathological traits are grouped into five broad higher-order domains, namely, negative affectivity, aloofness, antagonism, and psychoticism.

For the exact definitions of these five domains and the 25 pathological traits, see the DSM-5 (APA, 2013). Pathological personality traits are maladaptive variants and extremes of general traits that can be used to describe any individual. The general traits are part of the well-established Five-Factor Model on which the DSM-5 is based. Section 2.5 discusses the Five-Factor Model in more detail.

Here is a brief overview of the Five-Factor Model. The five factors are neuroticism (low emotional stability), extraversion, openness to new experiences (intellectual autonomy), altruism (kindness), and conscientiousness (orderliness). This gives us a Five-Factor Profile. Each individual and personality can be described using a Five-Factor Profile (Section 2.5.2).

The boxes below show an example of the characteristic pattern of pathological traits in obsessive-compulsive and avoidant personality disorders.

Avoidant personality disorder is expressed by three of the following four pathological traits: anxiousness, social withdrawal, anhedonia, avoidance of intimacy; anxiousness must always be present. Full definitions can be found in the DSM-5 (APA, 2013).

Case study Oliver Rhine

A 50-year-old psychiatrist came to therapy. He had treated many clients with depression and burnout, often highly educated professionals, often highly talented because of their education and their autonomous profession. After an extensive learning history and the development of a case conceptualization, it emerged that his father had not been able to complete higher education due to his background, but had found status very important and had dealt with the notable people in his village. This lack of education turned out to be a taboo in the family; his father reacted angrily when his grandson asked about his education and schooling. Oliver himself achieved excellent results with the highly educated patients and was much sought after within his field. When I suggested that he might be gifted despite his dyslexia, the client replied that he found the idea ridiculous. He had only got through grammar school in one go through hard work and perseverance and considered himself a mediocre student. On the Mental Health Index (see Section 2.4.5) he was found to have a 1-1-1-1 profile and only moderate problems (level 2) with his view of self, which was unfairly negative. He thought of himself as stupid and a moderate psychiatrist. His identity became the chosen problem in CBT, as did the fear of failure that arose when he gave training and presentations, even though he was known as a valued trainer.

Commentary

So Mr. Rhine did not have a personality disorder, but moderate impairment (a score of 2) on the identity component. This problem with his view of self seemed to be the result of invisible loyalties to his father which he was not allowed to overcome, or only silently. This made it difficult for him to 'just' succeed without fear of failure and to evaluate himself realistically and positively. Calling himself gifted, as the therapist suggested, would widen the gap with his father. Given his achievements at work and at school, the therapist considered it possible that the man was gifted. He met seven of ten aspects of the definition of giftedness. New colleagues who had taken a CBT course with him were also impressed and thought highly of him. The CBT was mainly aimed at improving the negative of self, and the therapist decided not to pursue the possibility that he might be a 'gifted person'. A view of self as showing cleverness and perseverance was more acceptable to the client and led to positive development.

In general, it is very important to assess the client's impairments in personality functioning (see Section 2.4.5). A dual diagnosis of a personality disorder and giftedness can be made only when there are moderate impairments in at least two areas of personality functioning. This dimensional DSM-5 diagnosis correlates highly with the DSM-5 classification of a personality disorder. The dimensional model provides a nuanced view of the healthy and problematic aspects of a person's personality functioning. The therapist can declare someone to be healthy while still having as a goal for treatment an unwarranted negative view of self. The client might recognize an accurate diagnosis but may not have a holistic view of themselves. If this is the case, explaining one's case conceptualization to the client will greatly strengthen the therapeutic relationship (see Section 3.2).

2.4.7   Giftedness and pathology

A traumatized gifted nurse with a score of 3–2–1–1 on the Mental Health Index (which implies a personality disorder), was found to have the following typical pathological traits.

- *Negative affectivity*

  - anxiousness
  - depression
  - restricted affectivity

- *Aloofness*

  - social withdrawal
  - avoidance of intimacy
  - anhedonia
  - depression
  - restricted affectivity

- *Antagonism*

  - none

- *Lack of inhibition*

  - rigid perfectionism

- *Psychoticism*

  - none

The above pattern of pathological traits corresponds to the characteristic pattern of pathological traits for an *obsessive-compulsive* personality disorder as well as for an *avoidant* personality disorder according to the DSM-5 (APA, 2013).

2.5   The Five-Factor Model and personality traits

People describe themselves and others in terms of distinctive individual traits. These traits may be related to character or temperament, or they may be cognitive in nature. For example, a person may be reliable, persistent, and intelligent, but also be opportunistic, extroverted, and have poor spatial reasoning.

Research into the so-called Big Five is based on the assumption that all significant individual differences are reflected in the language (Costa & McCrae, 1992). Out of the millions of words in a language, there are about five thousand that describe personality traits and five hundred that are most commonly used for this purpose. These five hundred words can be reduced to 30 aspects of characteristics and to five factors: the Big Five. Independent research has consistently and repeatedly identified these five basic factors in eight different languages and cultures to date (De Raad & Doddema-Winsemius, 2006).

2.5.1   The content of the five factors and 30 facets

The Big Five consists of the following five factors (Costa & McCrae, 1992; De Raad & Doddema-Winsemius, 2006).

1 *neuroticism* (N): emotional instability
2 *extraversion* (E): an outward-looking attitude
3 *openness* (O): open to new experiences, being intellectually autonomous and creative
4 *altruism* (A): being other-oriented, kind, and gentle
5 *conscientiousness* (C): being orderly and conscientious in planning and carrying out tasks

Each of these five factors is a continuum with two poles, and individuals can score high, medium, or low on them compared to a norm group. One pole – e.g., high openness (O) – is not better than the other pole – low openness – but does have different consequences. Most people have an average score rather than an extreme score at either pole.

Each of the five factors can be further distinguished into six underlying aspects that represent different nuances of the factor's domain. There are therefore in total *30 facets*, described in Table 2.4.

Although the Big Five model primarily describes a 'healthy' personality, it relates well to the more extreme personality traits and thus to the traits of personality disorders. The Five-Factor Model is also consistent with the idea of 'syndrome continuity', that is, the 'normal' personality transitions smoothly into the more extreme and one-sided traits associated with the personality disorder (see Millon & Everly, 1985, Section 2.4.1).

The NEO-PI-3 (Costa & McCrae, 1992) is a psychological test developed to measure the five factors and the 30 facets (general traits). Tables 2.3 and 2.4 compare the profiles of high and low scorers on the factor and facet scales of the NEO-PI-3 across personality disorders. 2.3 shows the five-factor profiles of 12 personality disorders or traits.

Table 2.3 Five-factor profiles for 12 personality disorders or traits

Personality disorder/trait	Five-factor profiles			
paranoid	N+	e–	A–	
schizoid	n+	E–		
schizotypal	N+	e–		
antisocial			A–	C–
borderline	**N+**		a–	c–
histrionic		E+		
narcissistic			A–	
avoidant	**N+**	E–		
dependent	N+			c–
obsessive-compulsive				c+
passive-aggressive[a]	N+		A–	c–
depressive[b]	N+	E–		c–

N Neuroticism; E Extraversion; O Openness; A Altruism; C Conscientiousness. This table is based on the meta-analysis by Samuel and Widiger (2008). The Big Five factors with a positive (+) and negative (–) correlation have a significant relationship with the personality disorder in question. A capital letter indicates an average correlation (> 0.30), a bold capital letter indicates a strong correlation (> 0.50), and a small letter indicates a below-average correlation (> 0.20).

[a] See Hopwood et al. (2009) and Dyce and O'Connor (1998).
[b] See Vachon et al. (2009).

This table is based on the meta-analysis by Samuel and Widiger (2008), reproduced with permission.

For practitioners, the link between the Big Five and everyday language is a great advantage when communicating within the profession and with clients, who almost always recognize the description of their personality.

Commentary

Four of the five factors are characteristic of the different personality disorders. Openness is not. However, high openness is a common characteristic of giftedness.

A further refinement of the facets, a name for the 30 general personality traits of the Five-Factor Model, yields Table 2.4.

2.5.2   The Five-Factor Model and screening for general characteristics of giftedness

Clinical assessment

The Five-Factor Model can be used as a frame of reference to provide a quick and efficient clinical assessment of the general and healthy characteristics of the gifted client. The clinician gives the client a plus, minus, or average score on the five factors. This provides a Five-Factor Profile.

Table 2.4 NEO facet profiles in personality traits

	N	E	A	C
paranoid	N+ 2,3; n+ 1,4,6	e− 1,2,6	A− 1; a− 2,3,4	
schizoid	n+ 3,4	E− 1,2,6; e− 3,4,5	a− 1	
schizotypal	N+ 3,4; n+ 1,2,6	e− 1,2,6	A− 1	
antisocial	n+ 2,5	e+ 5	A− 2,4; a− 1,3	C− 6; c− 1,3,5
borderline	N+ 1,3 to 6;	e− 1,6	a− 1,2,4	c− 1,3,5,6
histrionic	**N+ 2**	E+ 2; e+ 1,3,4,5,6		
narcissistic	n+ 2		A− 2,5; a 1,3,4	
avoidant	N+ **1,3,4,6** n+ 2	E− 1,2,3,6; e− 4,5	a− 1; a+ 5; o− 4	c− 1,5
dependent	N+ 1,3,4,6	e− 3		c− 1,5
obsessive-compulsive				c+ 2,3,4,5,6
passive-aggressive[a]	N+ 2		A− 2,4	C− 1,3,5
depressive[b]	N+ 1,3,4,6	E− 1 to 6	A− 1,6; A+ 5	C− 1,4

[a,b] For passive-aggressive[a] personality disorder see Dyce and O'Connor (1998) and for depressive[b] personality disorder see the study by Vachon et al. (2009).

Neuroticism: N1: anxiety N2: anger N3: depression N4: shame N5: impulsiveness N6: vulnerability
Extraversion: E1: warmth E2: sociability E3: dominance E4: energy E5: adventurousness E6: cheerfulness
Openness: O1: fantasy O2: aesthetics O3: emotions O4: change O5: ideas O6: values
Altruism: A1: trust A2: sincerity A3: caring A4: accommodating A5: modesty A6: compassion
Conscientiousness: C1: efficiency C2: orderliness C3: reliability C4: ambition C5: self-discipline C6: thoughtfulness
This table is based on the meta-analysis by Samuel and Widiger (2008).
Facets with a positive (+) and negative (−) correlation have a significant relationship with the personality disorder in question. A capital letter indicates an average correlation (> 0.30), a bold capital letter indicates a strong correlation (> 0.50), and a small letter indicates a below-average correlation (> 0.20). Each personality disorder has a meta-analytically determined five-factor profile.

Case study Jerome Bath

Jerome Bath is an artist in his fifties; he paints and writes novels, all at a high level. He dropped out of high school without a diploma because of his impulsiveness and drug use in a pop band, which he considered more important than his studies. His IQ was high, and he could have easily kept up with his classmates. Socially, he was shy and withdrawn, avoiding feelings, including numbing them with drugs and alcohol. He smoked hashish daily. He expected to have a great career in the arts.

He is now in CBT for recurrent depression and alcoholism. He lives alone with his faithful dog in a cluttered studio. His traits include being highly introverted; strict and unfriendly; disorganized and chaotic; neurotic and emotionally unstable; and highly intellectually autonomous, critical, and creative. His Five-Factor Profile is N+ E− O+ A− C−. His therapist thinks he has avoidant, narcissistic, and depressive traits, partly because he does not do his assignments of writing down positive events and thought patterns. He scores 2-2-1-2 on the Mental Health Index (limitations in personality functioning).

Commentary

Jerome's scores of high neuroticism (N+) and low extraversion (E−) reflect low emotional stability and high introversion, respectively (see Table 2.3), suggesting avoidant traits. His low score on the altruism factor may indicate narcissism (see Table 2.4). In addition, high neuroticism (N+) and low extraversion (E−) combined with low conscientiousness (C−) fit the profile for depressive traits. So his therapist's working hypothesis is correct. The Mental Health Index determines whether there is a dual diagnosis of a personality disorder. Based on clinical judgment, he seems to have a score of 2–2–1–2 (see Section 2.4.5), with good empathy (slightly limited, 1). This is the profile of an avoidant personality disorder with atypical features of depression and grandiosity.

2.5.3   Giftedness and healthy characteristics

Traits can be both healthy and pathological. We will discuss this in relation to perfectionism, narcissism, and the regulation of emotions.

The Mental Health Index (see case study in Section 2.4.5) determines whether there is a personality pathology by measuring the level of limitation in the functioning of the personality. A personality disorder is indicated by a score of moderate (score 2) or more severe (score 3 or 4) in two of the four areas measured by the index (identity, self-management, empathy, and intimacy). In other words, one score of 2 and three scores of 1, or four scores of 1, indicate a healthy functioning personality. The list of 25 pathological traits discussed above (see Section 2.4.6) provides a further concretization of the pathological traits.

Giftedness and healthy perfectionism

Unhealthy perfectionism has been well described in the literature. For the five most characteristic automatic thoughts of obsessive-compulsive disorder (Beck et al., 2003, 2014), see Section 2.6. For the characteristic pattern of pathological features of the obsessive-compulsive personality disorder, see the DSM-5 (APA, 2013).

Differential diagnosis of obsessive-compulsive traits and healthy perfectionism

Giftedness is often accompanied by perfectionism (Roger & Silverman, 1997). This is reflected in the Five-Factor Model as a high score for conscientiousness which corresponds with the obsessive-compulsive traits in the DSM−5. The pathological trait which is part of the obsessive-compulsive personality disorder in the DSM-5 is described as *rigid* perfectionism (see APA, 2013). The perfectionism of many gifted people is however often flexible, open, intense, and creative.

This distinction is important for differential diagnosis. High openness in the Five-Factor Profile is usually a counterargument for rigid perfectionism. I will now give two examples: a case of flexible perfectionism and a case of rigid perfectionism, both professors.

Case study Robert Oaktree

Robert Oaktree is a professor of physics. He represents the university at home and abroad during consultations and visits. He is the reliable and competent face of the university and a pleasant and visible guest and host. He is natural and pleasant in contact with others and is an extrovert. He is always the natural chairperson, emotionally intelligent in balancing content and relationships. His credo is to treat everyone with respect and empathy and not to hurt anyone. Outside work, he is active in charities and nature conservation.

On the Mental Health Index he has a 1–1–1–1 profile; there are at most minor limitations in his personality functioning; he is a perfectionist but not perfect. His identity, self-direction, empathy, and intimacy are all positive. He is also down-to-earth and highly intelligent, but certainly not highly sensitive. His Five-Factor Profile is N− E+ O+ A+ C+. So he is highly emotionally stable, highly extroverted, highly open and intellectually autonomous, highly altruistic and kind, and highly conscientious. His perfectionism is flexible and there are no pathological traits. The Five-Factor Model gives a good, nuanced description in 'general' terms. His Five-Factor Profile is N− E+ O+ A+ C+, which provides us with a brief description of his giftedness in relation to his general personality traits (Big Five) and also that the trait of high sensitivity is not present.

Case study Steven Strong

Steven Strong is a professor of medieval Dutch. He appears formal and intelligent. He is obstinate and completely autonomous. He ironically rejects old friends who try to reconnect with him. He is widely respected and considered brilliant in his field. He works hard and has a prolific output of books and journal articles. He calls his family faithfully on their birthdays. However, he is not happy in his own family. He condemns the liberal views of his son and daughter. He is unable to build intimate relations either within or outside his family. He compensates for this with his talents and communicates in the 'together/above' or 'together/against' position, which results in others failing to connect with him and withdrawing. Even his jokes come across as devaluing and unintentionally hurtful. Less-educated people are quick to see this as arrogant narcissism and typical behavior for a professor. His perfectionism, together with his giftedness in his field, leads to exceptional performance, but is rigid and unhealthy, especially for his interpersonal relationships.

On the Mental Health Index, he has particular problems with empathy (2, moderate) and intimacy (3, severe). However, he has an adequate positive view of self and his self-direction is good. His score is 1–1–2–3. He has three pathological traits: rigid perfectionism, avoidance of intimacy, and restricted affectivity (see APA, 2013). He has a dual diagnosis of obsessive-compulsive personality disorder in addition to giftedness. His Five-Factor Profile is N+ Eav O− Aav C+. He is high in neuroticism, average in extraversion, low in openness to new experiences, average in friendliness, high in conscientiousness, and high in giftedness and sensitivity. His high sensitivity is concealed by his low affectivity.

These two cases illustrate the difference between healthy and unhealthy perfectionism, which can easily be confused, leading to misdiagnosis. The case of Robert Oaktree is an example of giftedness and a healthy personality. The case of Steven Strong is an example of giftedness and an obsessive-compulsive personality disorder, a double diagnosis. The Five-Factor Model provides a description for both – and all – cases. The Mental Health Index (criterion A) and one or more pathological traits (criterion B) determine whether a personality disorder is present.

Trait 2 of an obsessive-compulsive personality disorder is perseveration (APA, 2013). A gifted person will often achieve their goals in creative ways, but someone with an obsessive-compulsive personality disorder will not be able to tolerate failure and will therefore keep going.

Trait 3 of an obsessive-compulsive personality disorder is avoidance of intimacy (APA, 2013). A gifted person is more concerned with maintaining autonomy, and the gifted person is statistically less likely to meet like-minded people (4% of the population) and develop intimacy.

Trait 4 of an obsessive-compulsive personality disorder is restricted affectivity (APA, 2013). Most gifted people are also highly sensitive and will therefore have an appropriate and proportional affective response to an eliciting situation; in this case, there is no restricted affectivity. Restricted affectivity could however be present to avoid an overly strong emotional responses due to the high sensitivity, which implies deep stimulus processing.

Giftedness and healthy narcissism

Unhealthy narcissism has been well described in the literature. For the five most characteristic automatic thoughts of narcissistic personality disorder (Beck et al., 2003, 2014), see Section 2.6. For the characteristic pattern of pathological features of narcissistic personality disorder, see the DSM-5 (APA, 2013).

Differential diagnosis of narcissistic traits and healthy narcissism

Giftedness and narcissism often co-occur (Webb, 2013). This is consistent with the narcissistic traits in the DSM–5. The most striking impression of the narcissist is that they act superior and grandiose (APA, 2013). The core behavior is to glorify oneself and devalue others. The DSM-5 refers to grandiosity and attention-seeking as pathological traits in the narcissistic personality disorder (APA, 2013). However, the narcissism of many gifted people, like their perfectionism, is often flexible, open, intense, and creative. This distinction is important in differential diagnosis. High empathy in the Five-Factor Model is usually a counterargument to pathological narcissism. The five facets or general traits of altruism highly correlated with narcissism are low scores on A1: trust, A2: sincerity, A3: caring, A4: accommodating, and A5: modesty (see Table 2.4). Conversely, high scores on these facets are incompatible with pathological narcissism. The environment might overestimate the pathology out of a sense of hurt. Webb (2013) suggests that for a gifted person to achieve exceptional performance, positive narcissism is required. Differentially, in healthy narcissistic traits, exceptional performance has often been realized, allowing the person to receive positive attention and appreciation from others, rather than seeking attention to compensate. See Chapter 6 for more details.

I will now give two examples: a case of healthy narcissism and a case of unhealthy or low empathic narcissism.

Case study Peter in the Fields

Peter in the Fields is a middle-aged mayor. He is seen as a well-liked person in his community. He is very helpful to his two elderly neighbors and is chairman of a charitable foundation related to the illness of one of his brothers. The first impression he makes is of being competent, quick-witted, and goal-oriented. His father was an unremarkable crafts-man and his mother a sturdy farmer's daughter who had been educated at home. Against all family expectations, the client had a successful school career followed by university, where he studied management while working full-time, graduating cum laude.

He applied for the post of mayor of a small town. At that time he was the director of a large company where he stood out for his integrity and overview, for being a versatile and creative man who was able to realize many projects. On the other hand, he was notable for his impatience with colleagues who, as highly gifted people, were slow to understand him, and for a certain compulsiveness towards people with different opinions. He could sometimes be blunt if people were not immediately ready for him or did not agree with him. At home with his wife, he can also be extremely short-tempered if his behavior and actions are not applauded or if his work with charities is not rewarded uncritically and with applause. He can then become narcissistic. Although his gift seems narcissistic to many people, his narcissism is positive and healthy. This is evidenced by the drop in his mental health score.

Commentary

Peter's personality can be described in the Five Factor Model as low neurotic and emotionally stable. He is a strong, stable man. As a friend he is highly extroverted. In addition, he is kind and friendly, open to new experiences, intellectually autono-mous, and reasonably conscientious. His Five Factor Profile is N− E+ O+ A+ Cav. On the Mental Health Index, his score indicates a healthy personality function-ing. He has a 1–1–2–1 profile for identity, self-direction, empathy, and intimacy. For definitions with all elements, see the DSM-5 (APA, 2013). The scores reflect impairment (moderate) in only one domain, that of empathy. For identity, he scores 1, indicating slight impairments. For example, his view of self is positive, but sometimes a little too self-confident. His self-confidence varies from too much to too little when criticized. His self-direction is good, although he is moderately impaired (2) in effective self-reflection. His empathy is moderately impaired (2). For example, his ability to integrate different views is moderately limited, although he can manage this in politics by compromising, but not really in his personal life.

In terms of intimacy, he also has the capacity for long-lasting friendships and a partner relationship. His intimacy is somewhat limited although within the healthy range. Looking at his 1–1–2–1 profile, there is no indication of a personality disorder, but of 'healthy' narcissistic traits due to poor functioning in the area of empathy in a man who is a constructive, highly gifted mayor.

Case study William Cook

William Cook is 30 years old and a successful pop singer. He arrives at an upscale detoxification clinic with a 12-year addiction to three grams of cocaine a day. He has no debts or physical problems, and he thinks alcohol is more harmful than cocaine. He is seeking treatment because he wants to live to a ripe old age and doesn't see how he can do it. He earns a lot of money and is able to get pure cocaine straight from Colombia. He travels a lot and performs abroad. He has no partner and few or no friends. He is very gifted, has an IQ of 155, studied biochemistry and pharmacology, and knows all about medicines and drugs. During the intake at the clinic, he has a critical and devaluing attitude towards the addiction psychologist, taking an above/against position in the interaction. He is extremely critical and lets it be known that he is exceptionally gifted. He is the only child of parents who always worked at a high scientific level and was brought up mostly by nannies. His parents were expats, living abroad and moving a lot, and William found it difficult to build connections due to the moves. He has had several hospital admissions for intoxication, but refused to provide information about these. A general practitioner's file cannot be requested either. About the addiction doctors in his previous clinic, which he left angrily against their advice, he says, 'What a low scientific level these addiction doctors had and how little they knew about their profession; I knew more than them with my IQ and my studies'. He comes across as narcissistic and antisocial. In his interactions with the psychologists and doctors at the addiction clinic, he acts in a superior and critical way, has no empathy, and is constantly devaluing. He has four of the five automatic thoughts that characterize narcissism (see box) as well as many antisocial thoughts. The therapist feels insecure because of his high level of intelligence and callous devaluation. In addition to attention-seeking and grandiosity, he also displays traits of recklessness, impulsiveness, irresponsible and unreliable behavior, manipulation, and hostile anger.

Clinical assessment: On the Five-Factor Model, he is rated as highly neurotic and emotionally unstable, highly extrovert, average for being open to new experiences, and low on being agreeable and altruistic, and for conscientiousness. On the Mental Health Index, he has a 3-3-3-3-3 profile, which reflects severe limitation in all four areas – identity, self-direction, empathy, and intimacy. These personality traits and limitations in his personality functioning are also present in the occasional periods over the last decade when he has not used cocaine. The traits of attention-seeking and grandiosity are present, as is a narcissistic talent. There is therefore a dual diagnosis of narcissistic personality disorder with antisocial features alongside giftedness and severe cocaine use. The result of his admission to the addiction clinic is that he again leaves feeling angry and hurt and again tries as a pop singer to win the admiration of the public.

On the Mental Health Index, his score is 3–3–3–3, reflecting severe impairments in all areas: identity (3, severe), self-direction (3, severe), empathy (3, severe), and intimacy (3, severe). He has an inflated, inappropriate view of self, his self-direction is severely limited in that he has no long-term goals, his empathy is zero, and intimacy with parents, friends, or a partner is completely absent. He has two of the following pathological traits: grandiosity and attention-seeking (APA, 2013). Definitions with all elements can be found in the DSM-5 (APA, 2013). He has a dual diagnosis of narcissistic personality disorder in addition to giftedness. He is highly neurotic, highly extrovert, moderately open to new experiences, low in friendliness, and low in conscientiousness, in addition to being gifted but not highly sensitive. His Five-Factor Profile is N+ E+ Oav A– C–.

These two cases show the difference between healthy and unhealthy narcissism, which can easily be confused, leading to misdiagnosis.

The case of Peter in the Fields is an example of giftedness and a healthy personality. The case of William Cook is an example of giftedness in combination with a narcissistic personality disorder, that is, a double diagnosis. The Five-Factor Model can be used to describe both – and in fact all – cases. The Mental Health Index or limitations in personality functioning (criterion A) and one or more pathological traits (criterion B) determine whether there is a personality disorder.

Trait 2 of a narcissistic personality disorder is attention-seeking; a pop musician usually has no shortage of this.

Giftedness, high sensitivity, and the healthy avoidance of emotions

An avoidant personality disorder is sensitive to rejection, withdraws from social and intimate situations, and experiences little enjoyment of life. See Table 2.5 in Section 2.6 and the full definition in the DSM-5 (APA, 2013).

The case study of Mary Dikeman is an example of unhealthy avoidance of emotions.

Case study Mary Dikeman

Mary Dikeman, 22 years old, contacts the mental health services because of depressive feelings. She often cancels meetings with fellow students because she is too anxious. She has trouble concentrating, and her grades in biology are very poor. She worries about everything and feels increasingly insecure. She spends most of the day worrying about how others see her. This has increased since her first boyfriend broke up with her after a short relationship. The client is the eldest of two daughters. On an intelligence test, taken while choosing a course of study in high school, she scored 140, which is remarkably high. Her father is an economist who she describes as a withdrawn man who works hard and can be irritable. Ten years ago he set up his own business and since then has drunk more alcohol than is good for him. She has never had a close relationship with him. She sees herself as more like her mother, who is a nurse. She describes her as busy, sensitive, quick, and somewhat chaotic. In their conversations, her mother has sometimes talked about having a negative view of herself, although in recent years she has become more at peace with herself.

Client's memories of home and school are not pleasant. The atmosphere at home was always tense. At school she got very good marks, but she did not feel comfortable with her classmates who often found her arrogant, stubborn, and nerdy. The feeling of being left out made her feel increasingly inferior. She suffered from stress and insomnia, and towards the end of high school her grades dropped significantly. Her mentor's support and intervention combined with a final push saved her from failing the year. The pattern of interpersonal contact from her childhood is repeated in social contacts and she has difficulties making good friends.

The client's score on the Mental Health Index is 2–2–1–2, indicating moderate impairments in identity (2, moderate), self-direction (2, moderate), empathy (1, mild), and intimacy (2, moderate). Definitions with all elements can be found in the DSM-5 (APA, 2013). She has a very negative view of self. Her self-regulation is moderately impaired. For example, she has no effective self-reflection. Her empathy is good. Intimacy with parents, friends, or a partner is moderately impaired. She has four of the following pathological traits which characterize an avoidant personality disorder (APA, 2013): anxiety, social withdrawal, anhedonia (even in non-depressive periods), avoidance of intimacy. A dual diagnosis of an avoidant personality disorder can be made in addition to giftedness.

Her Five-Factor Profile is N+ E− Oav A+ C+. She is highly neurotic and highly introverted, moderately open to new experiences, highly agreeable, and highly conscientious, as well as highly gifted and highly sensitive.

Differential diagnosis of healthy and unhealthy avoidance traits

Healthy and unhealthy avoidance of feelings regularly correlates with giftedness and high sensitivity (see also Section 2.10). This corresponds with the avoidant traits described in the DSM−5. The most striking impression of the avoidant person is that of shyness. The core behavior is the avoidance of emotions and/or social situations.

For many gifted and highly sensitive people, avoidance is flexible and creative and can be a healthy way of coping with overly intense feelings. It also reduces the risk of over-sensitivity and chronic stress.

High extraversion in the Five-Factor Model is usually a counterargument to excessive avoidance. The optimal stimulus level of extroverts is higher than that of introverts (Cain, 2012). Fast and divergent thinking and idealism are more likely to lead gifted people to think of negative events and 'disasters', which increases anxiety. Experiencing too little joy in life is at odds with the gifted person's broad and intense interest in specific engaging situations. Differential diagnosis should examine the possibility that the client is temporarily depressed because, in that case, stimulating and encouraging the broad range of interests can be used in the treatment of depression.

Although social withdrawal and avoidance of intimacy often seem pathological, this is not always the case. Gifted people are statistically deviant and therefore find it difficult or impossible to connect with friends and partners because few people are like-minded enough (in terms of interests and worldview, and often also in terms of high sensitivity) and of approximately the same level of intelligence to enable sufficiently satisfying attachments to be built. When in doubt, we should not be too quick to judge avoidance as pathological, but first analyze the function and work through the pros and cons of the avoidance with the client.

Giftedness and healthy autonomy

The gifted person's strong sense of justice and autonomy may resemble passive-aggressive traits or the core behavior of passive resistance associated with a personality disorder. The Mental Health Index determines whether a personality disorder is present and whether autonomy is a healthy or pathological trait.

2.6   Beck's cognitive model

The *cognitive theory* of psychopathology and personality traits or disorders is based on selective information processing, specifically selective processes regarding attention, memory, and interpretation. This selective information processing both influences the development of the personality disorder and maintains it. The memory stores *schemas*, a term derived from Piaget, which are structures of knowledge that are mostly implicit (Piaget, 1926). Assumptions can be made about the schemas that are present based on the *overt behavior,* the output in the form of thoughts, feelings, and actions. Beck calls the concrete content of a schema an assumption: a fundamental, articulated assumption made by the person about the self, others, and the world (Beck et al., 1990, 2003, 2014).

A good example is shyness. Most people are shy as children; usually a person overcomes their shyness. For a small group of people, the shyness becomes a personality disorder. Their view of self is that of a 'shy' person, and they behave as such. They do not accept an invitation to a party, and they continue to feel and act shy. The view of self is thus inadvertently maintained, becomes stronger over time, and can develop into an avoidant personality disorder with a negative view of self.

The *cognitive model* suggests that people's emotional and behavioral responses are influenced not by the objective situation, but by their subjective perception or understanding of the situation. This is a constructivist view (Beck, 1964; Beck, 1995). The person subjectively constructs the situation and responds accordingly.

An illustration of the cognitive model is learning to operate a computer or a car. The first time you have a lesson in how to use a computer or a driving lesson, you may automatically start thinking, 'This is too difficult for me, I'll never understand it or be able to do it'. This creates a feeling of fear and discouragement, leading to avoidance of the computer or driving lesson (behavior) and pain in the neck (physical response). The automatic negative thinking is triggered at a deeper level by schemas which developed from early experiences, the basic assumptions (core thoughts) and intermediate assumptions (beliefs). Beck's cognitive model is shown in Figure 2.7.

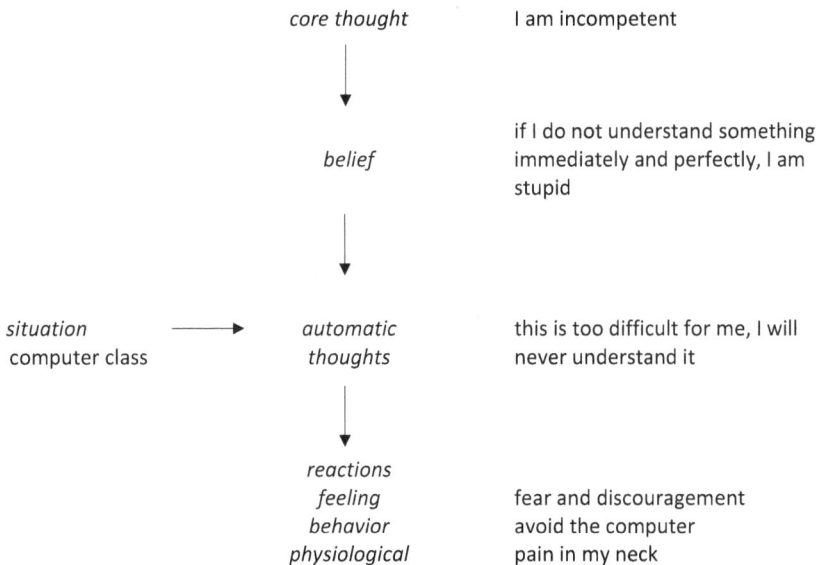

	core thought	I am incompetent
	↓	
	belief	if I do not understand something immediately and perfectly, I am stupid
	↓	
situation computer class →	*automatic* *thoughts*	this is too difficult for me, I will never understand it
	↓	
	reactions *feeling* *behavior* *physiological*	fear and discouragement avoid the computer pain in my neck

Figure 2.7 Beck's cognitive model applied

A gifted person with personality traits or a personality disorder may be aware (sometimes after self-observation) of the automatic thoughts that arise in his or her consciousness, but does not usually have insight into the deeper and more fundamental assumptions (view of self and view of others).

As an example, the automatic thoughts of a person with a *narcissistic* personality disorder, as summarized by Beck, are given in the box below (Beck et al., 1990). There are fewer automatic thoughts in a person with narcissistic personality traits than in a person with a narcissistic personality disorder; it is a continuum.

1 I am a very special and important person.

2 Because I am superior to others, I am entitled to preferential treatment.

3 I am not bound by the rules that others have to follow.

4 It is very important to be recognized, praised and admired.

5 If others do not respect my special status, they should be "punished" for it.

6 Others must provide for all my needs.

7 Others must realize how special I am.

8 It is intolerable if I do not get the respect I deserve or what I am entitled to.

9 Others don't deserve the admiration and wealth they receive.

10 Others have no right to criticize me.

11 The needs of others should not interfere with mine.

12 Because I am so talented, others must adapt to support my career.

13 Only people as special as I am will understand me.

14 I have every reason to look forward to a great future.

Beck et al. (1990) reproduced with permission

The automatic thoughts of a person with an *obsessive-compulsive* personality disorder have been described by Beck as follows (Beck et al., 1990). A person with obsessive-compulsive personality traits has fewer automatic thoughts than a person with an obsessive-compulsive personality disorder; it is a continuum from one trait to many traits or a personality disorder.

1 I am fully responsible for myself and others.

2 It is up to me to do the things that need to be done.

3 Others are often careless, lazy, incompetent, and often behave irresponsibly.

4 It is important to do everything perfectly.

5 Only with order, a system, and fixed rules can I do a job properly.
6 If I have no system, everything will be chaos.
7 Even a small shortcoming or mistake in my actions can have terrible consequences.
8 It is important to maintain the highest standards at all times, otherwise everything will go wrong.
9 I think it is important to have complete control over all my emotions.
10 Others have to behave the way I do.
11 If I do not perform at the highest level, I am actually a failure.
12 Weaknesses, shortcomings, and mistakes are unacceptable.
13 Details are very important.
14 My way of doing things is generally the best.

Beck et al. (1990) reproduced with permission

The five most discriminating items on the PDBQ have been empirically examined for five personality disorders (Beck et al., 2003). I refer to these five automatic thoughts as 'the top five'. These five items can be administered quickly in a clinical interview or with the PDBQ.

For example, for obsessive-compulsive personality disorder, the items would be:

1 Details are extremely important.
2 It is important to do a perfect job on everything.
3 People should do things my way.
4 I need order, systems, and rules in order to get the job done properly.
5 If I don't have systems, everything will fall apart.

Beck et al. (2003) reproduced with permission

During development from child to adult, there are different ways that can lead to the development of personality traits. According to Beck, some behaviors develop *unilaterally* while others, often contrasting behaviors, remain underdeveloped (Beck et al., 1990). For example, with paranoid personality traits, excessive vigilance, mistrust, and suspicion become overdeveloped, and harmony, trust, and acceptance are underdeveloped. Specific personality traits develop through interaction with significant others, such as parents or siblings, who reinforce basic behavioral patterns (basic strategies). Fear reduction can also be an important source of negative reinforcement. In addition, identification with significant others (learning by example or *modeling*) and an inherited disposition (temperament) are important factors. Often there are several different factors are at work simultaneously.

The view of self, of others, and of the world, and negative beliefs (which together form core beliefs) lead to core behaviors.

For example, a gifted person with an *avoidant* personality disorder may see themselves as socially ridiculous (view of self) and therefore vulnerable to disapproval and rejection (Beck et al., 2003). This is compounded by the person's perception of the other person as critical and demeaning. In addition, the person believes that rejection is catastrophic and that if people really get to know you, they will reject you as inferior. The person also believes that they cannot tolerate unpleasant feelings. These beliefs lead to two main strategies or core behaviors: avoiding situations where judgment might occur and avoiding uncomfortable feelings. The therapy plan aims to work with transforming the socially avoidant, vulnerable, and inhibited behaviors and to teach more assertive and group-oriented behaviors, enabling the underdeveloped side to become more developed.

Another example, a gifted person with an *obsessive-compulsive personality disorder* sees himself as responsible and competent (view of self) and therefore responsible for all mistakes, including the smallest things (Beck et al., 2003). This belief is reinforced by the view of others as irresponsible, incompetent, and nonchalant. The person believes that failure is catastrophic and that one must succeed. The person also believes that they cannot tolerate imperfection. These beliefs lead to the core behavior of overdoing it. The therapy plan aims to work with and transform the responsible, orderly, and controlling behavior and to teach playful, humorous, and spontaneous behavior, enabling the underdeveloped side (Beck et al., 1990) to become more developed.

An example of a case with both obsessive-compulsive and avoidant traits is Michael Moors.

Case study Michael Moors

Michael Moors is in his fifties, gifted, and very sensitive. He was bullied in primary school, and this continued until he was in the second year of secondary school. He reacted strongly and sensitively. He developed avoidant and obsessive traits. His view of others was that people were quick to make fun of him, find him strange, and look at him critically. He quickly saw this judgment in the eyes of others. This led him to avoid critical and dominant people on the one hand, and to try to be ahead of others with his quick thinking on the other. He also tried very hard to avoid social 'mistakes'. This resulted in chronic stress. Others cannot keep up with his fast thinking and talking and feel 'outclassed'.

A gifted person with a *narcissistic* personality disorder sees himself as unique, superior, and special (view of self) and therefore claims the right to special treatment (Beck et al., 2003). This is reinforced by the view of the other person as inferior or admiring. The person believes that being hurt is catastrophic. Another belief is that they do not have to follow the rules. These beliefs lead to the following core behavior: exalting oneself and devaluing others. The therapy plan aims to work with and transform the self-aggrandizing and rivalry behaviors and teach sharing and group-identifying behaviors, enabling the underdeveloped side (Beck et al., 1990) to become more developed.

The DSM-5 (APA, 2013) classifies 11 groups of personality traits and disorders. Each specific personality disorder or group of personality traits has its own salient impression. The researcher begins the phase of forming an hypothesis with the most striking impression made by the gifted client. The person stands out because they always respond in the same way. The 'way of responding' is a broader concept than only observable behavior, including the characteristic emotions and thought patterns in the most striking impression. This 'way of responding' provides clues for the diagnostician when considering certain personality traits.

Table 2.5 (Beck et al., 2003) presents the 11 personality disorders and groups of personality traits with main strategy, main beliefs, and view of self and of others.

Diagnosing the view of self and the view of others is an important step in diagnosing specific personality traits or a specific personality disorder. To provide more clarity regarding this schema (Padesky, 1994), the therapist asks the client, 'What does this event say about how you tend to see yourself? What does this event say about how you tend to see others'?

The gifted client will respond to questions about his or her view of self and view of others with *general* gifted core cognitions (see Table 2.6) and/or with specific core cognitions belonging to personality traits or personality disorders (see Table 2.5). It is therefore important for the clinician to be aware of and inquire about the core cognitions associated with the specific personality traits. Again, the diagnosis of self-esteem is twofold: view of self in general giftedness and view of self in specific personality traits, from the group of 11 traits.

Core behaviors (main strategy) and core cognitions (main beliefs) for the gifted personality are shown in Table 2.6.

The diagnosis of view of self is of great importance, on the one hand to improve self-esteem through cognitive-behavioral therapy, and on the other hand to understand its content, which is doubly determined by general giftedness and specific personality traits.

2.7 Young's schema-focused model

Young's schema-focused cognitive therapy builds on Millon's ideas about the two main criteria of personality pathology, namely, adaptive rigidity and vicious circles with self-destructive consequences (Young, 1994; Millon & Everly, 1985).

Table 2.5 Cognitive profiles of personality disorders

Personality disorder	View of self (COV)	View of others (COV)	Main beliefs	Main strategy (CAR)
Paranoid	Righteous Innocent, noble Vulnerable	Interfering Malicious Discriminatory Abusive motives Intrusive	"Others' motives are suspect." "I must always be on guard." "I cannot trust people."	Be wary Look for hidden motives Accuse Counterattack
Schizoid	Self-sufficient Loner		"Others are unrewarding." "Relationships are messy, undesirable."	Stay away
Schizotypal	Unreal, detached, loner Vulnerable, socially conspicuous Supernaturally sensitive and gifted	Untrustworthy Malevolent	(Idiographic, odd, superstitious, magical thinking; for instance, beliefs in clairvoyance, telepathy, or "sixth sense" are central in the belief structure.) "It's better to be isolated from others."	Watch for and neutralize malevolent attention from others Stay to self Be vigilant for supernatural forces or events
Antisocial	A loner Autonomous Strong	Vulnerable Exploitative	"I'm entitled to *break rules*." "Others are patsies, wimps." "I'm better than others."	Attack, rob Deceive, manipulate
Borderline	Vulnerable (to rejection, betrayal, domination) Deprived (of needed emotional support) Powerless Out of control Defective Unlovable Bad	(Idealized) Powerful, loving, perfect (Devalued) Rejecting, controlling, betraying, abandoning	"I can't cope on my own." "I need someone to rely on." "I cannot bear unpleasant feelings." "If I rely on someone I'll be mistreated, found wanting, and abandoned." "The worst possible thing would be to be abandoned." "It's impossible for me to control myself." "I deserve to be punished."	Subjugate own needs to maintain connection Protest dramatically, threaten, or become punitive towards those that signal possible rejection Relieve tension through self-mutilation and self-destructive behavior. Attempt suicide as an escape

(Continued)

Table 2.5 (Continued)

Personality disorder	View of self (COV)	View of others (COV)	Main beliefs	Main strategy (CAR)
Histrionic	Glamorous Impressive	Seducible Receptive Admirers	"People are there to serve or admire me." "People have no right to deny me my just deserts." "I can go by my feeling."	Use dramatics, charm; temper tantrums, crying; suicide gestures
Narcissistic	Special, unique Deserve special rules; superior Above the rules	Inferior Admirers	"Since I'm special, I deserve special rules." "I'm above the rules." "I'm better than others."	Use others Transcend rules Manipulate Compete
Avoidant	Vulnerable to depreciation, rejection Incompetent Socially inept	Critical Demeaning Superior	"It's terrible to be rejected, put down." "If people know the 'real' me, they will reject me." "I can't tolerate unpleasant feelings."	Avoid evaluative situations Avoid unpleasant feelings or thoughts
Dependent	Needy Weak Helpless Incompetent	(Idealized) Nurturant Supportive Competent	"I need people to survive, be happy." "I need to have a steady flow of support, encouragement."	Cultivate dependent relationships
Obsessive-compulsive	Responsible Accountable Fastidious Competent	Irresponsible Casual Incompetent Self-indulgent	"I know what's best." "Details are crucial." "People should do better, try harder."	Apply rules Perfectionism Evaluate, control "Shoulds", criticize, punish
Passive-aggressive	Self-sufficient Vulnerable to control, interference	Intrusive Demanding Interfering Controlling Dominating	"Others interfere with my freedom of action." "Control by others is intolerable." "I have to do things my own way."	Passive resistance Surface submissiveness Evade, circumvent rules

Beck et al. (2003), reproduced with permission

Table 2.6 Core behaviors and core cognitions of the gifted personality

core behavior	quick and creative in finding solutions
core emotion	intense excitement, thrill, stress, fear of failure
view of self	exceptional, outsider, special, clever, quick thinker, autonomous, intense, sensitive, strange
view of others	belong, ordinary, admire me
core reinforcement	(self) esteem, acceptance, admiring attention, creative kick, satisfying interest
core theme	fear of failure, isolation, being an outsider, rejection

Their excellent self-help book (Young & Klosko, 1994) deals with 11 'pitfalls' which the client can identify for himself/herself by completing the Schema Questionnaire (YSQ) (Young et al., 2003). Eighteen schemas are distinguished in Young's Schema Questionnaire (Young et al., 2003). Clients with personality pathology usually have more than one of these schemas or core beliefs. Young distinguishes the 18 schemas into five main areas of human psychological development. For definitions, see Young et al. (2003).

These 18 pitfalls overlap with the core themes of personality disorders. For example, the schemas of being demanding or of grandiosity are present in the client with narcissistic personality traits, whose core theme is the fear of being hurt and humiliated. Strict standards are schemas of the client with obsessive-compulsive personality traits, whose core theme is the fear of uncontrollable failure. Social isolation is common in avoidant personality traits where the core theme is fear of rejection.

Schemas are reinforced and maintained in three ways (Young, 1994): through surrender, avoidance, and overcompensation. These are called the three modes of coping.

Schema surrender means that the person selectively processes information through the lens of the schema and so gets confirmation of what they already thought. From the schema of unrelenting standards or strict norms, the gifted person sees all sorts of people around them behaving nonchalantly, carelessly, and lazily. Surrendering to the schema can also lead to self-fulfilling behavior in interactions with others. When the gifted person with social isolation and failure schemas behaves according to those schemas, this increases the chance of failure, for example, at work. His colleagues react to his schemas automatically by not taking him seriously, passing over him, and giving more attention to someone else, thus confirming the schemas.

Schema avoidance can manifest itself in the areas of feelings, thoughts, and behavior. A gifted person with the schemas of social isolation and failure may avoid feelings of sadness and anger about failure and social isolation with cannabis or alcohol. A gifted person with passive-aggressive traits will forget or avoid thinking about failure. A person with a schema of entitlement may avoid this schema by being overly modest so as not to feel the intense anger that would occur if his many demands were not met.

Overcompensation of schemas means that the person behaves in a way that is contrary to the basic schema. A gifted person with histrionic or dependent traits behaves in such an exaggeratedly autonomous and independent manner that the separation anxiety schema is masked and compensated for. A gifted person with schemas of emotional deficit and mistrust may behave in an overly naive and trusting manner, again becoming a victim of abuse. A person with antisocial traits and the schema of inadequate self-control may behave in a very controlled and inhibited manner until the bomb explodes to the surprise of those around them.

The schema mode model was developed for borderline and narcissistic personality disorders in particular. The definition of a mode is an instantaneously changing state of feeling and coping. There are four types of 'schema modes' (Young et al., 2003), namely:

1   child modes
2   dysfunctional parenting modes
3   dysfunctional coping modes
4   the healthy adult mode

The large number of variables – namely, 18 schemas, three forms of coping, and various modes – allows for a complex case conceptualization that is highly individualized. Young's model is more dynamic and transdiagnostic than the DSM-5 model. A relative limitation is the cognitive perspective, which sees the core behavior and its consequences as deriving from the schema.

Another advantage of the schema model is that it is dimensional and extends on a continuum from the healthy person with their schemas to the more one-sided, dominant, and more frequent schemas in personality disorders.

The following is a case study from Schema Therapy.

Case study Jerry Thunder

Jerry Thunder is 35 years old when he applies for Schema Therapy. He lives with his girlfriend, works as a project manager for a management consultancy firm, and has recently graduated from business school with honors. He studied in the evenings while working full-time. Jerry wants to do schema therapy himself because his girlfriend has benefited from it. He has studied the treatment and recognizes patterns in himself that have been holding him back in his life for years. Jerry has strong feelings of mistrust, fear of commitment, separation anxiety, fear of getting sick, and a constant threat of losing what he has worked so hard to build, such as his relationship, but also material things and his money. This fear was exacerbated by a burnout and the temporary loss of work, combined with a crisis in his relationship due to his girlfriend's affair with another man. They had previously been in couples therapy, which they look back on with satisfaction. They are both committed to their relationship of 16 years, but his girlfriend expects him to change.

Jerry says he looks good on the outside, but inside he still feels anxious, depressed, and often extremely tired. He can become so frustrated by these persistent symptoms that six months ago he briefly felt he would rather die, for example, by driving his car into a viaduct.

During the intake, it becomes clear that Jerry has been traumatized by a broken family, the change in the relationship with his father, with whom he initially felt close, but increasingly felt not seen or understood, and who he experienced as intrusive and unreliable. His father wanted him to be a 'real man' and forced him to do things he was afraid of, often without any preparation. Jerry was a sensitive boy and suffered from asthma and eczema from an early age. He was regularly overwhelmed by bouts of wheezing and severe itching. His school career was hampered by these physical problems and the resulting frequent absences. At school, Jerry felt like an outsider and was bullied. As a result, he became more withdrawn.

Jerry could feel the growing tension between his parents and it worried him. Eventually it emerged that his father had a secret second life with a sex addiction and debts. His mother decided to divorce his father when Jerry was 18, leading to Jerry and his younger brother having to live independently due to financial and housing problems. The boys were separated from their mother and sister and contact with their father was broken.

Jerry was forced to quickly become independent, take care of himself and his younger brother, and accept that the family had broken up. His first boss saw his talent but also took a paternal interest in him, taking him under his wing and sometimes helping him financially and to find better accommodation.

Jerry 'pulled himself together', became strict with himself, and developed an invulnerable facade of hard work, perfectionism, and fear of rejection. He began to compensate for his fragile health with a compulsively healthy lifestyle and lots of fitness training. At the same time, he met his girlfriend, who was a few years younger and also wanted to escape an unstable home situation. He took her and his younger brother under his wing.

Screening for giftedness

All ten characteristics of giftedness (Section 2.1) are present, and the work-related assessments included IQ measurements, resulting in a score of around 130 for Jerry. This case provides an illustration of a case conceptualization based on the schema therapy model. Based on the intake, his life story, and the specific schema therapy questionnaires, the following early maladaptive thinking and feeling schemas were identified as having developed in Jerry:

Unrelenting standards/overly critical: as a result of his striving to become invulnerable and infallible, to be in control and to control everything. The iron discipline with which he controls his asthma and eczema, but also his fears.

Vulnerability to illness and danger: due to the severe suffering caused by his chronic asthma and eczema, and later the danger of the breakup of his family, the fear of lack of money and not having a roof over one's head. Behaving as if he is invulnerable is an overcompensation of this schema and obsessive control of lifestyle and relentless exercise is an avoidance of the schema.

Abandonment/instability: resulting from the family breakdown and abandonment by father and mother. Activation of this schema is avoided by clinging to his partner and employer, making it difficult for him to move on in his career.

Mistrust/abuse: due to his father's role, which led to his trust being betrayed, but also due to bullying by peers at school. This pattern is avoided by withdrawal and emotional inhibition, which prevents the possibility of his vulnerability being exploited. Jerry may also sometimes choose a counterattack as the best defense.

Emotional inhibition: as a solution to his high sensitivity and emotionality in an insecure family situation.

From the Schema Mode Inventory (SMI) (Young et al., 2007), the interactions with the therapist and the analyzed interactions around problem situations that Jerry brings in during the intake phase, the following *schema mode* emerge:

- The 'angry child' who feels betrayed, abandoned and misunderstood
- The 'detached protector' or hermit in him

- The 'self-glorifier' who distracts by finding something else to do that feels better
- the 'compulsive overcontroller' who needs to control everything
- The 'demanding side' or the uncontrollable booster/pusher

The 'healthy adult' side, the side that should be in control of the different moods, is often quite overwhelmed by the above modes. However, the 'healthy adult' side also enables Jerry to make use of a good mind, excellent self-reflection, and social skills.

Later in treatment, the 'vulnerable child mode' comes to the fore, feeling misunderstood, abandoned, bullied, and rejected for who he is.

This case was successfully treated and provides a good example of how screening can be enriching in schema therapy when giftedness is suspected.

2.8   Interaction diagnosis

2.8.1   The Rose of Leary

Timothy Leary developed a useful and practical model for quickly classifying interactions, the so-called 'Rose of Leary' (Leary, 1957). He distinguishes two main dimensions: together and opposed, and above and below. This leads to four communication positions: below/together, above/together, below/opposed, and above/opposed. Often a person has a preference for one of these four positions. Alternating preferences for two (or more) positions are also possible. For example, the person with dependent personality traits will have a preference for the below/together position. The client with narcissistic personality traits prefers the above/together position when at rest, but switches to the above/opposed position after being hurt. People with diverse personality traits are also likely to have a preference for changeable positions. The person with both narcissistic and passive-aggressive traits will alternate between the above/together, above/opposed, and below/opposed positions. The person with histrionic and dependent traits will sometimes be in the above/together position and sometimes in the below/together position. Finally, the person with borderline traits, whose main characteristic is instability in interpersonal relationships, alternates between all four interaction positions.

The communication position of one person will stimulate a complementary or opposite (symmetrical) interaction position in the other: above evokes below, below evokes above, together invites together, and opposed provokes opposed. These are the rules according to which communicative behavior, and therefore also interactional dysfunction, occur. The therapist quickly notices this behavior in his own reaction and in the interaction position that is imposed on him, so to speak. It is therefore desirable for the therapist to engage in self-analysis (Section 5.4).

Figure 2.8 classifies four personality traits according to the Rose of Leary.

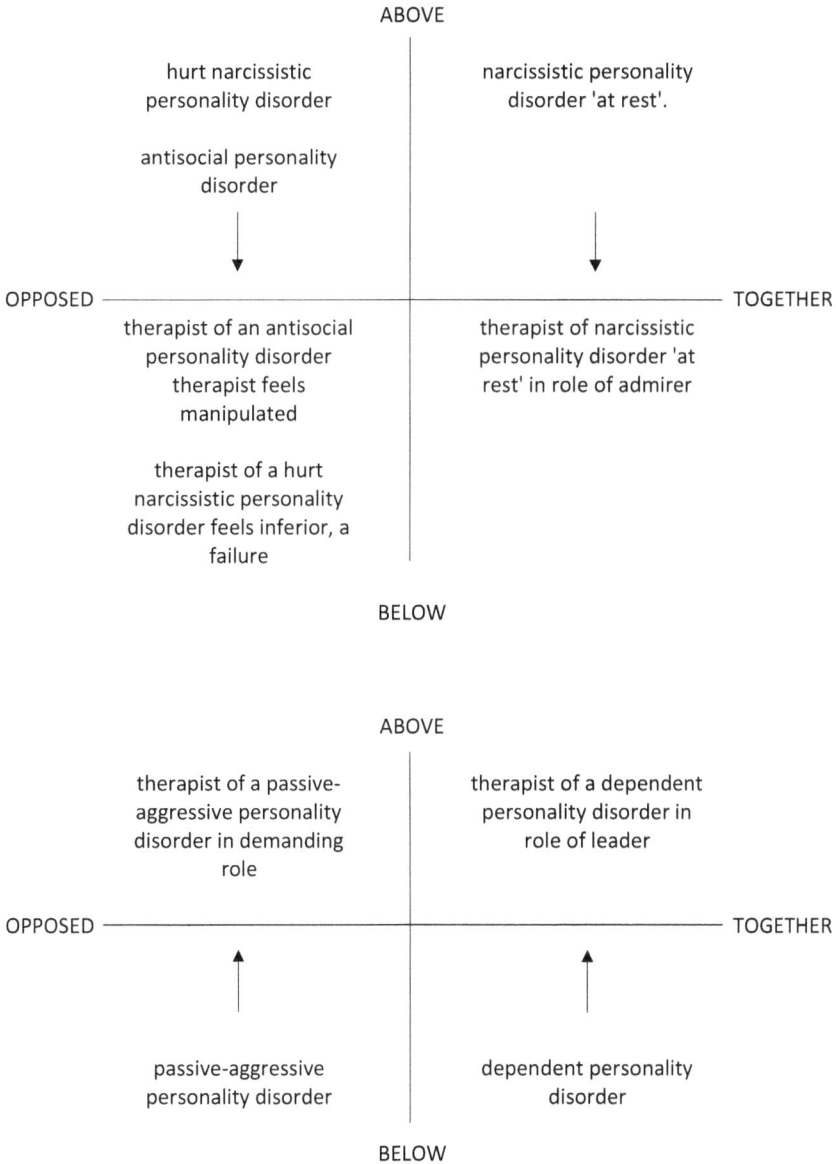

Figure 2.8 The Rose of Leary and the application of four personality traits

2.8.2   *Attachment*

Although the Rose of Leary is a quick and practical way of classifying interactions into two dimensions, I would like to add the degree of attachment as a third dimension. Interpersonal behavior (and therefore interactional dysfunction) cannot be properly explained without this third dimension, and the dimension of attachment provides greater depth in understanding interpersonal behavior. Horney (1939) already described three basic patterns in interactions between people, namely, moving towards, against, and away from others. The latter, in her case, refers to the aloof personality. Millon's model (Section 2.4.1) builds on Horney's proposal and chooses a classification whereby the focus is on the self (independent), on the other (dependent), on both (ambivalent), or on neither (detached). If we reduce the many complicated theoretical models to the basic dimensions, interpersonal attachment behavior is an essential behavioral dimension.

This model (the Rose of Leary and interpersonal attachment) combines well with Beck's cognitive model as well as possible avoidance of intimacy and fear of rejection and abandonment. We will proceed following Millon's model.

Attachment behavior is a continuum, ranging from

- (extreme) attachment and complete focus on the other, *via*
- secure attachment *to*
- ambivalent attachment *to*
- (extreme) detachment and focus on self

Attachment includes both the together dimension and the opposing dimension. Consider, for example, the person with histrionic personality traits who may be jealously attached and the person with passive-aggressive personality traits who may be ambivalently attached in their defiance and resistance. My proposal is to assess the person's preferred position in dealing with significant others (past and present) and thus with the diagnostician or therapist along three bipolar dimensions:

1 together versus opposed
2 above versus below
3 overly attached via ambivalently attached to detached

This gives us an evaluation of 12 possible positions in three dimensions. These positions have been visualized in Figure 2.9.

The abbreviations in Figure 2.9 refer to the different personality traits (APA, 2013), where SZT stands for schizotypal and SZO for schizoid personality traits. The numbers indicate different positions that can be taken. For example, the histrionic personality is often above/together and excessively attached (HIS1), but also ambivalently attached (HIS2). The obsessive-compulsive personality is ambivalently attached, but switches from above/together (OC1) to

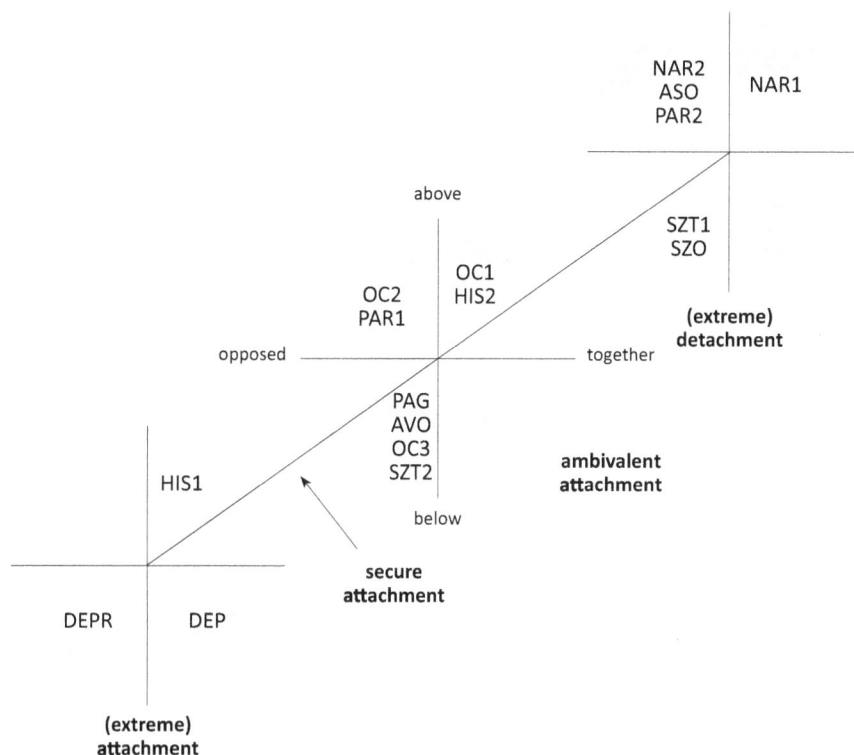

Figure 2.9 Personality traits and three attachment quadrants

above/opposed (OC2) to below/opposed (OC3). DEPR stands for depressive, DEP for dependent, HIS for histrionic, OC for obsessive-compulsive, PAR for paranoid, PAG for passive-aggressive, AVO for avoidant, NAR for narcissistic, and ASO for antisocial. The remaining personality traits are described in Table 2.7.

Of the three more severe personality disorders (Millon & Everly, 1985), borderline personality disorder can move along a continuum from extreme attachment through ambivalent attachment to extreme detachment. Paranoid personality disorder is somewhere between ambivalent and detached. Schizotypal personality disorder is more on the detached side, but not as extreme as schizoid, and also more ambivalent than schizoid.

The characteristic style of interaction within and outside of therapy can lead to an interpersonal or interactional diagnosis based on the client's interactional disorders and is an indicator of a possible personality disorder.

The therapeutic relationship is an eliciting event (CS/Sd) that triggers attachment (or detachment) behaviors. These attachment behaviors can facilitate or

Table 2.7 Interaction positions and types of attachment in personality traits

Personality trait	Interaction position and attachment type
paranoid	above/opposed, ambivalently attached to detached
schizoid	below/opposed, detached
schizotypal	below/opposed, detached to ambivalently attached
antisocial	above/opposed, detached
borderline	all quadrants
histrionic	above/together, overattached to ambivalently attached
narcissistic	above/together or above/opposed, detached
avoidant	below/opposed, ambivalently attached
dependent	below/together, overly attached
obsessive-compulsive	above/together or above/opposed or below/opposed, ambivalently attached
passive-aggressive	below/opposed, ambivalently attached
depressive	below/opposed, overly attached

disrupt the therapeutic process and therefore need to be consciously managed by the therapist on a regular basis.

2.9   Cloninger's temperament model

Cloninger has developed a psychobiological model of personality (Cloninger et al., 1993). He identifies four dimensions of temperament: novelty seeking (NS): the search for new situations; harm avoidance (HA): avoidance of distress, misfortune, and negative feelings; reward dependent (RD): sensitivity to rewards and recognition; and perseverance.

According to Cloninger (2000), these dimensions of temperament are hereditary and independent of environmental influences. They correspond to different neurotransmitter systems. They are bipolar and can be assessed by the clinician using the TCI test. The clinician can also assess a client's first three temperament dimensions in a clinical interview.

Characteristics of the Temperament Dimensions: novelty seeking, for example, easily bored and impulsive; harm avoidance, for example, pessimistic and phobic; and reward dependent, for example, social and dependent. For a full definition, see Cloninger (2000).

In addition, Cloninger distinguishes three character dimensions that people have learned as adults on the path to self-understanding: self-directedness: being an autonomous individual; cooperativeness: being part of humanity; and self-transcendence: being part of the universe.

In general, a low desire for stimulation combined with low social orientation indicates cluster A personality traits, a low desire for stimulation with high avoidance of suffering indicates cluster C personality traits, and a high desire for stimulation indicates cluster B personality traits. The profile indicates personality traits, not necessarily personality disorders, for which more is needed. See Section 2.4.

2.9.1   Self-assessment with tests

The seven dimensions mentioned can be measured with the psychological test TCI (Temperament and Character Inventory) (Cloninger, 1994).

Psychologists often underestimate the limitations that temperament factors place on the client's ability to change. The practical value of Cloninger's model is considerable, because it provides a better basis for diagnosis. It is also important for a workable and realistic treatment plan to distinguish between the immutable fact of the temperament factors and the therapeutic changeability of the personality and personality disorder.

2.9.2   Temperament and giftedness

Giftedness is partly shaped by temperament, which is inherited. The following four examples illustrate this.

Example of antisocial temperament

John is gifted and has antisocial traits. He is always restless and wants to explore new situations and meet new people. He is careless and unconcerned about danger and possible accidents. He is also insensitive to criticism and has no experience of fear or guilt. As a result, he does not learn and is not susceptible to external correction by the police and the courts. He has many fines and accidents to his name.

Because of his temperament, he is a strong stimulus-seeker, scores low in distress avoidance, and is socially inept. This is the basic temperament of the antisocial person.

Example of a dependent and avoidant temperament

Anita is also gifted, with mostly dependent and avoidant traits.

She prefers to keep things the way they are, takes as few risks as possible, is very cautious, and sees danger, illness, and disaster everywhere. She has many fears and easily feels guilty and inadequate. She has learned to quickly create safe and predictable situations and often anticipates rejection and criticism too quickly.

She is temperamentally low in stimulus seeking, high in distress avoidance, and highly sociable. This is the basic temperament of the dependent and avoidant person.

Example of a schizoid temperament

Henry is schizoid and gifted. He keeps his distance in relationships and is single. He does not seek stimulation and avoids new situations and people. He has no social needs and is introverted. He is also insensitive to praise and criticism. He is detached from possible danger and misfortune.

Because of his temperament, he is a low stimulus-seeker, scores low in distress avoidance, and is low in social orientation. This is the basic temperament of the schizoid person.

Example of a histrionic temperament

Lotte is gifted and has histrionic traits and an irrepressible need for social interaction. She is very extroverted, has 20 real friends, not to mention all her Facebook friends. She is always looking for new stimuli and people. She sees no danger and is downright careless, which, due to her flair, usually ends well for her. She is very focused on recognition and admiring attention.

Her temperament is high in stimulus-seeking, low in distress avoidance, and highly social. This is the basic temperament of the histrionic person.

2.9.3 Giftedness in relation to temperament

Giftedness helps John to be quick-thinking, creatively antisocial, and resourcefully manipulative. It helps Anita to be cleverly adaptable and to avoid being particularly intelligent. Henry is also clever and autonomous in finding seclusion. And Lotte knows how to charm and captivate many friends and acquaintances intensely and skillfully because she is so broadly interested. The general characteristics of giftedness (see Section 2.1) play an important role in the screening definition.

The different temperaments indicate a tendency and also influence the giftedness and the direction this person seeks: new or familiar situations, avoiding or not avoiding suffering and mischief, sensitive or not to appreciation and criticism. Temperament should be assessed separately; high curiosity (characteristic 6 of the screening definition, see Section 2.1) in giftedness is associated with both high and low stimulus-seeking behavior. High sensitivity is often associated with high avoidance of distress.

2.10   High sensitivity as a personality trait

Aron and Aron (1997) introduced the term *high sensitivity* in 1997, defining it as 'an innate temperament with a strategy of processing information carefully before acting, resulting in an awareness of subtle differences and a tendency to become over-excited quickly'.

In facets of the Five-Factor Model (see Section 2.5), high sensitivity can be formulated as having the following traits: thoughtful, conscientious, cautious, and non-impulsive action.

- deep processing
- overstimulation
- emotionality
- thoughtful action
- sensitivity

Overstimulation occurs via deep processing or high sensitivity and excessive sensitivity to stimuli, resulting in emotionality (Van Hoof, 2016).

The prevalence of high sensitivity is 20% in humans and animals (see Section 1.1), explained in evolutionary terms as being traits which are perceptive and cautious and therefore good for the survival of the whole group.

Aron (1996) developed a self-test for high sensitivity, some items of which follow:

- I am aware of subtle cues in my environment.
- During stressful days I feel the need to retreat to my bed or a dark room or other place where I can be alone and undisturbed.
- I am easily overwhelmed by things like bright lights, strong smells, coarse fabrics, or loud sirens.

For all items in the self-test, see Aron (1996).

2.10.1   Elaboration

Someone who answers 'yes' to 14 questions in the self-test is probably highly sensitive (Aron, 1996). Since high sensitivity is an inborn personality trait (see definition at the beginning of this section), the criteria of trans-temporal: present from early childhood and visible in the learning history, and of trans-situational: expressed in many current situations apply here, as with giftedness (see Figure 2.10).

This test is psychometrically not very strong, but it is clinically relevant. This is because the research population was initially limited to students, but this test probably captures three different components. This was suggested when Smolewska et al. (2006) examined the dimensionality of the questionnaire in a study. High sensitivity was not found to be a single construct, but the self-test for high sensitivity (Aron, 1996) was found to measure three different things.

The first factor was described as 'becoming easily overstimulated by internal or external demands'. The second was described as 'aesthetic awareness' and the third as 'unpleasant sensory arousal' due to external stimuli (negative affect). What struck Smolewska et al. was that half of the questions in the 23-item questionnaire were about the first factor: the degree of overstimulation.

2.10.2   Overexcitability (OE) and the Five-Factor Model

Based on Dabrowski's (1972) disintegration theory, Webb et al. (2016) distinguishe five types of overexcitability (OE), whereby a high intensity is at the core of giftedness:

1   sensory
2   imaginative
3   psychomotor
4   intellectual
5   emotional

In her study, Van Hoof (2016) found that high sensitivity along with giftedness is highly correlated with all OE scales *except* psychomotor OE. Giftedness without high sensitivity has high correlations with sensory, imaginative, and intellectual OE. High sensitivity seems to make the difference for excessive sensitivity to emotional stimuli when giftedness (in 80% of cases, see Section 1.1) co-occurs with high sensitivity.

Vuyk et al. (2016) advocate renaming the OE scales as the corresponding facets of the openness to experience (O) factor from the scientifically well-researched Five-Factor Model (see Section 2.5). They examined the correlations between the O facets and the OE scales and found strong similarities.

2.10.3   Self-assessment with a test focusing on overexcitability (OE)

The OEQ-II (Falk et al., 1999) is a self-administered test that measures these five OEs.

Figure 2.10 shows the functional analysis of general giftedness (see also Chapter 3) together with high sensitivity.

2.10.4   High sensitivity and stress

Relevant to stress is the evolutionary view of the stress system according to Hoogendijk and De Rek (2017). Humans have an outdated stress system that goes

TRIGGERING EVENT
(CS/sd)
complex and
engaging situation

thinking process
fast, complex, highly
associative, divergent,
creative, and autonomous

behavior (CAR)
thinking up quick and creative
solutions

thoughts (COV)
- I am autonomous, quick
  thinking, and creative
- I am different from others
- I am curious and have many
  and intense interests
- I am responsible
- I need to be competent
- everything has to be
  perfect and fair
- I want to make things (the
  world) better
- I want to be fair and just (or
  am disillusioned)
- I am clever but lack social,
  sporting, or artistic skills
- different rules apply to me
- others are different,
  smarter or less smart,
  jealous or admiring, more
  social or sporty
- it is not possible for me to
  just be normal and
  participate
- I am an exception and I am
  not one of them
- others exclude me
- others don't like me
- others find me strange

consequences (C)
advantages
+C+ pride, self-esteem
+C+ appreciation,
     acceptance, admiration
     from others
+C+ satisfaction, flow, kick
+C+ creativity
-C- dullness diminishes

disadvantages
-C+ less sense of belonging
-C+ others drop out
+C- negative reactions
     from others, insecurity,
     jealousy, irritation

emotional process
intense, usually overexcitable,
and highly sensitive

0C+ no resistance
+C- social isolation
+C- lack of understanding
+C- haste, impatience
+C- stress, tiredness
+C- frustration,
     dissatisfaction

feeling (CER)
driven, intense excitement,
stress, fear of failure

Figure 2.10 Functional analysis (general) of giftedness

back five hundred million years in evolution when fish appeared. In the shadow of a shark, the fish was stressed to the point where it could flee quickly. What is new in human history is the vague chronic stress from digital (virtual) sources. Through the stress hormone axis, psychological stressors work physically and people feel uncomfortable or stressed. Stress is healthy, but chronic stress is not, because it increases the risk of anxiety, depression, and burnout. Cognitive behavioral therapy also works physically through the stress hormone axis. Conversely, body-oriented techniques (e.g., yoga) also work psychologically and improve feelings. In the stress system, body and 'soul' come together.

In the case of high sensitivity, this means that more self-care is needed, as well as attention to stimulus reduction and recovery time from chronic stress (see Chapter 4). An additional burden is the vague virtual, digital stress, as a person receives five times more information today than 25 years ago (Levitin, 2014). The gifted person, who is estimated to think four times faster and is usually highly sensitive, is therefore at increased risk.

2.11   Integrating ten-step giftedness and personality diagnostics into a case conceptualization

The ten steps listed in Table 2.8 in this chapter are recommended for the assessment of personality with giftedness.

Table 2.8 Steps in personality analysis for giftedness

1		screening ten personality traits general giftedness	
2		12 sets of specific personality traits	
3		Mental Health Index	
	decision: personality disorder	<=>	decision: no personality disorder
4	25 pathological traits DSM-5 (APA, 2013)		▼ ▼
5		general 30-facets Five-Factor Model	
6		Beck's cognitive screening of view of self, other, world	
7		Young's schemas	
8		interaction diagnosis	
9		temperament	
	decision: highly sensitive	<=>	decision: not highly sensitive
10		case conceptualization	

Reference list

APA, American Psychiatric Association. (2013). *Diagnostic and statistical manual of mental disorders* (5th ed.). American Psychiatric Press.

Aron, E. N. (1996). *The highly sensitive person – how to thrive when the world overwhelms you.* Carol Publishing Group.

Aron, E. N., & Aron, A. (1997). Sensory-processing sensitivity and its relation to introversion and emotionality. *Journal of Personality and Social Psychology, 73*(2), 345–368.

Baron-Cohen, S., & Wheelwright, S. (2004). The empathy quotient: An investigation of adults with Asperger syndrome or high functioning autism, and normal sex differences. *Journal of Autism and Developmental Disorders, 34*(2), 163–175.

Bartholomew, K., & Horowitz, L. M. (1991). Attachment styles among young adults: A test of a four-category model. *Journal of Personality and Social Psychology, 61*, 226–244.

Beck, A. T. (1964). Thinking and depression: II. Theory and therapy. *Archives of General Psychiatry, 10*, 561–571.

Beck, A. T., Davis, D. D., Freeman, A., Arntz, A., Beck, J. S., Behary, W. T., Brauer, L., David, A. C., Daniel, O. D., DiTomasso, R. A., Fournier, J. C., Fusco, G. M., Gündüz, A., Hilchey, C. A., Mankiewicz, P. D., Mitchel, D., Padeksy, C. A., Rebeta, J. L., Reinecke, M. A., (…), Treadway, M. T. (2014). *Cognitive therapy of personality disorders* (3rd ed.). Guilford Press.

Beck, A. T., Freeman, A., Davis, D. D., Arntz, A., Beck, J. S., Butler, A. C., Fleming, B., Fusco, G., Morrison, A. P., Padesky, C. A., Pretzer, J. L., Renton, J., & Simon, K. M. (2003). *Cognitive therapy of personality disorders* (2nd ed.). Guilford Press.

Beck, A. T., Freeman, A., & Pretzer, J. (1990). *Cognitive therapy of personality disorders.* Guilford Press.

Beck, J. S. (1995). *Cognitive therapy: Basics and beyond.* Guilford Press.

Cain, S. (2012). *Quiet: The power of introverts in a world that can't stop talking.* Crown Publishing.

Cloninger, C. R. (1994). *Temperament and character inventory (TCI).* Center for Psychobiology of Personality, Washington University.

Cloninger, C. R. (2000). A practical way to diagnosis personality disorder: A proposal. *Journal of Personality Disorders, 14*(2), 99–108.

Cloninger, C. R., Svrakic, D. M., & Przybeck, Th. R. (1993). A psychobiological model of temperament and character. *Archives of General Psychiatry, 50*, 977–991.

Costa Jr., P. T., & McCrae, R. R. (1992). *NEO-PI-R: Professional manual.* Psychological Assessment Resources.

Dabrowski, K. (1972). *Psychoneurosis is not an illness: Neuroses and psychoneuroses from the perspective of positive disintegration.* Gryf Publications.

De Raad, B., & Doddema-Winsemius, M. (2006). *De Big 5 persoonlijkheidsfactoren: Een methode voor het beschrijven van persoonlijkheidseigenschappen.* Nieuwezijds.

Dyce, J. A., & O'Connor, B. P. (1998). Personality disorders and the five-factor model: A test of facet-level predictions. *Journal of Personality Disorders, 12*, 31–45.

Falk, F., Lind, S., Miller, N. B., Piechowski, M. M., & Silverman, L. K. (1999). *The overexcitability questionnaire-two (OEQ-II): Manual, scoring system, and questionnaire.* Institute for the Study of Advanced Development.

Hermans, D., Raes, F., & Orlemans, H. (2018). *Inleiding tot de gedragstherapie* (7th ed.). Bohn Stafleu van Loghum.

Hofstee, W. K. B. (1990). Het diagnostisch proces. In F. Luteijn, B. G. Deelman & P. M. G. Emmelkamp (Eds.), *Diagnostiek in de klinische psychologie.* Houten/Diegem: Bohn Stafleu van Loghum.

Hoogendijk, W., & De Rek, W. (2017). *Van big bang tot burn-out.* Balans.

Hopwood, C. J., Morey, L. C., Markowitz, J. C., Pinto, A., Skodol, A. E., Gunderson, J. G., Zanarini, M. C., Shea, M. T., Yen, S., McGlashan, T. H., Ansell, E. B., Grilo, C. M., &

Sanislow, C. A. (2009). The construct validity of passive-aggressive personality disorder. *Psychiatry Fall*, *72*, 256–267.

Horney, K. (1939). *New ways in psychoanalysis*. W.W. Norton & Co.

Hutsebaut, J., Berghuis, H., Kaasenbrood, A., De Saeger, H., & Ingenhoven, T. (2015). *Semi-gestructureerd interview voor persoonlijkheidsfunctioneren DSM-5*. Kenniscentrum Persoonlijkheidsstoornissen. StiP5.1. Retrieved August 26, 2024, from www.kenniscen-trumps.nl/wp-content/uploads/2023/03/STIP-5.1a_A4_spreadsNW.pdf

Hutsebaut, J., Feenstra, D. J., & Kamphuis, J. H. (2016). Development and preliminary psychometric evaluation of a brief self-report questionnaire for the assessment of the DSM-5 level of personality functioning scale: The LPFS Brief Form (LPFS-BF). *Personality Disorders*, *7*(2), 192–197.

Krueger, R. F., Derringer, J., Markon, K. E., Watson, D., & Skodol, A. E. (2012). Initial construction of a maladaptive personality trait model and inventory for DSM-5. *Psychological Medicine*, *42*(9), 1879–1890.

Kuipers, W., & Van Kempen, A. (2007). *Verleid jezelf tot excellentie!* Lecturium.

Leary, T. (1957). *Interpersonal diagnosis of personality*. Ronald.

Levitin, D. (2014). *The organized mind: Thinking straight in the age of information overload*. Dutton.

Millon, T., & Everly Jr., G. S. (1985). *Personality and its disorders: A biosocial-learning approach*. Wiley.

Padesky, C. A. (1994). Schema change processes in cognitive therapy. *Clinical Psychology & Psychotherapy*, *1*, 267–278.

Piaget, J. (1926). *The language and thought of the child*. Harcourt, Brace.

Rogers, K. B., & Silverman, L. K. (1997). *Personal, medical, social and psychological factors in 160 + IQ children*. National Association for Gifted Children 44th Annual Convention.

Samuel, D. B., & Widiger, T. A. (2008). Meta-analytic review of the relationships between the five-factor model and DSM-IV-TR personality disorders: A facet level analysis. *Clinical Psychological Review*, *28*, 1326–1342.

Smolewska, K. A., McCabe, S. B., & Woody, E. Z. (2006). A psychometric evaluation of the Highly Sensitive Person Scale: The components of sensory-processing sensitivity and their relation to the BIS/BAS and "big five". *Personality and Individual Differences*, *40*(6), 1269–1279.

Spek, A. (2019). Talenten van mensen met een autismespectrumstoornis. *Gedragstherapie*, *4*, 319–332. Amsterdam: Boom.

Vachon, D. D., Sellbom, M., Ryder, A. G., Miller, J. D., & Bagby, R. M. (2009). A five-factor model description of depressive personality disorder. *Journal of Personality Disorders*, *23*, 447–465.

Van Hoof, E. (2016). *Hoogsensitief*. LannooCampus.

Vuyk, A., Krieshok, T. S., & Kerr, B. A. (2016). Openness to experience rather than overexcitabilities: Call it like it is. *Gifted Child Quarterly*, *60*(3), 192–211.

Webb, J. T. (2013). *Searching for meaning – Idealism, bright minds, disillusionment, and hope*. Great Potential Press.

Webb, J. T., Amend, E. R., Beljan, P., Webb, N. E., Kuzujanakis, M., Olenchak, F. R., & Goerss, J. (2016). *Misdiagnosis and dual diagnoses of gifted children and adults: ADHD, Bipolar, OCD, Asperger's, depression, and other disorders* (2nd ed.). Great Potential Press.

Young, J. E. (1994). *Cognitive therapy for personality disorders: A schema-approach* (Rev. ed.). Professional Resource Exchange.

Young, J. E., Arntz, A., Atkinson, T., Lobbestael, J., Weishaar, M. E., Van Vreeswijk, M. F., & Klokman, J. (2007). *The schema mode inventory (SMI)*. Schema Therapy Institute.

Young, J. E., & Klosko, J. S. (1994). *Reinventing your life*. Penguin Group.

Young, J. E., Klosko, J. S., & Weishaar, M. E. (2003). *Schema therapy: A practitioner's guide*. Guilford Press.

Case conceptualization and functional analysis of dual core behavior in giftedness and personality

Summary

This chapter examines both the process of cognitive behavioral therapy and the practice of developing a *case conceptualization* of giftedness in seven stages. The case conceptualization provides the link between the diagnosis of symptoms, giftedness, and personality on the one hand and therapy on the other. This provides an overview as well as focuses on how the general core behavior of giftedness relates to the core behavior of specific personality traits. In addition, the *functional analysis* of both of these (general and specific) core behaviors in giftedness is used as a prelude to the treatment plan.

3.1 The process of cognitive behavioral therapy: the seven stages

In the therapy of a gifted client with specific personality traits, we follow the cognitive behavioral process in seven phases (Brinkman, 1978; Schacht et al., 2007). It begins with an inventory of the problems: both the symptoms and the advantages and disadvantages of, for the client, often automatic, core behaviors.

The therapist actively involves the client in exploring how the symptoms (e.g., anxiety) and problems at work or in relationships (e.g., loneliness and social isolation) relate to the core behaviors of giftedness and personality traits, childhood experiences, and learning history to create a preliminary case conceptualization or case conceptualization. The therapist then presents the client with the preliminary case conceptualization.

At the end of the diagnostic phase, the case conceptualization is further evaluated and both the core and symptom behaviors are identified. Treatment plans are agreed based on the functional analyses of these symptom and core behaviors and the order of treatment is determined. Treatment of the selected behaviors is then implemented according to this plan and then evaluated. The box below shows the seven stages.

DOI: 10.4324/9781003423287-4

The seven stages of the process of cognitive behavioral therapy

1   problem inventory
2   preliminary case conceptualization
3   the tested case conceptualization
4   functional analysis of core behaviors
5   treatment plan with problem selection
6   implementation phase of therapy
7   evaluation

Within the cognitive behavioral framework, therapy is semi-structured and goal-oriented and is conducted according to the so-called process of cognitive behavioral therapy (Brinkman, 1978; Schacht et al., 2007). One of the characteristics of cognitive behavioral therapy is that it is process-based and/or protocol-based.

Because of the success and scientific support for protocol-based treatments, CBT is often mistakenly considered to be non-process-based. However, cognitive behavioral therapy for both personality disorders and giftedness is primarily process-based and only partly structured. As many gifted people score high on the personality trait autonomy, highly structured protocols are ineffective and the therapist needs to be flexible and adaptable in order to provide the optimal amount of structure for the client by balancing how much to direct and how much to follow.

Another element of the therapeutic process is the functional analysis. In cognitive behavioral therapy we assume that, through a learning process, problem behavior, like healthy and desirable behavior, has acquired a function. A functional analysis is a hypothesis about the factors that trigger and maintain the problem behavior. These factors may precede (antecedent), coincide with (concurrent), or follow (consequent) the problem. Cognitive behavioral therapy is characterized by accepting tasks to practice outside of the therapy (or motivating the client to do so) and as much as possible using techniques shown in empirical (evidence-based) research to be effective. The implementation of the treatment thus becomes an experiment to see whether the hypothesis about the problem behavior is correct and, if necessary, adjusting and retesting the hypothesis in the therapy. The final test of whether the functional analysis is correct and whether the treatment has been effective occurs when there is a therapeutic change in feelings, thoughts, and behavior.

The core behaviors of a client with (general) giftedness and specific personality traits are by definition self-evident to them and insight into both the behaviors and their costs and benefits is not present. Nevertheless, the CBT process can be used for treating the core behaviors of a client with giftedness combined with (specific) personality traits, for example, quick and creative solution-finding together with avoidance of feelings and social situations in the gifted client with avoidant traits.

The process of cognitive behavioral therapy is summarized in seven phases (Brinkman, 1978; Schacht et al., 2007). In the case of giftedness combined with personality traits, the cognitive behavioral therapist begins with the problem inventory, the first phase of the process of cognitive behavioral therapy.

3.1.1   Stage 1: Problem inventory

In this phase, the cognitive behavioral therapist explores the possibility of comorbidity for the gifted client of the symptomatic behaviors, such as anxiety or mood and eating disorders, with specific personality traits (Section 2.3). In addition, the cognitive behavioral therapist assesses the extent of dysfunctional interactions in relationships, work, leisure, and with the therapist and assesses whether the client may have a dysfunctional view of themselves and of others.

It is advisable to actively involve the client in the problem inventory by providing homework such as registration exercises. Self-sufficiency in general, and self-registration or self-reflection in particular, are forms of operant behavior that can be learned using learning principles, for example, a therapist providing positive intermittent (occasional) reinforcement in the form of positive attention and appreciation for a client with avoidant or obsessive-compulsive traits.

Topographical analysis and baseline measures

A topographical analysis describes the concrete and specific situations in which the symptom behaviors and core behaviors do or do not occur. This topographical analysis is combined with a baseline assessment. A baseline measure determines how strongly and how often certain feelings, behaviors, or thoughts currently occur. Determining the current level, the baseline, provides an opportunity to assess after therapy the extent to which feelings, behaviors, and thoughts have changed. For a client with a combination of giftedness and personality traits, it is important to measure the current baseline level of core behaviors, characteristic feelings, and automatic thoughts. Through self-reporting and a cognitive journal, the client becomes aware of the frequency and intensity of his or her core behaviors, feelings, and beliefs.

For example, the cognitive behavioral therapist might ask a client with avoidant traits to do a registration task where they track their core behavior of avoidance and the core feeling of fear or shame. The triggering event, the automatic thoughts, how convincing the thoughts are, and the consequences of the core behavior are also registered.

3.1.2   Stage 2: Preliminary case conceptualization

Once an inventory of the problems and the symptoms has been made with the client and the classification (determination) of giftedness in relation to the personality has been discussed, the cognitive behavioral therapist makes a diagram of a draft case conceptualization. The case conceptualization is used to clarify for the client the relationship between their symptom behaviors, background problems, giftedness, core behaviors, and personality traits. The therapist puts the draft of the case conceptualization on paper and asks the client to think about it at home with the aim of discussing it again in the next session.

3.1.3   Stage 3: The tested case conceptualization

Further testing and assessment of general (five-factor) personality traits, temperament, and personal coping style provide specific diagnostic data, as well as the identification of limitations in personality functioning and pathological traits. This data is incorporated into the tested case conceptualization. How this case conceptualization can be created in practice is explained in Section 3.2.

3.1.4   Stage 4: Functional analysis

The topographical analyses of the symptom behavior and the core behavior provide information for the functional analysis of the core behavior and an analysis of the meaning of the core feeling. When both giftedness and personality traits have been identified, the functional analysis examines the core behavior of the client, such as quickly creating solutions, in combination with avoidance in the client with avoidant personality traits, adapting and seeking support in the client with dependent personality traits, and with trying too hard in the client with obsessive-compulsive personality traits.

The therapist organizes the data from the baseline measurements in the scheme of the three-factor model (Hermans et al., 2018) using learning psychology terms, namely, the thoughts (COV = covert operant), feelings (CER = conditioned emotional response), and behavior (CAR = conditioned avoidance or approach response) evoked by the eliciting event (CS/Sd) and maintained by the disadvantages and advantages of the behavior as well as the effects or consequences (C). The functional analysis is a hypothesis about the 'elicitors' and 'maintainers' of the problem behavior and is formulated at a higher level of abstraction than the topographical analysis, which describes the concrete situations in which the problem behavior does or does not occur. The functional analysis is discussed in detail with examples in Section 3.3. The (partial) treatment plan is drawn up based on the functional analysis.

3.1.5   Stage 5: Treatment plan and problem selection

In the treatment plan, the concrete goals are formulated and the techniques to achieve these goals are selected. Table 3.1 gives an example of the five foci of the cognitive behavioral model with specific treatment goals for a gifted client with narcissistic personality traits. Also listed for each therapy goal are specific techniques that can be used in the process (see Section 4.2). These specific goals and techniques can be seen as concrete suggestions for the development of a treatment plan.

Table 3.1 Treatment plan for narcissistic traits

Starting point	Treatment goals	Techniques
triggering event (CS/Sd)	• hurt • humiliation	• gradual exposure • temporary avoidance • the stop rule
thoughts (COV)	• I am good as I am, even if I am ordinary • I am good as I am, even if I am criticized or hurt • being ordinary has advantages • others are equal • when others are critical or jealous, they feel hurt • others are allowed to criticize, I may learn from it	• continuum techniques • cognitive diary • historical test
feeling (CER)	• fear of humiliation and being ordinary • feeling the anger and transforming it • counter-issue: self-love	• downward arrow technique • counterconditioning • relaxation • hypnosis • EMDR
behavior (CAR)	• reciprocal behavior • doing/being normal • reducing the tendency to hurt back and devalue • learning to stand up for yourself without hurting the other person	• behavioral experiments • role play • self-control techniques • assertiveness training
consequences (C)	• increase in disadvantages • decrease in advantages	increasing awareness and other forms of (self) reinforcement

As giftedness has two core behaviors, one general (being quick to find solutions) and one specific (belonging to the 12 personality traits), we will make a treatment plan for both. For the treatment plan for general giftedness, see Section 4.1.1, and for the treatment plan for specific personality traits, see Section 4.1.2.

The treatment plan also includes a choice of which problems to address and in what order (problem selection). The client's wishes are important, together with the personality problems identified in the case conceptualization. Brinkman provides guidelines for the order in which to address problems (Brinkman, 1978):

1 the probability value of the problem, that is, the extent to which the client and the therapist agree that the problem exists
2 the problem value for the client (the extent to which it is a problem for the client)
3 the centrality of the problem in the case conceptualization
4 the treatability of the problem
5 the concreteness of the problem

Few clients seek help directly for personality change. They do so, for example, when the symptoms have already subsided, but the client is aware of the need for structural change, possibly because of frequent relapses in the past. For example, a gifted person with obsessive-compulsive personality traits will often relapse into burnout. To prevent relapse, it is important to treat the obsessive-compulsive personality traits in conjunction with the gifted personality traits.

3.1.6   Stage 6: Implementation of therapy

The therapy is carried out based on the treatment plan. Together with the client, techniques are applied within and outside the therapy sessions and practiced in exercises at home or elsewhere. The client uses self-registration to monitor changes.

Section 4.2 describes a number of specific cognitive behavioral techniques adapted to giftedness.

3.1.7   Stage 7: Evaluation of therapy

After the implementation of the therapy, the evaluation follows. In this phase, the changes in core behaviors, core feelings, and core thoughts are compared with their baseline levels, measured and evaluated in terms of whether the client has changed in the desired direction. Tests and self-reports are used for this purpose.

In summary, the process of cognitive-behavioral therapy has four main parts:

I   Classification and Diagnosis (C & D – phase 1)
II   the behavior Analysis (A – phases 2 to 5)
III   implementation of Therapy (T – phase 6)
IV   the Evaluation (E – phase 7)

3.2   Manual for developing a case conceptualization of giftedness

3.2.1   Features of a case conceptualization

This section discusses a practical model of a case conceptualization. Abstractly, a person receives an *input* in the form of a stimulus (S), the experience of which is influenced by the person or organism (O means intra-organism), leading to an *output* in the form of a reaction (R, an emotion or behavior) that has consequences (C, consequences). This is known as the SORC model.

The SORC model forms the *horizontal* line in the case conceptualization model. This model provides a functional analysis for both the core behavior and the symptom or problem behavior. Each behavior is the focus of a functional analysis. This immediately allows for multiple functional analyses and multiple partial treatment plans for the individual core and symptom behaviors. This helps enormously in the *problem selection phase* and in ordering the implementation of the partial treatment plans.

The timeline is the *vertical* line of the model. There are three categories: 'early', 'middle', and 'late'. This three-way division is based on Hermans et al. (2018). At the top is *early*: the learning history of how the symptom behaviors and core behaviors were learned through conditioning. This is also known as the historical case conceptualization and is divided into ten-year periods.

Below this is *middle*: current and recent situations that affect the core behavior. These are current and recent situations of support and stress. At the bottom is the *late*: here the specific trigger of the symptom and the background stress are linked to the current symptom behavior in a functional analysis.

The balance of advantages and disadvantages becomes more negative and the functioning less adequate with the onset or worsening of symptoms, such as depressive withdrawal or anxious avoidance behavior. This is the moment when clients are often referred for therapy. This is because, in addition to the disadvantages of the core behavior, their symptomatic behavior now has more disadvantages and fewer advantages; they are "in the red" in terms of energy.

The short definition of giftedness as a high-frequency, trans-situational, and trans-temporal core behavior of rapid and creative solution-finding is integrated into this model of a case conceptualization (Table 3.2). The timeline or trans-temporal aspect is accommodated vertically, and the trans-situational aspect is accommodated horizontally in the 'middle' category.

The O-factor can be filled in with the personal coping style, the general traits of the Five-Factor Model, the 12 groups of personality traits of the DSM-5 classification, the pathological traits of the DSM-5, the core cognitions (Beck et al., 2003, Table 2.5) and schemas (Young et al., 2003), the core theme, temperament, the personality dysfunctions of the DSM-5 (identity, self-direction, empathy, and intimacy), somatic, and intelligence. This incorporates the dimensional DSM-5 into the case conceptualization. Building a case conceptualization requires a system and

Table 3.2 General model of a case conceptualization of giftedness and personality traits

	S	O	R	C
early	• trauma • support • models • unilateral (learning) situations	O	emotional/behavioral response	disadvantages/ advantages (reinforcements)
middle	• stress • support	O	• core behavior • general giftedness combined with core behavior of specific personality traits	disadvantages/ advantages
late	specific symptom trigger	O	symptom behavior/ problem behavior	disadvantages/ advantages

Table 3.3 The process of building a case conceptualization

I. late	R	>	S	>	C	>	O
II. early	S	>	R	>	C	>	O
III. middle	R	>	S	>	C	>	O

a sequence for filling in the cells. This sequence is shown in Table 3.3. The following subsection elaborates on these three series or steps.

3.2.2   Building a case conceptualization

Case study Madeleine Clergyman

Madeleine Clergyman is 45 years old and contacts the practice with a request for a personality analysis for previously diagnosed giftedness following complaints of depression. The client grew up in the South Netherlands as the eldest child in a large Catholic family. Her childhood was overshadowed by her father's illness, he was diagnosed with multiple sclerosis when she was 12 years old. Her youngest sister has Down's syndrome. To make matters worse, her younger brother had to undergo lengthy rehabilitation after a serious car accident. As the eldest, she had to take care of the 'little ones'. She always felt tension and an underlying fear of her father's illness.

Madeleine studied law initially, followed by a degree from the academy for art and design. She enjoyed student life immensely, but often felt lonely and different. As an associate in a large law firm, she excelled because of her empathy and intelligence. It was here that she met her husband, a widower with two children. She stopped working after the birth of their first child. Her husband is a director of a large company, and they have a good life together, including materially. She describes him as stable, loyal, and cheerful. However, he does not really understand her intensity and sensitivity.

What has been bothering her for some time is her giftedness, her intense way of feeling and reacting, and her fast rate of thinking. When she was 23, she was a member of Mensa for a short time. Although she liked the confirmation of her high IQ, she often found the members too introverted and did not feel a connection. Now she is seeking therapy for her depressive symptoms and to clarify for herself what kind of meaningful and creative work she could do in the future.

On the Mental Health Index (see Section 2.4.5), Madeleine scores 1–1–1–2; she is thus a healthy person with moderate limitations (2) in intimacy, specifically that there is insufficient reciprocity in intimate relationships. She has the giving position without receiving reciprocal support, attention, and understanding, and she does not experience deep connection in her friendships. She also has all ten characteristics of giftedness.

Her Five-Factor profile is Nav. E+ O+ A+ C+. She has average emotional stability and is very open, extroverted, friendly, and conscientious. Descriptively, she has obsessive-compulsive and theatrical traits with complaints of a mild depressive disorder, intimacy problems, and creative stagnation.

With a score of 14 out of 23 on Aron's screener (Aron, 1996), high sensitivity is evident. On the Schema Questionnaire she scores high on self-sacrifice and high on ruthlessness and entitlement. On the RSES (Rosenberg, 1965) she scores high on self-esteem, indicating high self-confidence. There are no outliers on the abbreviated pathological traits scale (PID-5), which means that she has no pathological traits.

Madeleine's case is shown in Figure 3.1 in the scheme of case conceptualization.

The creation of a case conceptualization is further illustrated below using this case study.

I.   Late

We start with the 'R-late' cell, which is the symptom/problem behavior. Here we describe in behavioral terms all the symptom disorders, based on the assessment of behavior.

POSSIBLE CATEGORIES OF SYMPTOM BEHAVIOR

- anxious avoidant behavior
- aggressive attacking behavior
- depressive withdrawal behavior
- bipolar approaching or attacking behavior
- addictive approach behavior (addictions, eating disorders, paraphilias)
- avoidance behavior of too many stimuli behavior (chronic fatigue syndrome [CFS] and burnout)
- hyperactive, distractible behavior (ADHD)
- bipolar approach behavior
- psychotic behavior

POSSIBLE CATEGORIES OF PROBLEM BEHAVIOR

- attachment problems
- partner choice problems
- partner relationship problems
- work choice problems
- creative stagnation
- difficulties making friends
- relationship problems at work

	S	O	R (CER/CAR)	C
EARLY	Learning history			
0–10 jr	eldest child sister with Down syndrome brother gets into an accident school is easy, makes an impression	gifted	caring

adapting | + appreciation
- exhaustion

+ appreciation
- focus too much on others |
| 10–20 | 12 years old - father diagnosed with MS extrovert and quick at school and as a student 18 years old - law school | | make an impression | **+ admiring attention**
- too externally focused |
| 20–30 | College of Art 23 years old – joins Mensa work in a legal office | creative | creating solutions quickly and creatively | + appreciation,
+ acceptance
- too independent
- to be ahead of others |
| 30–40 | marriage blended family first child housewife | self-sacrifice | | |
| 40–50 | 45 years old - housewife | a need for depth and intimacy | depressive withdrawal | + saving energy
+ reflection
- brooding, stress
- feeling lonely |
| **MIDDLE** | Stress or support, expected or actual | Coping, traits, core cognitions, etc. | Core behavior | Balance of costs (-) and benefits (+) |
| | *Stress*
1. illness in the family

2. abandonment

3. being ignored

4. fascinating **situation**

Support
husband | *Coping style*
proactive compensation surrender

Pathological traits DSM-5*
none

General DSM-5-traits
histrionic and compulsive traits

Five factors
N-E+O+A+C+

Core cognitions/ Schemas
self- sacrifice emotional deprivation vulnerability to harm and illness unrelenting standards

Core theme
illness in family attention seeking | 1. caring

2. adapting

3. make an impression

4. creating solutions quickly and creatively | + appreciation
- exhaustion

+ appreciation
- focused too much on others

+ admiring attention
- too externally focused

+ appreciation,
+ acceptance
- too independent
- be ahead of others |
| **LATE** | Specific symptom triggers | | Symptomatic behavior | Balance of costs (-) and benefits (+) |
| | *Specific symptom triggers*
midlife and no mean-ingful work, lack of intimacy

Background stress
illness in family of origin | *Interaction diagnosis*
above/together excessive and ambivalent attachment

Temperament
NS+HA-RD+ histrionic temperament

Dysfunctional personality*
identity 1 self-direction 1 empathy 1 intimacy 2

Somatics
none

Intelligence
high | 5. depressive withdrawal

6. lack of intimacy

7. creative stagnation | + saving energy
+ reflection
- brooding, stress
- feeling alone

+ own desires
+ new relationship goals

+ new life goals
+ reflection
- frustration, stress |

Figure 3.1 Example of a case conceptualization with a gifted client

The second step is to consider the situations (S) in which the symptom/problem behavior occurs. The consequences (C) are the third step and involve the benefits and disadvantages of the symptom/problem behavior. These can be divided into consequences within the person, such as anxiety reduction, as well as how the environment responds, such as support or rejection. The fourth step is to fill in the many categories of O, the internal factors. See Section 3.2.1 for the description of the O factor from personal coping style to intelligence.

The order of completion is summarized: R > S > C > O (for an example, see Table 3.4).

POINTS TO CONSIDER WHEN COMPLETING THE LATE

- Use keywords.
- Work horizontally ('park' your vertical ideas).
- There is often more than one symptom behavior; a rule of thumb is one to four.
- Distinguishing between core and symptom/problem behaviors can be difficult, but make a choice.
- Put your diagnostic findings that are identical for the cell O-late and O-middle into the O-factor. See also Step III. Middle.

II. Early

We start with the cell 'S-early' and fill in all the situations that have influenced the person's development. These include examples from father, mother, and grandparents (modeling), the behavior of siblings towards the client, traumas and peak experiences, stress and support, the behavior of peers at school or work towards the client, and the behavior of friends and later partners and children. This learning history is divided into periods of ten years up to the present time.

The second step is to fill in the 'R-early' cell, responding with feelings and behaviors, with symptoms and with core developing behaviors. The third step is the consequences (C) of responding in this way. This is where patterns of reinforcement become apparent, as well as excessive or insufficient learning of certain core behaviors (see Section 2.6). The fourth step is to fill in the many categories of O, the internal factors present in the person.

The order is summarized as follows: S > R > C > O (for an example see Table 3.5).

POINTS TO CONSIDER FOR COMPLETION OF EARLY

- Are there any gaps in the learning history that need to be reviewed?
- Is any other additional assessment needed, for example, developmental?
- Use key words.
- Work horizontally ('park' your vertical ideas).

Table 3.4 Example of a 'late' row according to the SORC model

S	O	R (symptom behavior)	C
Stress	*Coping style*		
1. illness in the family	proactive compensation of schemas	5. depressive withdrawal	+ saving energy + reflection
2. abandonment	schema surrender		− brooding, stress
3. being ignored			− feeling alone
4. fascinating situation	*Pathological traits DSM-5* none	6. lack of intimacy	+ own desires + new relationship goals
	General DSM-5 traits histrionic and compulsive traits	7. creative stagnation	+ new life goals + reflection
	Five factors N-E+O+A+C+		− frustration, stress
	Core cognitions/Schemas self-sacrifice emotional deprivation vulnerability to harm and illness unrelenting standards		
	Core theme illness in family seeking attention		
	Interaction diagnosis above/together excessive and ambivalent attachment		
	Temperament NS+HA-RD+ histrionic temperament		
	Dysfunctional personality * identity 1 self-direction 1 empathy 1 intimacy 2		
	Somatics none		
	Intelligence high		

Table 3.5 Example of an 'early' row according to the SORC model

S	O	R (core behavior)	C
eldest child sister with Down syndrome		caring	+ appreciation − exhaustion
brother gets into an accident school is easy, makes an impression	gifted	adapting	+ appreciation − focus too much on others
12 years old − father diagnosed with MS extrovert and quick at school and as a student		make an impression	+ admiring attention − too externally focused
18 years old − law school College of Art	creative	creating solutions quickly and creatively	+ appreciation, + acceptance − too independent − to be ahead of others
23 years old − joins Mensa work in a legal office marriage blended family first child 45 years old − housewife	self-sacrifice	depressive withdrawal	+ saving energy + reflection − brooding, stress − feeling lonely

III. Middle

In this row, the cell 'R-middle', the *core behavior*, is filled in first. In addition to the general core behavior of creative problem solving, there are several specific core behaviors that need to be screened and identified (see also Sections 2.4.2, 2.6, and 3.3). The second step is to identify, in descending order of frequency, which situations trigger these core behaviors. A good rule of thumb is to include one to three specific core behaviors (top 3) in the case conceptualization. The third step is to identify the consequences (C) of the core behaviors (see Section 3.3). The fourth step is to fill in the many categories of O, the internal factors present within the person. See the description above of the O factors from personal coping style to intelligence.

The order of completion is summarized below: R > S > C > O (for an example, see Table 3.6).

POINTS TO CONSIDER WHEN COMPLETING MIDDLE

- Use keywords.
- There are often several core behaviors; a rule of thumb is 1 to 3 (maximum 4).
- Giftedness includes the core behavior of finding solutions quickly and creatively.
- It may be difficult to distinguish between core and symptom/problem behaviors.
- Go through the many categories of the O-factor which are identical for the cell O-middle and O-late. See also Step I, Late.
- Create case conceptualization, functional analyses, and (partial) treatment plans.

Table 3.6 Example of a 'middle' row according to the SORC model

S	O	R (core behavior)	C
Stress 1.illness in the family	*Coping style* proactive compensation surrender	1.caring	+ appreciation − exhaustion
2.abandonment	*Pathological traits* DSM-5	2.adapting	+ appreciation − too much focus on others
3.being ignored	none	3.impress	+ admiring attention
	General DSM-5-traits histrionic and compulsive traits		− too externally focused + appreciation
4.stimulating situation		4.creating solutions quickly and creatively	+ acceptance − too independent − be ahead of others
	Five factors N-E+O+A+C+		
	Core cognitions/Schemas self-sacrifice emotional deprivation vulnerability to harm and illness unrelenting standards		
	Core theme illness in family attention seeking		
	Interaction diagnosis above/together excessive and ambivalent attachment		
	Temperament NS+HA-RD+ histrionic temperament		
	Dysfunctional personality identity 1 self-direction 1 empathy 1 intimacy 2		
	Somatics none		
	Intelligence high		

In the case study of Madeleine Clergyman, seven functional analyses are given:

1 Caring
2 Adapting
3 Making an impression
4 Creating solutions quickly and creatively
5 Depressive withdrawal behavior
6 Intimacy deficit
7 Creative stagnation

Seven (sub-) treatment plans can be formulated; a protocol is available for symptom behavior 5 (Barlow et al., 2017; Keijsers et al., 2011) and for core behaviors 1, 2, 3, and 4. See treatment plans in Sections 4.1.1 and 4.1.2.

3.3 Choice of functional analysis of dual core behavior in giftedness in combination with personality traits

Dual core behavior is an important concept in giftedness. Giftedness involves general core behaviors combined with specific personality traits and specific core behaviors. The general core behavior of gifted people is to create solutions quickly and creatively, and this is colored by the specific personality traits, for example, avoidant or obsessive traits.

Figure 3.2 shows the functional analysis of general giftedness.

COMMENTARY

In addition to content, the process of feeling and the process of thinking are particularly important in the general functional analysis of giftedness. The content of thoughts and feelings is colored by the functional analysis of specific personality traits.

Table 2.5 shows the core behaviors (main strategies) of the specific personality traits. For example, a client with histrionic traits is over-the-top, exaggerates, and is charming, whereas a client with schizoid traits is distant and a client with avoidant traits avoids feelings or social situations. These core behaviors have a clear function. A functional analysis is a hypothesis about both the eliciting and maintaining factors of certain behaviors and, in the case of personality traits, the core behaviors associated with these traits. Functional analyses of obsessive-compulsive and narcissistic personality traits are illustrated here.

TRIGGERING EVENT
(CS/sd)
complex and
engaging situation

thinking process
fast, complex, highly
associative, divergent,
creative, and autonomous

behavior (CAR)
thinking up quick and creative
solutions

thoughts (COV)
- I am autonomous, quick
  thinking, and creative
- I am different from others
- I am curious and have many
  and intense interests
- I am responsible
- I need to be competent
- everything has to be
  perfect and fair
- I want to make things (the
  world) better
- I want to be fair and just (or
  am disillusioned)
- I am clever but lack social,
  sporting, or artistic skills
- different rules apply to me
- others are different,
  smarter or less smart,
  jealous or admiring, more
  social or sporty
- it is not possible for me to
  just be normal and
  participate
- I am an exception and I am
  not one of them
- others exclude me
- others don't like me
- others find me strange

consequences (C)
advantages
+C+ pride, self-esteem
+C+ appreciation,
     acceptance, admiration
     from others
+C+ satisfaction, flow, kick
+C+ creativity
-C- dullness diminishes

disadvantages
-C+ less sense of belonging
-C+ others drop out
+C- negative reactions
     from others, insecurity,
     jealousy, irritation
0C+ no resistance
+C- social isolation
+C- lack of understanding
+C- haste, impatience
+C- stress, tiredness
+C- frustration,
     dissatisfaction

emotional process
intense, usually overexcitable,
and highly sensitive

feeling (CER)
driven, intense excitement,
stress, fear of failure

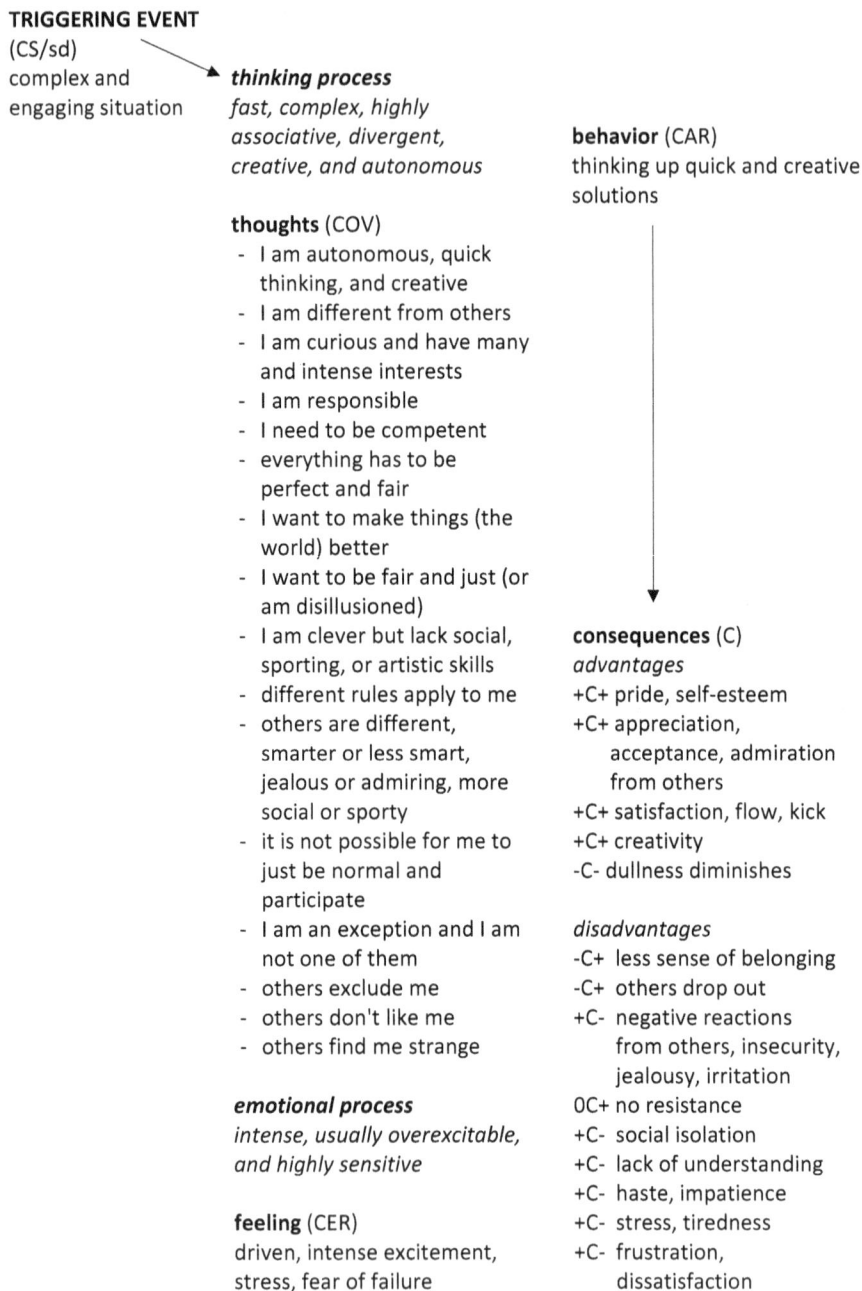

Figure 3.2 Functional analysis (general) of giftedness

Case study Joannie Bead

Joannie Bead is 40 years old and reports symptoms of burnout. She is very worried about her children, 10-year-old twins, who, since her divorce live with her and her ex-husband alternately. She also struggles to control her eating (binge eating) and drinking, although she is very disciplined in other areas. Sometimes she is overwhelmed by vague anxieties.

She grew up as the only child of an older father with bipolar disorder who was periodically explosive and aggressive. He was a bank manager and was feared for his impatience and sharpness. Her mother, a housewife, could offer little in the way of resistance or family structure. She idealized her friends' families.

Joannie was well suited to the Montessori method of education. She did her homework on time and almost flawlessly. This left her time to pursue her passion for drawing cartoons. Due to her fear of failure, she scored low on her assessment test at the end of primary education, but still received a high recommendation for secondary school.

She appeared to combine her schoolwork with gymnastics at a high level with ease. In reality, however, the combination was too hard and, partly due to family stress, she became overburdened in her final exam class. She was excused from attending classes and by studying at home was able to pass her final exams with flying colors. She did not choose to go to college but chose a teacher training program because she felt it was more structured. She found the course to be inferior and decided to start a jewelry business with a very good friend after graduation. This became a great success, partly due to her creativity and taste.

The behavior of clients with obsessive-compulsive traits is characterized by excessive effort. When faced with a triggering event (CS/Sd) such as imminent, imagined, or actual failure, this client becomes anxious, irritable, guilty, and gloomy (CER). This client will think that they are responsible and competent and that others are sloppy and will assume that if anything goes wrong it will be a disaster and that it will be their fault (COVs). These thoughts lead them to try even harder. The consequences (C) support this behavior and reinforce perfectionist behavior: these clients feel valued by others and feel increased self-esteem, a positive consequence

that increases (+C+), as well as avoiding criticism and failure, a negative consequence that decreases (−C−). Because of these benefits, compulsive behaviors can
become 'addictive' and persist, becoming stronger and stronger. This vicious circle
can sometimes be broken by a favorable environment. More often, long-term CBT
is required. Figure 3.3 summarizes the above.

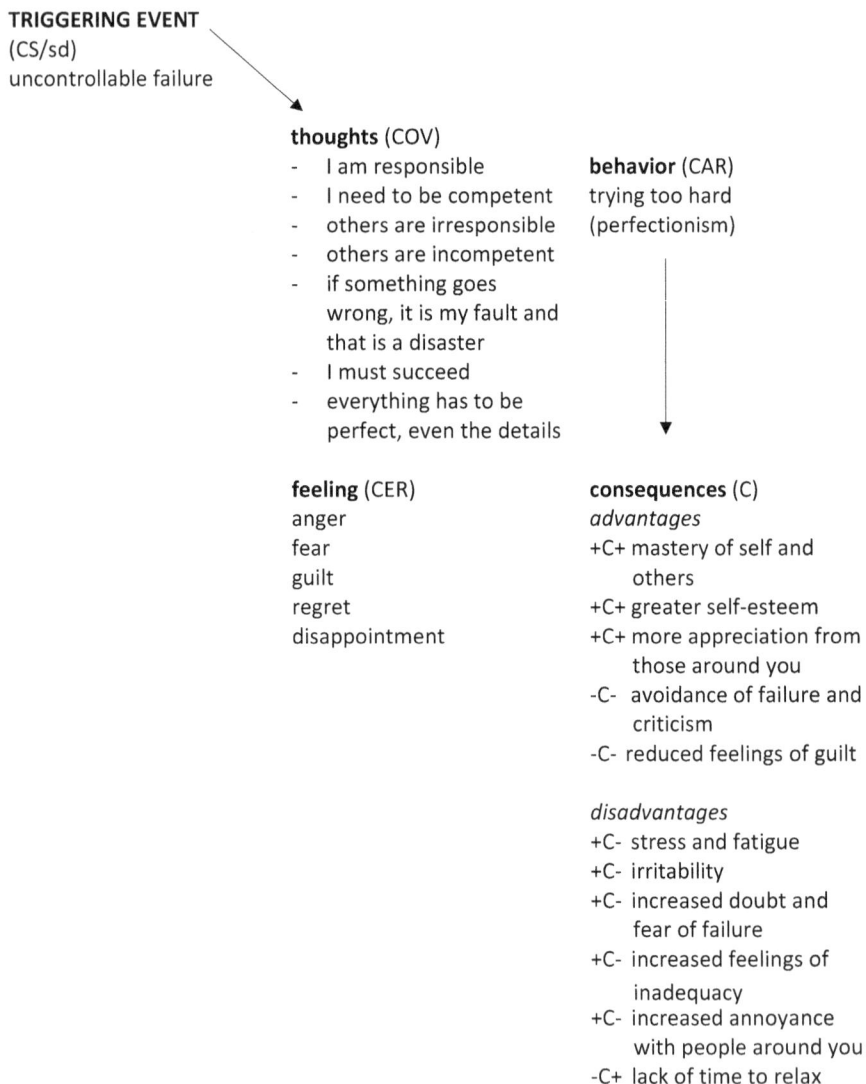

TRIGGERING EVENT
(CS/sd)
uncontrollable failure

thoughts (COV)

- I am responsible
- I need to be competent
- others are irresponsible
- others are incompetent
- if something goes
  wrong, it is my fault and
  that is a disaster
- I must succeed
- everything has to be
  perfect, even the details

behavior (CAR)
trying too hard
(perfectionism)

feeling (CER)
anger
fear
guilt
regret
disappointment

consequences (C)
advantages
+C+ mastery of self and
      others
+C+ greater self-esteem
+C+ more appreciation from
      those around you
-C- avoidance of failure and
      criticism
-C- reduced feelings of guilt

disadvantages
+C- stress and fatigue
+C- irritability
+C- increased doubt and
      fear of failure
+C- increased feelings of
      inadequacy
+C- increased annoyance
      with people around you
-C+ lack of time to relax

Figure 3.3 Functional analysis of obsessive-compulsive personality traits

Case study Remco Bread

Remco Bread graduated from university two years ago. He starts treatment for a generalized anxiety disorder. He is tired, physically tense, and chronically worried about almost everything. He is very critical of himself. He sees himself as someone who can do a lot and has a great future, but that in reality he is unable to achieve any of this. He considers himself serious and enjoys philosophical and deep conversations. He has been repeatedly turned down for jobs for which he has applied, which gives him a constant sense of humiliation. When the therapist looks at his attitude in a role play of an interview situation, his behavior is downright devaluing. He is condescending towards and critical of the people on the interview panel, adopting the attitude of: 'It's pure coincidence that you are sitting on the other side of the table, I could have just as easily been sitting there. It is a coincidence that you are inside and I am still outside'. He comes across as extremely critical. When he is rejected he even considers lodging a complaint about the procedure. This interaction has happened repeatedly over the past two years, leading to Remco becoming depressed. As a result he is more open to feedback from the therapist. The therapist discusses his behavior and explores the reasons for his devaluing attitude. The repeated rejection of a job application touches on a core theme of humiliation. The client reacts with pride, but also with jealousy, and from this feeling he begins to devalue the other person. The admiration he feels for himself suppresses the core theme of humiliation. One of the consequences of his devaluing behavior is that the environment reacts negatively. The hiring committee does not welcome a difficult employee who is also highly narcissistic, and it uses its power to reject him. The appreciation and admiration for the talents that this academic certainly possesses are not expressed, and his anger, frustration and, in the long run, depression increase (see the functional analysis in Figure 3.4). He believes that others should admire him and not criticize him. He also thinks he is so special that he is entitled to special treatment and should be hired without an application process.

COMMENTARY

The gifted client with narcissistic traits (Beck et al., 2003) has as a core behavior the elevation of oneself and devaluation of others. This leads to taking advantage of, using, or competing with others. This behavior is triggered by both admiration from others and feeling hurt by others, real or perceived. Admiration evokes feelings of pride and hurt evokes feelings of anger and envy. The client with narcissistic personality traits thinks that he or she is unique, special, and superior to others, who are inferior and jealous of their special status. The client thinks that they do not have to play by the rules and that they are entitled to special treatment, even in therapy. These feelings and thoughts lead to devaluing behavior, behavior which has the benefit of affirming the client's uniqueness and superiority and avoiding any feelings of being hurt. The disadvantages are that the environment often reacts negatively, and the client becomes increasingly dependent on their own and others' admiration. This leads to increasing compensatory behavior, increasing anger and, in the long term, the risk of depression. If the advantages are greater than the disadvantages, these consequences are reinforced and perpetuate the core behavior. Figure 3.4 shows the functional analysis of narcissistic personality traits in general terms.

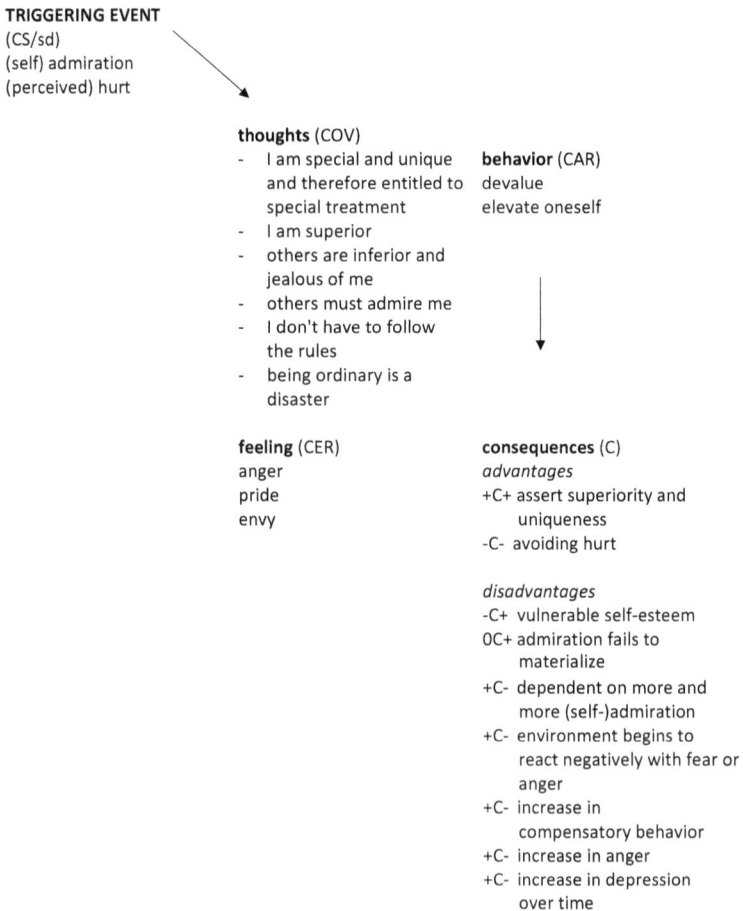

TRIGGERING EVENT
(CS/sd)
(self) admiration
(perceived) hurt

thoughts (COV)
- I am special and unique
  and therefore entitled to
  special treatment
- I am superior
- others are inferior and
  jealous of me
- others must admire me
- I don't have to follow
  the rules
- being ordinary is a
  disaster

behavior (CAR)
devalue
elevate oneself

feeling (CER)
anger
pride
envy

consequences (C)
advantages
+C+ assert superiority and
     uniqueness
-C- avoiding hurt

disadvantages
-C+ vulnerable self-esteem
0C+ admiration fails to
     materialize
+C- dependent on more and
     more (self-)admiration
+C- environment begins to
     react negatively with fear or
     anger
+C- increase in
     compensatory behavior
+C- increase in anger
+C- increase in depression
     over time

Figure 3.4 Functional analysis of narcissistic personality traits

For the 11 different groups of personality traits or personality disorders in the DSM-5, see Section 2.4.2. Every person has personality traits, usually a mixture of different traits. A personality disorder is present only when the personality traits become dominant and one-sided and the balance of pros and cons weighs negatively (see Section 2.4.1). There is therefore a continuum from personality trait to personality disorder without a clear distinction.

Because many personality disorders are 'mixtures', they have several core behaviors that occur with varying frequency in reality. A practical recommendation is to rank the core behaviors in order of frequency and then to focus on the top three or at most four core behaviors. These are the core behaviors that will be the focus of treatment and will be reflected in the therapeutic relationship, and each of them needs a functional analysis and a (partial) treatment plan. For example, a client has avoidant, depressive, and narcissistic traits and a top three of corresponding core behaviors in descending frequency.

3.4   The dual core theme of giftedness

The human organism reacts meaningfully to a meaningful situation (definition of learning according to Hermans et al. [2018]). Why one person always reacts in an antisocial and aggressive way and another is submissive and dependent can be understood from the individual's temperament, learning history, and current cognitions and personality traits. A core theme is constructed as a result of many similar experiences. This provides a 'verbal label' that indicates the type of emotional experience that has occurred repeatedly and is stored in emotional memory (Lang, 1985).

The case study of Remco Bread in Section 3.3 is an illustration of the analysis for narcissistic personality traits. This is a client with narcissistic personality traits who has experienced a lot of humiliation in his past. This core theme of humiliation causes him to react with anger to any perceived hurt or when he is not treated with complete respect and the expected admiration is not forthcoming. Admiration is therefore an inhibitory stimulus, a situation that prevents the core theme of humiliation in the emotional memory from being triggered. Hurt, on the other hand, is an excitatory stimulus that leads to feelings of anger and rivalry and to devaluing behavior by arousing and further stimulating the core theme of humiliation.

Case study Peter Eastman

Peter Eastman is in his early fifties and head of accounting. He has very critical parents. He never learned to be satisfied with himself and always tried very hard. His father was hot-tempered and did not tolerate any resistance or even a simple 'no'. As a result, Peter never did resist and is always there for everyone. This has led to complaints of overwork and burnout. Peter does his best in every situation to avoid uncontrollable failure. He is always anxiously tense and annoyed when others are casual and sloppy, but is afraid to say anything about it, which adds to his tension. When a new computer system is introduced at work, which he can no longer supervise, and his unreliable, alcohol-addicted director blames him for a failed project, he collapses and ends up on sick leave. His core issue has been activated, and his compensatory behavior of doing his best is no longer adequate.

COMMENTARY

Peter is a client with obsessive-compulsive personality traits in which failure and uncontrollability are core themes. These are evoked by situations in which he is in danger of failing or being out of control.

The core theme of uncontrollability is inhibited by functioning flawlessly and perfectly. When the core theme is activated, the client reacts with anxiety and annoyance and his behavior is to try even harder.

The consequences are the same as those mentioned in the functional analysis of obsessive-compulsive personality traits (see Section 3.3).

3.5   From functional analysis to treatment plan and problem selection

A cognitive behavioral therapy (CBT) treatment plan contains concrete treatment goals and techniques to achieve these goals (see also Sections 4.1 and 4.2). These goals are concrete and realistic and are determined in part by the baseline assessment. The baseline assessment determines the frequency and severity of complaints, core beliefs, core feelings, or core behaviors at the start of therapy. It is a measurement that precedes the implementation of the treatment plan. Baseline assessment allows for evaluation after the implementation of the technique during the implementation phase of therapy.

There are five types of treatment goals:

1 reduction of symptoms
2 self-acceptance of giftedness
3 increasing coping skills
4 changing core cognitions, personality traits, or personality disorder
5 reinforcing therapy-supportive behaviors

For the client with giftedness and specific personality traits, all five goals are necessary and important. A therapy plan is based on both the case conceptualization of general giftedness and specific personality traits in addition to the scientific research literature, because the empirically proven effectiveness of a technique is important.

For example, scientific research shows that exposure and COMET (Competitive Memory Training) are effective for anxiety. EMDR (Eye Movement Desensitization and Reprocessing) has been shown to be effective for trauma and trauma-related anxiety. If the core cognition of a particular client with a personality disorder is of an anxious nature, we can use these techniques: exposure for expectancy anxiety and EMDR for anxiety with a traumatic onset (Stöfsel & Mooren, 2015).

Good and effective treatments have been developed for negative view of self, such as De Neef's positivity journal (2015).

Mindfulness or mindfulness combined with stress reduction or cognitive therapy works well for chronic pain and negative emotions (Kabat-Zinn, 1990/2004), for anxiety disorders (Brantley, 2014), to prevent relapse for recurrent depression (Mark et al., 2007; Segal et al., 2018), and for destructive thoughts and feelings and a lack of self-compassion (Germer, 2009).

The treatment plan and techniques are discussed in Chapter 4.

Reference list

Aron, E. N. (1996). *The highly sensitive person – how to thrive when the world overwhelms you*. Carol Publishing Group

Barlow, D. H., Farchione, T. J., Bullis, J. R., Gallagher, M. W., Murray-Latin, H., Sauer-Zavala, S., Bentley, K. H., Thompson-Hollands, J., Conklin, L. R., Boswell, J. F., Ametaj, A., Carl, J. R., Boettcher, H. T., & Cassiello-Robbins, C. (2017). The unified protocol for transdiagnostic treatment of emotional disorders compared with diagnosis-specific protocols for anxiety disorders: A randomized clinical trial. *JAMA Psychiatry, 74*(9), 875–884.

Beck, A. T., Freeman, A., Davis, D. D., Arntz, A., Beck, J. S., Butler, A. C., Fleming, B., Fusco, G., Morrison, A. P., Padesky, C. A., Pretzer, J. L., Renton, J., Simon, K. M. (2003). *Cognitive therapy of personality disorders* (2nd ed.). Guilford Press.

Brantley, J. (2014). *Angst beheersen met mindfulness: Hoe aandacht en compassie je kunnen bevrijden van angst en paniek*. Nieuwezijds.

Brinkman, W. (1978). Het gedragstherapeutisch proces. In J. W. G. Orlemans, P. Eelen & W. P. Haaijman (Eds.), *Handboek voor gedragstherapie (H. A1 t/m A14)*. Van Loghum Slaterus.

De Neef, M. (2015). *Build your confidence with CBT*. Open University Press.

Germer, C. (2009). *The mindful path to self-compassion: Freeing yourself from destructive thoughts and emotions*. The Guildford Press.

Hermans, D., Raes, F., & Orlemans, H. (2018). *Inleiding tot de gedragstherapie* (7th ed.). Bohn Stafleu van Loghum.

Kabat-Zinn, J. (1990/2004). *Full catastrophe living*. The Bantam Dell Publishing Group.

Keijsers, G. P. J., Van Minnen, A., & Hoogduin, C. A. L. (2011). *Protocollaire behandelingen voor volwassenen met psychische klachten, deel 1 en 2*. Boom.

Lang, P. J. (1985). The cognitive psychophysiology of emotions: Fear and anxiety. In A. H. Tuma & J. D. Maser (Eds.), *Anxiety and the anxiety disorders*. Lawrence Erlbaum Associates.

Mark, J., Williams, G., Teasdale, J. D., Zindel, V., & Kabat-Zinn, J. (2007). *The mindful way through depression: Freeing yourself from chronic unhappiness*. Guilford Press.

Rosenberg, M. (1965). *Society and the adolescent self-image*. Princeton University Press.

Schacht, R., De Raedt, R., & Rijnders, P. (2007). Evidence-based stepped care in de gedragstherapeutische praktijk. *Gedragstherapie, 40*, 85–110.

Segal, Z. F., Williams, J. M. G., & Teasdale, J. D. (2018). *Mindfulness-based cognitive therapy for depression*. Guilford Press.

Stöfsel, M., & Mooren, T. (2015). *Diagnosing and treating complex trauma*. Oxfordshire: Routledge.

Young, J. E., Klosko, J. S., & Weishaar, M. E. (2003). *Schema therapy: A practitioner's guide*. Guilford Press.

Cognitive behavioral therapy for giftedness and personality

Treatment plan, techniques, and process

Summary

Chapter 4 addresses the implementation and evaluation of cognitive behavioral therapy (CBT) for giftedness. We examine the process of problem selection for clients with giftedness and also with specific personality traits. The therapy is based on a concrete treatment plan that includes specific goals as well as techniques adapted for giftedness. The treatment plan builds on the case conceptualization, which includes functional analyses of the symptom behaviors and core behaviors of giftedness and specific personality traits. Many well-known psychotherapeutic techniques can be adapted to giftedness and high sensitivity.

4.1 Treatment plan and problem selection for giftedness

The treatment plan formulates the concrete goals for treatment and the chosen techniques to achieve these goals. Section 4.1.1 and Table 4.1 describe the five foci of a cognitive behavioral functional analysis and, building on that, a general treatment plan for a client with giftedness. Section 4.1.2 provides a treatment plan for specific personality traits, another aspect of general giftedness.

Finally, Section 4.1.3 lists appropriate or adapted techniques for each goal. These concrete and specific therapy goals and techniques for the gifted can be seen as concrete suggestions for the creation of a treatment plan. Figure 4.1 shows the functional analysis of general giftedness.

A complex and engaging situation (S) stimulates 'content-related' thoughts (COV) and feelings (CER) through a gifted thought process and (often) a highly sensitive feeling process, which lead to core behaviors (CAR), which themselves have positive and negative consequences (C+ and C−) or advantages and disadvantages. This is a functional analysis.

4.1.1 General giftedness treatment plan

The treatment plan is based directly on the functional analysis with its five levels or intervention points. For each of the five levels, goals can be formulated with appropriate techniques. The treatment plan for giftedness is shown in Table 4.1.

DOI: 10.4324/9781003423287-5

Table 4.1 The treatment plan for giftedness

Starting point FA	Therapy goals	Techniques
triggering event (CS/Sd)	decrease the number of complex and engaging situations and the number and breadth of interests	temporary avoidance stop mechanism self-control response prevention
thought process	*simplify complexity slow down the fast, highly associative thinking from diverging to converging from autonomous to empathic*	task concentration training cognitive diary convergence training
thoughts (COV) content of specific features	improve view of self thoughts on specific traits	positive journaling, COMET cognitive therapy
feeling process	*intense usually overexcitable and highly sensitive*	de-intensifying desensitization recovery time
feeling (CER) generally	reduce the feeling of being driven and of intense arousal stress ▼ fear of failure ▼ impatience ▼	relaxation self-hypnosis EMDR mindfulness heart coherence
feeling (CER) related to specific traits	improve feelings related to specific traits	COMET relaxation hypnosis imaginary rescripting role play EMDR
behavior (CAR) create solutions quickly and creatively	improve creative stagnation create fewer problems but solve more	self-registration role play slow, attentive slowing down mindfulness self-exposure cognitive therapy
consequences (C)	reduce disadvantages increase advantages > see Functional Analysis	awareness and other forms of (self) validation to improve the balance of advantages and disadvantages

TRIGGERING EVENT
(CS/sd)
complex and
engaging situation

thinking process
fast, complex, highly
associative, divergent,
creative, and autonomous

behavior (CAR)
thinking up quick and creative
solutions

thoughts (COV)
- I am autonomous, quick
  thinking, and creative
- I am different from others
- I am curious and have many
  and intense interests
- I am responsible
- I need to be competent
- everything has to be
  perfect and fair
- I want to make things (the
  world) better
- I want to be fair and just (or
  am disillusioned)
- I am clever but lack social,
  sporting, or artistic skills
- different rules apply to me
- others are different,
  smarter or less smart,
  jealous or admiring, more
  social or sporty
- it is not possible for me to
  just be normal and
  participate
- I am an exception and I am
  not one of them
- others exclude me
- others don't like me
- others find me strange

consequences (C)
advantages
+C+ pride, self-esteem
+C+ appreciation,
     acceptance, admiration
     from others
+C+ satisfaction, flow, kick
+C+ creativity
-C- dullness diminishes

disadvantages
-C+ less sense of belonging
-C+ others drop out
+C- negative reactions
     from others, insecurity,
     jealousy, irritation
0C+ no resistance
+C- social isolation
+C- lack of understanding
+C- haste, impatience
+C- stress, tiredness
+C- frustration,
     dissatisfaction

emotional process
intense, usually overexcitable,
and highly sensitive

feeling (CER)
driven, intense excitement,
stress, fear of failure

Figure 4.1 Functional analysis (general) of giftedness

4.1.2 Treatment plan for specific personality traits

In the treatment plan, specific goals are formulated and the techniques to achieve these goals chosen. Table 4.2 describes the five foci of the cognitive behavioral model with specific therapy goals for a client with obsessive-compulsive personality traits. Specific techniques that could be used to achieve each goal are also listed and are described in more detail in Section 4.2. These concrete and specific therapy goals and techniques can be seen as concrete suggestions for creating a treatment plan.

4.1.3 Problem selection in giftedness

The treatment plan includes the choice of problems to be treated and the order in which they will be treated (problem selection), based on the client's wishes and input regarding personality problems from the case conceptualization by the

Table 4.2 The treatment plan for obsessive-compulsive personality traits

Starting point	Therapy goals	Techniques
triggering event (CS/Sd)	failure lack of control	gradual exposure temporary avoidance stop mechanism
thoughts (COV)	• I am not solely responsible • others are also responsible and competent • making mistakes is a learning experience and not a disaster • I am good as I am • success is fun but not essential • criticism can be instructive and is often meant to be constructive	continuum techniques cognitive diary historical test pie chart technique IBSR (Inquiry-Based Stress Reduction)
feeling (CER)	fear of lack of control fear of failure counter theme: relaxation and control	downward arrow technique COMET relaxation IBSR hypnosis EMDR
behavior (CAR)	making mistakes reduce checking reduce overload	behavioral experiments role play response prevention self-exposure
consequences (C)	reduce disadvantages increase advantages > see Functional Analysis	awareness and other forms of (self) reinforcement

cognitive behavioral therapist. Guidelines for addressing problems include (Brinkman, 1978):

1 the probability value of the problem, that is, the extent to which client and therapist agree that the problem exists
2 the problematic value of the problem for the client
3 the centrality of the problem in the case conceptualization
4 the treatability of the problem

These four criteria will here be applied to giftedness. In the first place, the screening determines that there is probable giftedness (1). For the client, this is often an ambivalent surprise that may evoke disbelief and resistance. This requires the patient provision of psychoeducation and further diagnostic underpinning by the therapist. The client usually recognizes themselves in the case conceptualization and functional analysis which eventually leads the client to revise their view of themselves. The client may previously have seen themselves as 'just' clever or even as stupid, for example, because of a mathematical disorder (recognizing and manipulating numbers and symbols) or dyslexia. The functional analysis concretizes the problematic value (2) of giftedness for the client through their individual balance of advantages and disadvantages. The client is psychologically 'in the red', for example, through agonizing creative stagnation, through overwork or burnout, through success in performance but failure in personal relationships, or through not wanting to deviate from family members or fellow students. Giftedness is given a central position in the case conceptualization (3); it is literally inescapable. This includes personality traits or any personality disorder or recurrent depression. Treatability (4) is closely related to the individual functional analysis and thus to the longer-term balance of advantages and disadvantages.

The client can choose to work on specific personality traits or symptoms or to accept their general level of giftedness and reduce the accompanying disadvantages.

In giftedness, the following are commonly chosen therapy goals:

• Overcome creative stagnation and become aware of and realize values.
• Develop autonomy and the ability to be critical.
• Reduce rapid and multifaceted thinking and the tendency to complicate and learn to simplify.
• Reduce social isolation.
• Make choices in partners, friends, and work more based on feeling.
• Increase awareness and improve interaction problems.
• Improve negative view of self.
• Make an overvalued (unjustifiably positive or unstable) view of self more realistic.
• Improve awareness and acceptance, and better coping with high sensitivity (OE) and intense feelings.

- Slow down when feeling driven.
- Take time to recover from overstimulation.
- Reduce impatience
- Replace negative coping with positive coping.
- Set goals related to improving aspects of personality dysfunction.
- Change personality traits.
- Move from thinking autonomously to acting autonomously.
- Replace disillusionment with idealism.
- Reduce fear of failure.
- Reduce strong sense of responsibility.
- Improve difficulties with planning and concentration.

Creative stagnation and values

As the core behavior of the gifted person is to create solutions quickly, creative stagnation can be a painful and frustrating problem. It is therefore important to discuss and try to resolve this problem by raising the client's awareness of their personal values and life goals. An artist or writer who is blocked may become depressed about it, and depression can lead to stagnation. The personal value in this case may be a high aesthetic awareness rather than a materialistic orientation. This may be one reason why many artists do not manage their affairs well; it simply does not interest them.

Autonomy and critical thinking

Autonomy of thought and autonomy of action are personality traits of the gifted which often lead to social isolation, lack of understanding, and anxiety in the client as well as irritation for others. The gifted person's critical response is automatic and well-intentioned, which can lead to them being shunned and resisted, for example, in the workplace, so that their creative value is not utilized and stagnates (see above). Dealing with one's own autonomy and one's own high level of being critical is an important problem to be chosen. Insight is the first step towards changing behavior.

Moving from thinking autonomously to acting autonomously is another therapy goal. This is more common in intelligent women who are overly dependent on avoiding rejection and abandonment.

Quick and versatile thinking and divergence

Thinking quickly and laterally and having rapidly diverse associations make it difficult for the gifted and those around them to follow a common thread, leading to frustration and giving up. One solution is to increase the client's awareness of how difficult it is for others to follow them and of the addictive rush that creative divergence gives, and to learn to think more convergently.

Social isolation

Because of the large deviation from the statistical average IQ of 100, the group of IQ-matched people is very small. A gifted person with an IQ of 130 has only a small proportion of the population in the IQ range of 120–140 as potential partners or friends (Kuipers & Van Kempen, 2007). The risk of social isolation is therefore much higher for this gifted person than for a person with an IQ of 100, who has 66 per cent of the population with an IQ between 90 and 110 as a 'target group'.

Difficulties in choosing or keeping partners, friends, and work

Similar to or complementary with other personality traits, empathy and social need also appear to play a role in social isolation or contact. Similarity, like-mindedness and interest are of great importance in the social lives of gifted people. For this reason, however, gifted people are more likely to end up isolated in work situations and therefore to perform below their potential. For the same reasons, finding and keeping a partner is also very important and finding the right match in practice is often like looking for a needle in a haystack, despite the possibilities provided by the Internet.

Interaction problems

Specific personality traits and core behaviors lead to specific interaction problems. Narcissistic self-exaltation evokes admiration or, conversely, anger, resentment, or distancing. Perfectionism often provokes anger and criticism from others. General traits of giftedness also lead to interactional problems, which can strengthen or inhibit additional specific personality traits. Autonomous thinking is inhibited by and clashes with dependent traits and excessive conformity. Quick and versatile thinking and unusually broad interests reinforce obsessive traits and excessive striving. Autonomy of thought and action can reinforce schizoid traits and aloofness, increasing social isolation.

Quick thinking and impatient reactions create insecurity or irritation in others, leading to avoidance of the gifted as an aversive stimulus. Idealism and a strong sense of justice cause less scrupulous people in the environment to drop out and withdraw. High sensitivity to stimuli is not taken into consideration by people who have low sensitivity, which can also lead to withdrawal.

Negative view of self

People with a negative view of self are easy to identify. Many situations trigger negative cognitions in them – 'You see, I am worth nothing, I am stupid, I am unattractive, I do not belong' or 'You see, I am not seen'– and thus a negative feeling. A negative view of self causes much distress and makes people vulnerable (De Neef, 2015). It can lead to gloom or depression, loneliness, brooding, anxiety, eating problems, somatic complaints, substance abuse, or aggression.

A negative view of self is common in giftedness and very common in personality disorders. In Beck's table (see Table 2.5), the view of self in the paranoid, schizotypal, borderline, avoidant, dependent, and depressive personality disorders or personality traits is negative in terms of content and valence. Alongside symptomatic and core behaviors, a negative view of self is or should be a frequently selected problem for therapy. Highly sensitive gifted clients in particular often have (unprocessed) traumas that are difficult to work through (see EMDR, Section 4.2). There are also often negative and traumatic childhood experiences (including pre-verbal), a history of bullying and loneliness, factors that have led to a negative view of self.

Overvalued (unjustifiably positive or unstable) view of self

In addition to a negative view of self, overcompensation can lead to an overly positive or unstable view of self, fluctuating sharply from very positive and superior to inferior and overly negative. Gifted people with narcissistic traits are particularly prone to this.

Counter-conditioning with the COMET technique and building a stable foundation with the positivity journal technique or using IBSR can help to eliminate overcompensation and build a stable and appropriate positive view of self.

Relaxation while feeling driven

Intensity, quick thinking, and drive bring haste and impatience. Relaxation and slow (not sluggish) living – for example, through mindfulness, living with attention in the here and now, and regularly focusing on yourself for three minutes – are important preventative skills.

Recovery time from stimuli for hyper- and oversensitivity

Highly sensitive people process stimuli deeply and therefore become overstimulated more quickly than others. Personality traits will impact how a gifted person deals with this, for example, whether they take a break in time or go on for a long time without a recovery period. Compulsive traits, frequent perfectionism, *and a high sense of responsibility* are traits that could play a role. In addition, the fast thinking and intense and driven desire to create also make the gifted person vulnerable to being slow to take time to rest and recover. If being creative is enjoyable, the tendency will be to carry on for longer.

Negative forms of coping

Millon and Everly (1985) distinguish two types of coping: reactive and proactive (see Section 2.4.1). Young et al. (2003) speak of three ways of coping with schemas: surrender, avoidance, and compensation (see Section 2.7). Developing less one-sided coping, which leads to a better advantage/disadvantage balance, can be an important therapeutic goal (Webb, 2013).

Goals for improving personality dysfunction

Working on improving identity, self-directedness, empathy, and intimacy (for definitions of these, see the DSM-5, American Psychiatric Association, 2013) are important goals which can be explicitly included in a treatment plan.

With regard to empathy and intimacy, gifted individuals who are very focused on the well-being of others (the caregivers or do-gooders) may also find that they completely ignore themselves in their caregiving tasks and fail to monitor their boundaries, at the expense of their own rest and recovery time.

Reducing the fear of failure

Fear of failure may be related to narcissistic traits, the grandiosity of always understanding everything quickly and outperforming others, and the fear of the pain of 'defeat'.

The compulsive gifted person has many opportunities to survey the playing field quickly, making them aware that it is 'always' possible to do things better (perfectionism), creating feelings of inadequacy and being 'not good enough'.

Fear of failure is reduced by improving the ability to plan. The 'absent-minded professor' is a common type.

Changing personality traits

Changing personality traits is the aim of much cognitive behavioral therapy. This usually involves changing pathological traits (see Section 2.4.6), such as rigid perfectionism, anxiety, social isolation, attention-seeking, distractibility, and so on, to more balanced traits with a more positive balance of advantages and disadvantages.

4.2 Cognitive behavioral techniques adapted to giftedness and high sensitivity

Many well-known psychotherapeutic techniques (Keijsers et al., 2011; Barlow et al., 2017) can be adapted to giftedness and high sensitivity. Here are some suggestions.

4.2.1 De-intensification by self-registration

The client can register their own intensive behavior on a scale of 0 to 10. This raises awareness of how often, how long, and how intensely the client is concretely engaged in an engaging activity. Self-control techniques and cognitive therapy can then help.

4.2.2   Heart coherence

Heart coherence is a promising self-help technique which uses neurofeedback to facilitate learning to reduce stress and improve the stress mechanism (Servan-Schreiber, 2005, 2017).

4.2.3   Inquiry-based stress reduction according to Byron Katie

The work of Byron Katie is also known as inquiry-based stress reduction (IBSR). It involves meditative thought inquiry with (four) set questions and alternative state-ments aimed at disengaging the automatic emotional, physiological, physical, and behavioral responses to an event or situation, by allowing the client to discover that those responses are not the result of the event itself, but of the thoughts about that event. One aspect is to let the client experience that other and even opposite interpretations of that event are also possible and valid, undermining the belief in the thought (Katie & Mitchell, 2003; Coumar, 2024).

4.2.4   Positivity journal for a negative view of self

So how can a client's view of themself be improved? Fumbling around with the negative view of self, trying to negate the negative belief usually has no lasting effect. Installing and reinforcing an alternative and competitive positive schema bears more fruit (Brewin, 2006; De Neef, 2015). This treatment, which involves keeping a positivity journal, is very concrete and structured and helps the client build a firm and nuanced positive view of self in a number of steps. Its simplicity makes the approach easy to explain in a self-help book (De Neef, 2015).

This treatment has three elements:

1 *Learning to look differently*, by keeping a journal of positive experiences and behaviors of which the client is proud and about which they are satisfied or happy (self-observation). Then they think of positive attributes of themselves and learn to eliminate the 'censorship' that leads to positive behaviors and attributes not being included in the positivity journal (self-assessment). The cli-ent empowers themselves for concrete behaviors (self-empowerment).
2 *Doing things differently*, namely, exhibiting behaviors that better fit the new positive view of self and new behaviors that the client wants to try.
3 *Inhibiting activation of the negative view of self* by paying special attention to lowering impossibly high demands and dealing with negative criticism.

4.2.5   Mindfulness with self-compassion

Mindfulness or attentiveness combined with self-compassion works well when there are very many destructive thoughts and feelings and a lack of self-compas-sion (Germer, 2009).

4.2.6   Accelerated eye movements in EMDR

Eye Movement Desensitization and Reprocessing (EMDR) (Stöfsel & Mooren, 2015) is an effective and client-friendly technique to treat core events and single and complex traumas. Core cognitions can also be positively changed with it. To put sufficient load on working memory in the fast thinking gifted person, faster eye movements and other tasks, such as head arithmetic, are applied.

4.2.7   ACT

Acceptance and commitment therapy (ACT) helps anxiety, depression, panic, emotional pain, negative thinking, brooding, and self-criticism (Hayes & Smith, 2005). ACT views pain and suffering as normal, inseparable parts of being human. It is precisely the avoidance or suppression of painful experiences that causes suffering. ACT works on the client's willingness to accept painful experiences and commit to actions that fit their values (Hayes & Smith, 2005).

4.3   The cognitive behavioral process: implementation and evaluation of therapy

In Chapter 3, the analyzing part of the CBT process was covered, culminating in a concrete treatment plan with goals and techniques. In the implementation phase, the treatment plan is realized. It involves learning desirable and unlearning undesirable feelings and thoughts through techniques aiming to improve the balance of advantages and disadvantages. The core behavior of quickly and creatively finding solutions obviously does not have to change, but the creative problem creation, if present, does.

For specific personality traits, we focus on core behaviors, core thoughts, and core feelings. These can be learned or unlearned. The triggering situations (S) and consequences (C) of traits are also important.

THE EVALUATION PHASE

In cognitive behavioral therapy, the aim is to change core behaviors, core feelings, and core cognitions, especially outside of the therapy sessions. The client keeps track by self-recording the extent to which his core behaviors and core cognitions change. If the treatment is effective, his core behavior becomes less frequent; the alternative, previously underdeveloped behavior becomes stronger. Situations that previously elicited these core behaviors do so less frequently. The same is true of negative feelings. These too become less automatically triggered and decrease in severity and frequency. Core thoughts change toward the new, alternative, and balanced beliefs. During effective treatment, the credibility of the old view decreases and the credibility of the new one increases.

An example is a client with mixed perceptions of compulsive and paranoid traits who had as an old conception the core cognition, 'If I make a mistake, I'll get

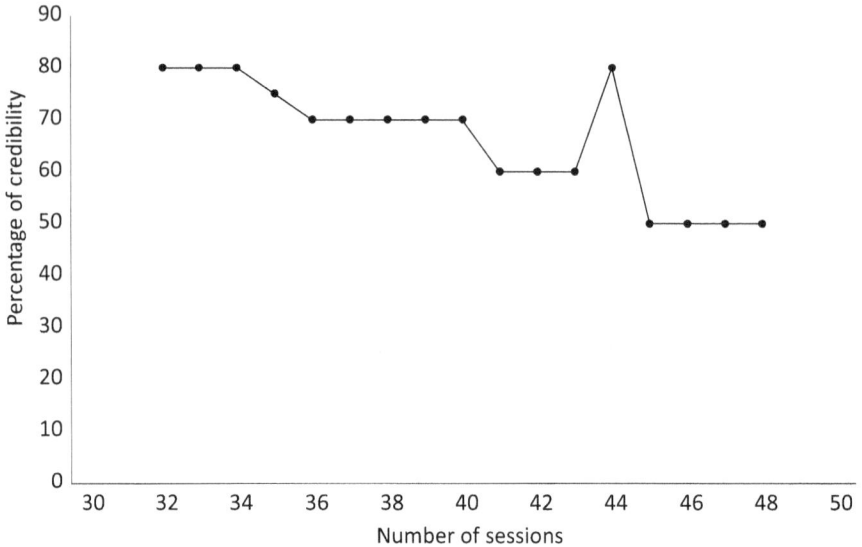

Figure 4.2 Registration credibility of a basic assumption or core cognition

caught for it'. The credibility of this view diminished during a 50-session cognitive behavioral therapy. The client scored the persuasiveness of this cognition.

Figure 4.2 shows the progression of the percentage credibility of this cognition during the second part of the therapy. The graph shows a decreasing trend across the board. The exception is the relapse in the final phase of therapy. In the preceding period, the client became involved in a conflict. After this, the positive trend recovers.

Reference list

American Psychiatric Association. (2013). *Diagnostic and statistical manual of mental disorders* (5th ed.). American Psychiatric Press.

Barlow, D. H., Farchione, T. J., Bullis, J. R., Gallagher, M. W., Murray-Latin, H., Sauer-Zavala, S., Bentley, K. H., Thompson-Hollands, J., Conklin, L. R., Boswell, J. F., Ametaj, A., Carl, J. R., Boettcher, H. T., & Cassiello-Robbins, C. (2017). The unified protocol for transdiagnostic treatment of emotional disorders compared with diagnosis-specific protocols for anxiety disorders: A randomized clinical trial. JAMA Psychiatry, 74(9), 875–884.

Brewin, C. R. (2006). Understanding cognitive behaviour therapy: A retrieval competition account. *Behaviour Research and Therapy, 44*, 765–784.

Brinkman, W. (1978). Het gedragstherapeutisch proces. In J. W. G. Orlemans, P. Eelen & W. P. Haaijman (Eds.), *Handboek voor gedragstherapie (H. A1 t/m A14)*. Van Loghum Slaterus.

Coumar, A. (2024). *Inquiry-based psychotherapy: Applying the work of Byron Katie in clinical settings*. Swayam Prabha Psychological Services.

De Neef, M. (2015). *Build your confidence with CBT*. Open University Press.

Germer, C. (2009). *The mindful path to self-compassion: Freeing yourself from destructive thoughts and emotions*. The Guildford Press.

Hayes, S. C., & Smith, S. (2005). *Get out of your mind and into your life: The new acceptance and commitment therapy*. New Harbinger Publications.

Katie, B., & Mitchell, S. (2003). *Loving what is: Four questions that can change your life*. Crown Publishing Group.

Keijsers, G. P. J., Van Minnen, A., & Hoogduin, C. A. L. (2011). *Protocollaire behandelingen voor volwassenen met psychische klachten, deel 1 en 2*. Boom.

Kuipers, W., & Van Kempen, A. (2007). *Verleid jezelf tot excellentie!* Lecturium.

Millon, T., & Everly Jr., G. S. (1985). *Personality and its disorders: A biosocial-learning approach*. Wiley.

Servan-Schreiber, D. (2005). *The instinct to heal – curing depression, anxiety, and stress without drugs and without talk therapy*. Rodale Books.

Servan-Schreiber, D. (2017). *Anticancer – a new way of life*. Penguin Books.

Stöfsel, M., & Mooren, T. (2015). *Diagnosing and treating complex trauma*. Routledge.

Webb, J. T. (2013). *Searching for meaning – Idealism, bright minds, disillusionment, and hope*. Great Potential Press.

Young, J. E., Klosko, J. S., & Weishaar, M. E. (2003). *Schema therapy: A practitioner's guide*. Guilford Press.

Chapter 5

The therapeutic relationship in giftedness combined with specific personality traits

Self-analysis and functional analysis

Summary

Chapter 5 starts by examining the interaction diagnosis of both the general core behaviors of giftedness and specific personality traits before looking at the functional analysis of the complex therapeutic relationship and the therapist's self-analysis of his or her own cognitions, feelings, and behaviors. In the therapeutic relationship, certain interactions and interaction disorders are manifested specific to the group of personality traits. The therapist can analyze and correct his or her own inappropriate responses, cognitions, and behavior, thereby influencing the client's symptom behavior, dual core behavior, and practice behavior.

5.1 Core behavior and interaction diagnosis

An interaction diagnosis can be made for each core behavior. This also applies to the general core behavior of creating solutions quickly and creatively. See Figure 5.1. This core behavior can also manifest itself in sub-behaviors: idealistic care, best effort, empathic adaptation, and quick and creative problem-solving.

In addition to an interaction diagnosis of the general core behaviors of giftedness, it is also possible to create interaction diagnoses for the core behaviors of each of the 11 groups of specific personality traits or personality disorders. See Sections 2.4.2 and 2.6 and Table 2.5. Figures 5.2, 5.3, and 5.4 (Beck et al., 2003) visualize core behaviors for different forms of disordered attachment. The core behaviors of the 11 groups of specific personality traits or disorders are thus placed in the preferred interaction positions.

These figures help the therapist to identify the specific core behavior of the personality traits of the client, in addition to the general gifted core behavior of quickly and creatively finding solutions or simply creating problems. In addition, being conscious as the therapist of one's own interactional position and that of the client is important to recognize possible interactional disorders in good time.

DOI: 10.4324/9781003423287-6

criticize devalue create problems quickly and creatively	create solutions quickly and creatively idealistically caring do one's best
autonomy resistance create problems quickly and creatively	empathic adaptation create solutions quickly and creatively

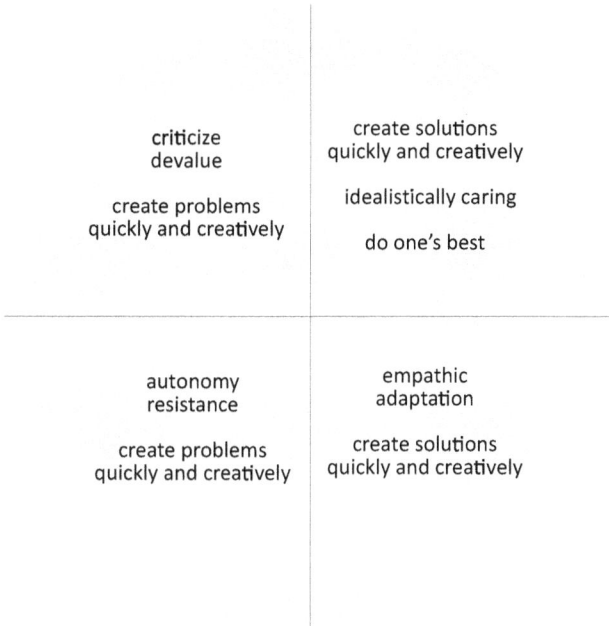

Figure 5.1 Core behaviors associated with giftedness

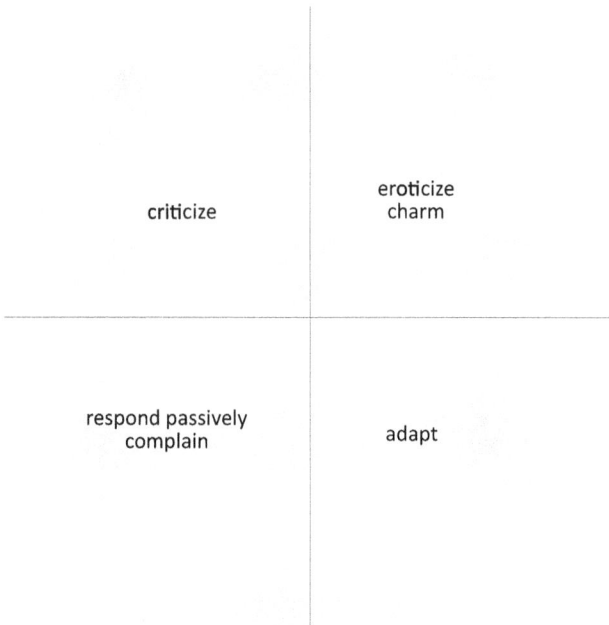

criticize	eroticize charm
respond passively complain	adapt

Figure 5.2 Core behaviors associated with excessive attachment

direct
force   do one's best

blame   amuse
distrust   exaggerate

resist

avoid
isolate

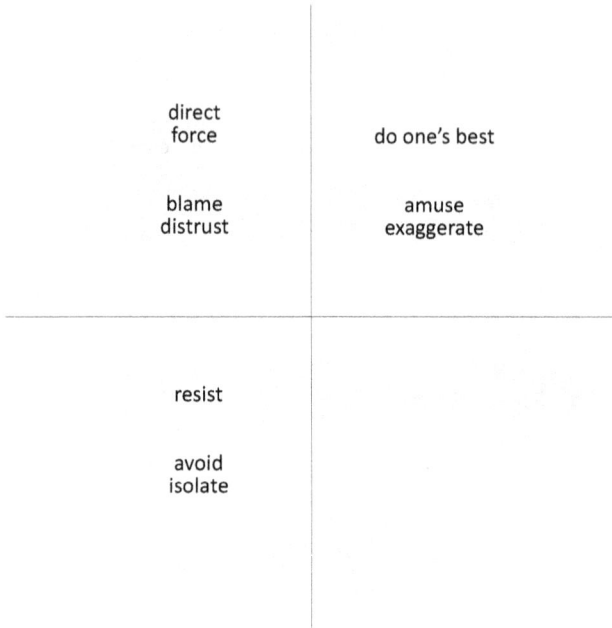

Figure 5.3 Core behaviors associated with ambivalent attachment

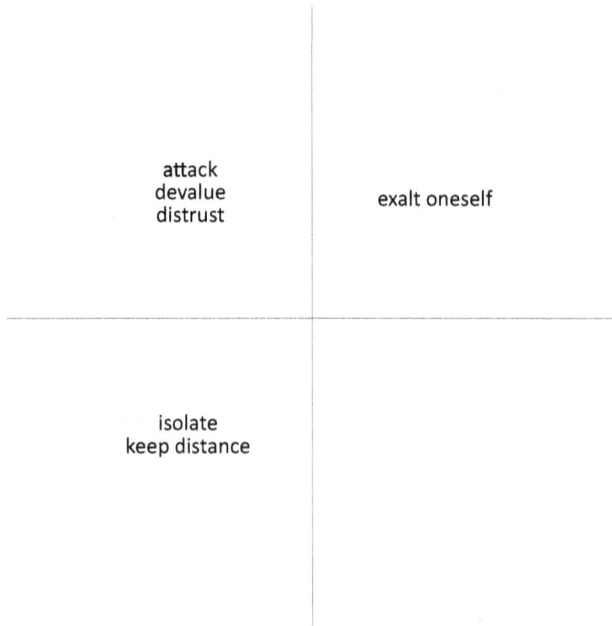

attack
devalue   exalt oneself
distrust

isolate
keep distance

Figure 5.4 Core behaviors associated with detachment

5.2   Core behavior and interactional disorders, also in cognitive behavioral therapy

As long as the gifted client with narcissistic personality traits feels admired, this client is 'calm'. This is also true in cognitive behavioral therapy. But sooner or later, the therapist falls short in their admiration of the client, or is even downright hurtful, and then the client with narcissistic personality traits reacts with anger. He then shoots into the above/against position and goes on the attack; he pushes the therapist into the below/against position and starts to hurt and devalue him. The therapist ends up in the position of feeling like a failure and inferior, despite pre-ferring the above/together or equal/together position. The therapist therefore finds themself, against their will, 'down' and in a struggle and feels first-hand the pulling power (the interactional attraction) of the client with narcissistic personality traits. This is exactly what other people around the client with narcissistic traits know so well. The client's colleagues might be afraid of the sudden switch to anger, as is the client's partner, or they might themselves become angry and begin to 'hit back'. Figure 5.5 illustrates this mutual positional game.

This disordered interaction is an illustration of the fact that, in a client with certain personality traits, the client's schema (image of the other) and preferred interactional position tend to provoke an untherapeutic response in the therapist. This perpetuates the characteristic behavior of the client with certain personal-ity traits, as this specific core behavior is reinforced by the environment and, in this case, also by the therapist. In this way, events that fit a particular pattern are absorbed effortlessly, but experiences that conflict with the pattern are rejected or distorted until they fit the pattern. Ambiguous situations are interpreted in a

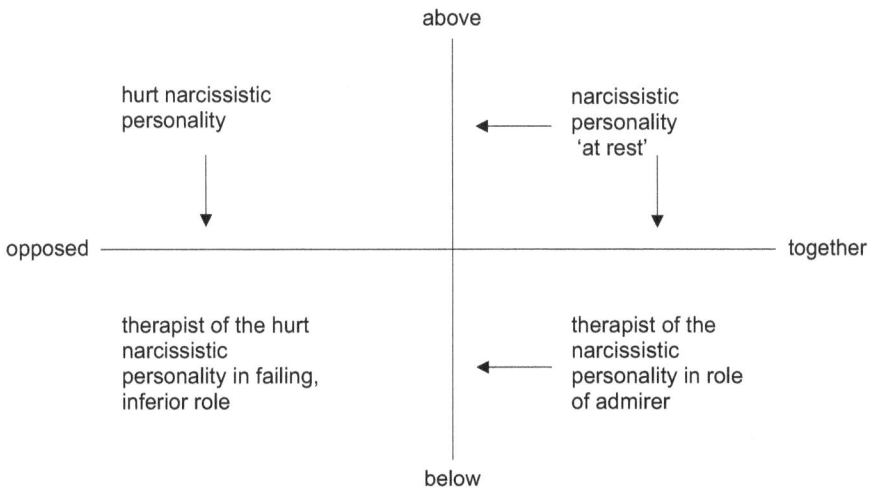

Figure 5.5 Interaction disorder in cognitive behavioral therapy for narcissistic personality traits

distorted way to fit the schema. So it is with clients with certain personality traits. There is an attentional bias, a prejudiced attention for the specific information and events that fit the schema of the client with, for example, narcissistic personality traits.

The client with passive-aggressive personality traits sees obligation everywhere, and the client with paranoid traits quickly sees conspiracy and betrayal in many situations. A one-sidedness in (schema) development has therefore occurred; a person's lens becomes tinted by a dominant color, causing them to distort information. This leads to one-sided reactions that do not 'fit' with the reality.

An interaction disorder should be distinguished from 'normal' resistance, which is common in symptom disorders without personality traits or personality disorder. For example, a client with persistent depressive disorder (dysthymia) does not do his homework, and in the next session the therapist responds with Brinkman's three A's: *accepting* the resistance, *analyzing* it, and coming up with an *alternative* (Brinkman, 1978). There are a number of possibilities: the client has been too gloomy in the past week and did not think that practicing would help anyway (depressive cognition), he did not understand the task properly due to inadequate explanation by the therapist, the task was not feasible, or the client's distress has decreased. Failure or incompletion of a task provides a great deal of information, and analyzing it is often more fruitful than therapy with practice tasks that proceed effortlessly and without resistance.

For the client with passive-aggressive personality traits, resistance to commitment and thus to exercise assignments is the central and recurring problem. Again, this is not an ordinary resistance, but a generalized one, which can lead to a disorder of interaction with the therapist. The therapist may become irritated by the resistance and procrastination of such a client and think, 'we won't get there this way' and 'in good therapy there must be practice outside of it'. This leads the therapist to prescribe even more homework, which leads to even more resistance and forgetting, resistance and procrastination on the part of the client. This creates a vicious circle and the therapy reaches a dead end. The solution is to switch to cognitive therapy, which focuses on the generalized resistance to obligation that occurs in all kinds of situations. Thus, each client with specific personality traits has his or her own type of resistance and interactional disorder. In the gifted client, highly developed autonomy is more likely to lead to critical resistance.

The therapist looks at past and present dysfunctions in interaction within and outside of cognitive behavioral therapy. A good assessment is necessary, based on the learning history of the relationship with parents, siblings, and other close relatives or friends. The therapist recognizes interactional patterns and is prepared for there to be interactional dysfunction. As indicated above, passive-aggressive personality traits are a predictor of a specific interaction dysfunction in the therapeutic relationship. The therapist can carry out a functional analysis of the therapeutic relationship and his/her own part in it, using self-analysis (see Section 5.4).

Both the therapist's and the client's reactions are evoked according to Leary's rules of communication (Leary, 1957):

- against evokes against
- together → together
- below → above
- above → below

We can call this the relationship definition aspect or relationship level. Every communication, in addition to a message of content, provides a message of how the relationship is defined by the 'sender' (Watzlawick et al., 1967).

Every client evokes an interaction-appeal on the therapist. For example the interaction-appeal from a dependent person is in the quadrant together/below. An antisocial person's is in the quadrant above/against. Clients have interpersonal impacts on the feelings, behaviors, and cognitions of the therapist. That is called objective countertransference (Hafkenscheid, 2003). Impact messages are generalizable across therapists (Hafkenscheid, 2005).

SELF-ASSESSMENT BY THE THERAPIST WITH TEST

The IMI-C (Impact Message Inventory) is a computer test (Hafkenscheid, 2012).

5.3   The therapist's evoked response to a specific personality trait

In addition to a position in the interaction quadrant, the therapist is forced into a specific role from the schema of the specific client with a personality trait. The client's reaction to the therapist is largely determined by the client's image of the other, as formulated by Beck (Beck et al., 2003). This view of others is specific to each personality disorder (see Table 2.5 in Section 2.6).

Because of the image the client with avoidant personality traits has of the other, the therapist becomes the demeaning, critical person. Psychoeducation about the desirability of self-disclosure and the fear of it because of the avoidant client's conditional assumption – 'if I show my feelings, I will be rejected' – is therefore an important element of the relationship-based therapy plan.

In his view, the client with narcissistic personality traits is entitled to special treatment, even in therapy, and is afraid to be ordinary. Sooner or later he will also feel hurt or unappreciated by the therapist and will see the therapist as inferior and failing.

The client with borderline personality traits will feel abandoned very quickly and then react with anger or auto-aggressive behavior. In his view, the therapist is dangerous, dismissive, untrustworthy, and out to abuse him.

The client with schizotypal personality traits will want very gentle contact, but will also feel vulnerable and will want to withdraw from time to time. The therapist becomes the threatening and untrustworthy other.

The client with dependent personality traits will want advice and support to survive their feelings, will not learn to act independently enough, and will become too attached to the therapist for fear of abandonment. The therapist is idealized as highly competent and supportive.

The image the client has of the other is projected onto the therapist and is specific to the various personality traits and personality disorders. The therapist knows which image to expect from a correct diagnosis and incorporates it into his or her relationship-oriented treatment plan.

5.4   Therapist's self-analysis of their response to giftedness combined with specific personality traits

It is time for self-analysis when the therapist becomes aware of disproportional feelings. The following is a therapist's self-analysis of her reactions to a gifted client.

Self-analysis of my behavior, thoughts, and feelings by a gifted client

The first thing I notice in myself is a positive countertransference: I feel challenged, it motivates me. One pitfall is that I get caught up in their tendency for divergent thinking. An issue could arise around who is leading, and this might appeal to another, more directive side in me. This could make it complicated, but also interesting.

Sometimes I feel discouraged because I make the mistake of thinking that someone with so much competence should still be able to benefit from therapy and yet is not taking what I see as the logical next steps. Alternatively, I get irritated because I am criticized or devalued. I also find it difficult to be idealized. I am tempted to enjoy it and sometimes find it difficult to use it therapeutically. I recognize the social isolation that often accompanies giftedness.

Overall, there are four possible therapist feelings in the therapeutic relationship:

1 the insecure therapist
2 the irritated therapist
3 the discouraged therapist
4 the over-involved therapist

These are disproportionate feelings on the part of the therapist that affect his or her behavior. Uncertainty leads the therapist to go along with the client's behavior too much. Irritation causes the therapist to react too strongly in opposition to the client's behavior. Discouragement leads the therapist to withdraw and disengage, 'moving away' or distancing instead of responding to the client's behavior. Over-involvement often leads to overcompliance and over-care.

But more combinations between the therapist's feelings and behavior are possible. An insecure feeling can lead to the therapist distancing themselves, and an irritated feeling can lead to going along with the client and caring too much. Over-involvement may provoke irritation and resistance toward the client, whereas discouragement can lead to compliance, effort, or similar resistance.

Once the therapist has done the functional analysis of the therapeutic relationship when a high-autonomy, gifted client, with or without passive-aggressive traits, fails to complete exercise tasks, the therapist simultaneously examines what feelings and thoughts are evoked in him and what specific behavior of the client elicits these feelings and thoughts. The following is a description of the self-analysis of an irritable therapist.

A common problem in cognitive behavioral therapy with gifted people is their autonomy and therefore their aversion and resistance to practical tasks.

Situation (A): The client has failed the homework again.
Therapist's thoughts: see Table 5.1.
Therapist's feeling (C): irritation.
Behavior of the therapist (C): controlling and demanding.
Alternative and balanced thoughts (E) of the therapist (true and helpful):

1   We are now at the heart of his autonomy problem.
2   Practice is a means, not an end.
3   When autonomy needs are too high, it happens all the time.
4   Relax and make fewer demands on yourself and the client.
5   My work is meaningful but not easy, especially with a smart client who also has passive-aggressive traits.
6   I can see his pattern of autonomy and resistance as the essence of his problems.

Therapist's goal (G):

• less anger and more calm
• less demanding

Table 5.1 Assessment of the irritated therapist's thoughts (Ellis, 1962)

Thoughts of the therapist (B)	Assessment (D)	
1. We won't get anywhere like this.	not true	not helpful
2. No improvement without practice.	not true	not helpful
3. This is the umpteenth time.	true	not helpful
4. I'm trying my best, but what's the result? Very little.	not true	not helpful
5. My work is useless.	not true	not helpful
6. I'm tired of these obvious gifted excuses.	true	not helpful

COMMENTARY

The aim of such self-analysis is to arrive at a more therapeutic response. The therapist also gains insight into his or her own schemas, aversions, and vulnerabilities. When therapy gets stuck, the therapist usually reflects on the therapeutic process and may bring the treatment into supervision. It is also useful to do some self-analysis in preparation. The automatic reactions of the therapist may be playing a role and might be antitherapeutic. In addition, the therapist's underlying schemas may also be repeatedly triggered. In this case, personal therapy for the therapist is the best solution. If the therapist knows himself well, he has insight into his own ways of reacting and the conditions under which certain reactions occur. In therapy, one of these conditions is primarily the client's core behavior. With a gifted client, it is also about the drive and creativity to find solutions. Autonomy, idealism, perfectionism, curiosity, higher intelligence, unexpected developmental delays, and high sensitivity are also common personality traits that may elicit counterreactions in the therapist.

It is important for the therapist to identify their most difficult gifted clients and use the self-analysis (Ellis, 1962) to pinpoint the essence of those clients' behavior: what is the A, the activating event or provoking event? Does it often evoke the same B's (beliefs) in the therapist, thoughts that in turn lead to a particular feeling or behavior (C) that may be disproportionate and have more to do with the therapist's view (B) of this client than with the objective behavior (A) of the client themself? These are cases where the therapist may be pursuing an important schema of their own.

Another common problem in cognitive behavioral therapy with the gifted is perfectionism, with a tendency towards completeness and perfection and towards being tough or persistent. As an example of self-analysis in the obsessive-compulsive gifted client, the following is a description of the self-analysis of a discouraged therapist.

After initially trying very hard with the client and then becoming insecure, the therapist becomes increasingly annoyed with the client and has fallen into the trap of the irritated therapist. Finally, the therapist becomes discouraged because the client is not making progress, and after two relapses continues to doubt that the treatment is working. The therapist decides to analyze their discouragement and arrives at the following self-analysis.

Situation (A): After two relapses, the client doubts that the treatment is working.
Therapist's thoughts: see Table 5.2.
Therapist's feeling (C): discouragement.
Behavior of the therapist (C): dropping out.
Alternative and balanced thoughts (E) of the therapist (true and helpful):

1 The relapse discourages her and me.
2 Most of the time I feel competent in my work.
3 Every job has problems.
4 These are hard, obsessive personality traits.
5 She was doing very well for a long time before the relapse.
6 I see no perspective for a while and feel discouraged.

Table 5.2 Assessment of the discouraged therapist's thoughts (Ellis, 1962)

Thoughts of the therapist (B)	Assessment (D)	
1. It's not going to work out with this client.	not true	not helpful
2. I'd better learn another profession.	not true	not helpful
3. I should look for another job with fewer problems.	not true	not helpful
4. How smart and tough this client is, she keeps on going.	true	not helpful
5. Maybe the client can't do it after all.	true	not helpful
6. I'm tired of this endless intelligent avoidance.	true	not helpful

Goal of the therapist (G):

- less discouragement and more confidence
- teach the client how to cope with the relapse

COMMENTARY

As a result of this self-analysis, the therapist overcomes his discouragement and tendency to give up, and he will calmly teach the client how to cope with her relapse and reduce her perfectionism.

When a client with histrionic personality traits is in therapy with a therapist with obsessive-compulsive personality traits, we see the following interaction disorder emerge. The histrionic client's exaggeration becomes annoying to the therapist and fits into his image of others as irresponsible and careless. The compulsive therapist is therefore particularly sensitive to this. The therapist wants to overcome his anger, redirect it, and make it productive. He traces the triggering event, namely, the careless and exaggerated behavior of the histrionic client. His thoughts (B) are automatically negative: 'How unreal, exaggerated, and careless this client is'. He cannot easily overcome his anger; it requires more, namely, self-analysis. Because the histrionic client feels the therapist's anger increasing and his acceptance decreasing, he begins to exaggerate even more. The client and the therapist thus become trapped in a vicious circle that brings the therapy to a standstill. After self-analysis, the therapist can see it differently and thinks: 'This is exactly the core of the client's problem, exaggerating in order to be accepted and admired. This is what therapy should be about, and now it can be seen concretely in our interaction and discussed with the client'.

5.5 Functional analysis of the therapeutic relationship in giftedness combined with specific personality traits

In addition to the individual functional analysis of the client with personality traits or a personality disorder, there is also a functional analysis of the therapeutic relationship, in other words the interaction between client and therapist. Extending the

TRIGGERING EVENT (CS/Sd)

EXPERIENCE CLIENT

client's thoughts
(COV)

client's feelings   client's behavior
(CER)   (CAR)

CLIENT'S INTRAPSYCHIC EFFECTS (C)

advantages

disadvantages

INTERACTION EFFECTS (C)
CLIENT (Cl) ⟷ THERAPIST (T)

EXPERIENCE THERAPIST

therapist's thoughts
(COV)

THERAPIST'S INTRAPSYCHIC EFFECTS (C)

therapist's feelings   therapist's behavior
(CER)   (CAR)

advantages

disadvantages

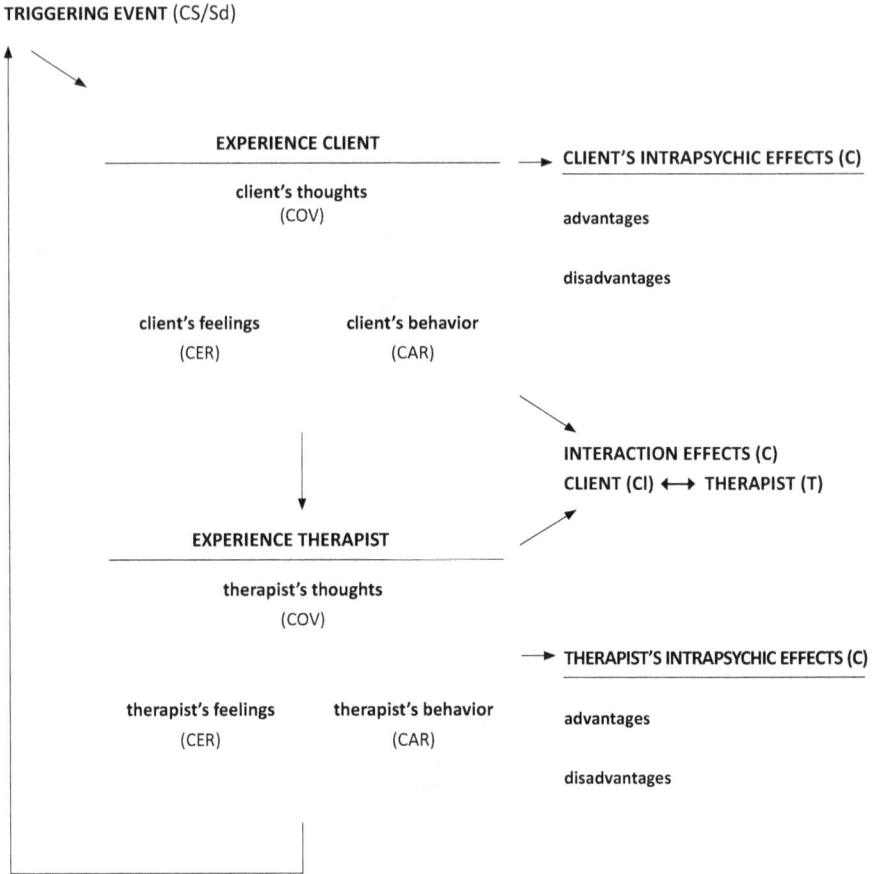

Figure 5.6 SORC model and therapist–client interaction

SORC model of the individual client with the SORC model of the therapist results in an interaction model as shown in Figure 5.6.

In the client, an eliciting event leads to thoughts, feelings, and behaviors. These behaviors have both intrapsychic and interactional consequences. The interactional consequences play a role in the therapeutic relationship. The client's behavior becomes an eliciting event for the therapist, who responds with thoughts, feelings, and behavior. The consequences of the therapist's behavior are also intra-psychic for the therapist and interactional for both the therapist and the client. The interactional consequences of the client's and therapist's behavior meet. In turn, the therapist's behavior becomes an eliciting event for the client and the (vicious) circle is closed.

As an example, the therapeutic relationship of a discouraged therapist with a gifted client with avoidant personality traits is presented (see also Figure 5.7).

TRIGGERING EVENT (CS/Sd)
(threat of) criticism and rejection

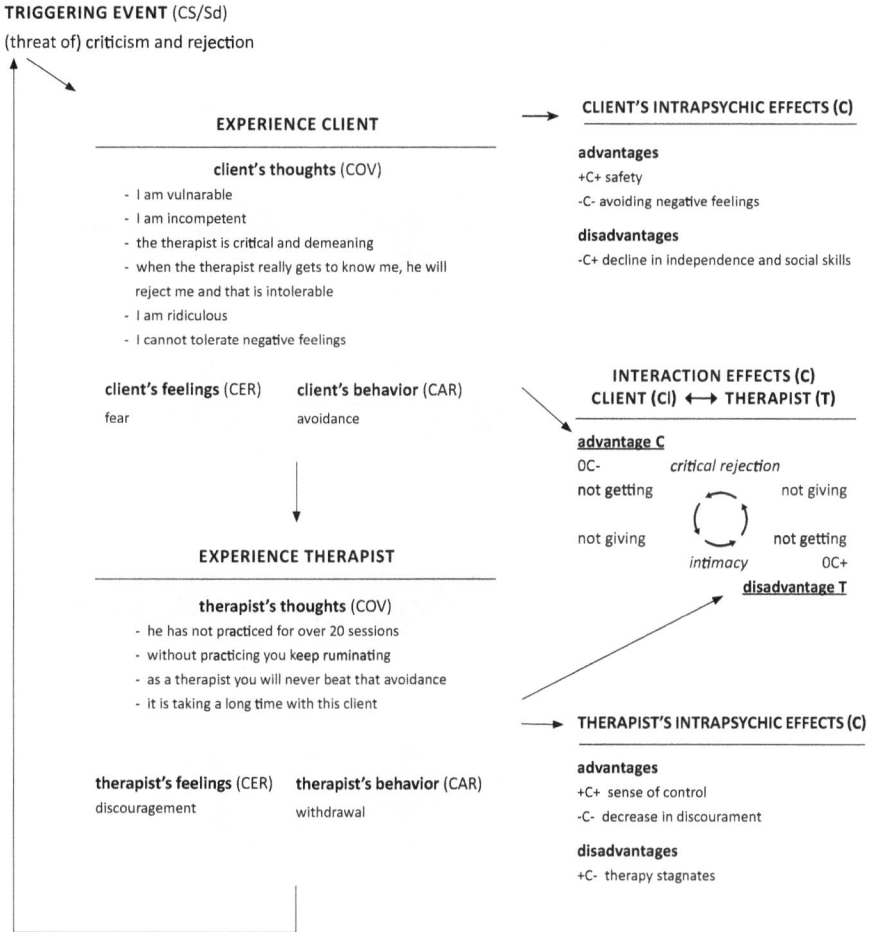

Figure 5.7 Functional analysis of a pitfall in the therapeutic relationship with avoidant personality traits: the discouraged therapist

Case study Ted Kline

Ted Kline is 28 years old and a musician. After briefly studying psychology, he followed his heart and joined the conservatory. It was here that he met his wife.

The reason for his referral is that he has all kinds of diffuse phobic complaints. From time to time he is also very depressed and is afraid that he might jump out of his fifth floor apartment. He has little faith in himself, in the future, in God, and in other people. He suffers from a generalized anxiety disorder and major depressive disorder. Previously, a liberal therapist had successfully treated him for stage fright with cognitive behavioral therapy.

As a small child, he brooded over all sorts of philosophical questions. He could rave about the universe and the afterlife and wanted to understand everything. His own mother thought he was a strange child, partly because he had few friends. His questions drove her crazy and, dominant as she was, she pushed him to play football and sports. His father, according to the client, had no say in the matter. During the short time he studied psychology, he felt lonely in a student flat. A fellow student developed schizophrenia, and from that time on he was afraid of going mad and brooded anxiously.

Ted avoided practicing exposing himself to his own brooding thoughts between therapy sessions at home. He put it off for a long time, with all sorts of reasons and rationalizations. The real motive, of course, was that he was trying to avoid anxiety. This procrastination discouraged the therapist, who thought, 'This is not going to work: the therapy isn't working, this avoidance is neither necessary nor good, and I have to get him to practice exposure anyway'. As a result, the therapist began to confront him more critically about his avoidance and tried to push him towards more exposure. After 20 sessions of cognitive behavioral therapy, the client still did not practice self-exposure to his anxious brooding.

The therapist decides to bring the stagnation into his peer group and, in preparation, makes the following self-analysis.

Situation (A): The client complains a lot about negative feelings, which he broods about, but does not practice the suggested tasks at home.
Therapist's thoughts: see Table 5.3.
Therapist's feeling (C): discouragement.
Behavior of the therapist (C): giving up.
Alternative and balanced thoughts (E) of the therapist (true and helpful)

1 Motivation to practice makes this client anxious and is a long-term problem.
2 Worrying is a form of avoidance and fits his personality disorder.
3 As the therapist, you need to motivate the client to gradually give up his avoidance.
4 A client with avoidant personality traits who is also gifted is a long process.

Table 5.3 Assessment of the discouraged therapist's thoughts (Ellis, 1962)

Thoughts of the therapist (B)	Assessment (D)	
1. He has not practiced for over 20 sessions.	true	not helpful
2. Without practicing you keep ruminating.	true	not helpful
3. You can never beat that avoidance as a therapist.	not true	not helpful
4. He always has very intelligent excuses.	true	not helpful

Goal of the therapist (G):

• less discouragement, more self-confidence
• motivate client to self-exposure

COMMENTARY

The therapist is at risk of giving up because of his growing discouragement. Through self-analysis he realizes that therapy is a long-term process. His peer group helps him to patiently find an effective approach to brooding by re-labeling it as a bad and senseless habit, like smoking. A self-control program is used to break this behavior. If the client broods too much, he breaks it by going for a walk or playing music. Figure 5.7 shows the pitfall of the discouraged therapist.

5.6   The therapist's own cognitions, feelings, and behavior in relation to giftedness: doing one's best, avoiding or opposing, or identifying oneself

The following are four examples of therapists who have developed a strong aversion to or affinity for gifted clients. We will then discuss four common patterns in the therapists' responses.

Case study Henry Wage

Therapist Henry Wage comes from a modest background. He was the first in a family of hardworking gardeners to attend college. Teachers, fellow students, and later colleagues saw him as gifted, which was not how he saw himself. He learned to look up to academics and quickly felt inferior among them. Even at the lyceum he quickly felt like a failure and suffered from an unjustified negative view of self. Gifted clients quickly arouse his feelings of inadequacy and make him insecure. So he avoids talking about giftedness. When this is pointed out to him by a colleague in his peer review group of fellow therapists, he says, 'It's like religion, it's better not to talk about it, it's a private matter'. It is also interesting that in his personal therapy he has been able to intelligently avoid this topic as well as his high sensitivity. His therapist helped him in this avoidance by not finding it an important topic and not being well-informed.

Case study Lisa Impatience

Therapist Lisa Impatience has a brilliant father, CEO of a large international company. He is very narcissistic and has remarkably little empathy for his daughter and his fellow human beings. He is proud of his two sons who, like him, are materially successful, the eldest as a banker and the second as a property developer. The mother is a docile, dependent woman who admires and cares for her husband. Lisa decided early on to do her own thing, expecting no support or real understanding from either parent. She chose to study psychology in order to gain real contact with and understanding of other people. Her gifted brothers and father did not understand this and devalued her choice as a hobby. Lisa has an aversion to gifted people, whom she sees as arrogant and often unempathetic. When she gets a client who thinks he might be gifted, she gets very irritated and thinks 'don't think so much of yourself, you are just a normal person', saying to the client 'the problem is just your symptoms and your personality'. She automatically goes against his thinking. The 'G-word' (gifted) immediately makes her nervous because of her experience with the men in her family.

Case study Annie Hunter

Annie is a highly sensitive therapist who works well with traumatized clients. She knows how to motivate vulnerable, dependent, and avoidant people to process and disclose their trauma with kindness and patience. As a child and adolescent, her sensitivity and ferocity were neither valued nor understood, but frowned upon and inhibited. Due to a chronically ill father, the family norm was sacrifice and avoidance of emotion. Because of her intelligence and empathy, Annie felt excluded from the family and ended up in the caring role. She was also humble and looked up to others in her studies and work. With gifted clients who thought and acted autonomously, she quickly became discouraged. Sometimes she would secretly think: 'What a complicated and stubborn client, who knows everything better. What are you doing here'? Excessive client autonomy offended and discouraged her. Her affinity is with trauma and vulnerability.

Case Study Ronald Aldonis

Ronald is a 'self-confessed' gifted therapist. Social isolation as the brightest boy in his class led to bullying and overcompensation. As a psychologist, he discovered the concept of giftedness and then better understood his own development. He became overly involved with gifted clients, identifying too much with them and engaging in boundless self-disclosure, suggesting 'we are both very special'. His colleagues felt that he worked too much from the 'uniformity myth': all problems were reduced to (mostly) unrecognized giftedness. These predictable interpretations also became boring.

Each therapist responds differently to giftedness. Does giftedness cause the therapist additional insecurity, irritation, discouragement, or over-involvement? What are his own perceptions of giftedness and his experiences of it in his family, at school and university, and among friends and colleagues at work? Does he automatically tend towards:

1 insecurity and avoiding
2 irritation and opposing
3 discouragement and dropping out
4 over-involvement and identifying

The therapist's reaction is partly determined by the influence of the specific personality traits from the 12 groups, such as avoidant, passive-aggressive, or narcissistic traits (see Section 2.4.2) on the general giftedness scale. Thus, the therapist responds to both the general and the specific traits (see also Figure 5.7), and he should distinguish his two responses in the therapeutic relationship. These functional analyses of the therapeutic relationship in general giftedness are shown in Figure 5.8, 5.9, 5.10, and 5.11.

TRIGGERING EVENT (CS/Sd)

complex and fascinating situation

CLIENT'S INTRAPSYCHIC EFFECTS (C)

advantages
+C+ kick
+C+ self-esteem
+C+ satisfaction

EXPERIENCE CLIENT

client's thoughts (COV)
- I am autonomous, quick, clever
- I am different, unusual, exceptional, strange
- I am an outsider, isolated
- others avoid me

disadvantages
+C- incomprehension
+C- stress
+C- frustration
+C- impatience

client's feelings (CER)
intense excitement,
driven, fear of failure

client's behavior (CAR)
quickly and creatively
creating solutions

INTERACTION EFFECTS (C)
CLIENT (Cl) ⟷ THERAPIST (T)

advantage C
+C+　　　esteem & acceptance
getting more　　　giving more

giving more　　　getting more
　　　esteem　　　+C+

advantage T

EXPERIENCE THERAPIST

therapist's thoughts (COV)
- I can't compete with her intelligence
- she thinks too fast for me
- her problems are so complex

advantage C
-C-　　　criticism
getting less　　　giving less

giving more　　　getting more
　　　esteem　　　+C+

advantage T

therapist's feelings (CER)
insecure

therapist's behavior (CAR)
go along with it

THERAPIST'S INTRAPSYCHIC EFFECTS (C)

advantages
+C+ sense of control
-C- decrease in insecurity

disadvantages
+C- therapy stagnates on the long term

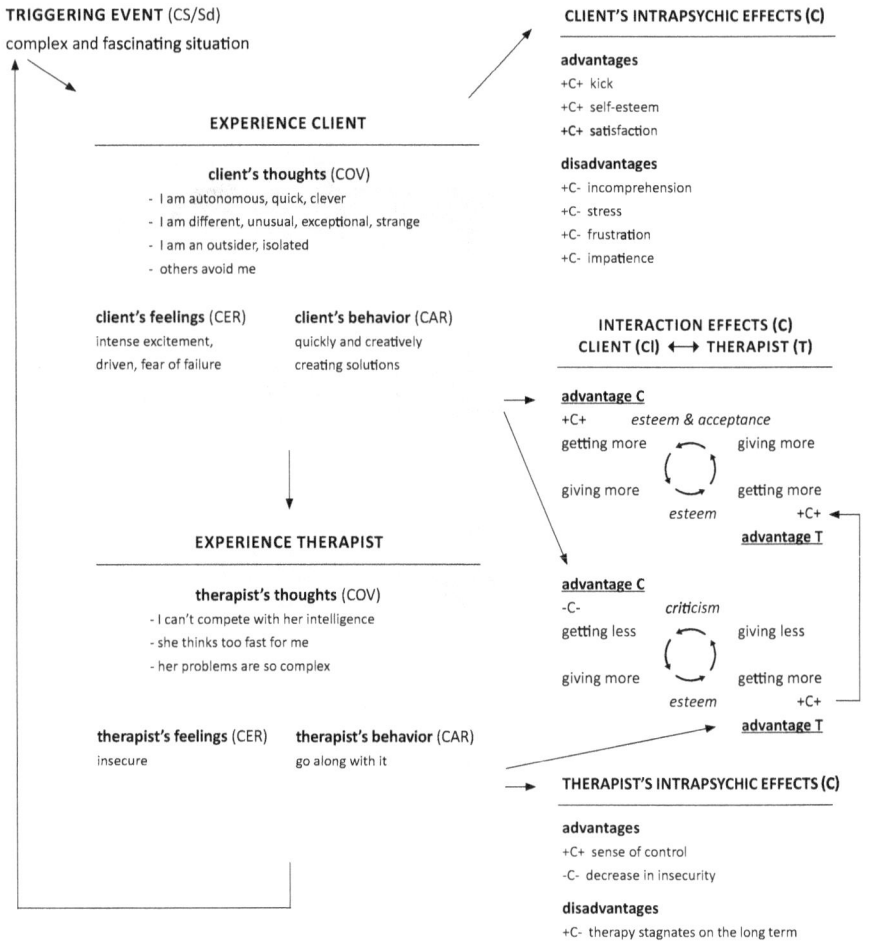

Figure 5.8 Functional analysis of a pitfall in the therapeutic relationship with gift-edness: the insecure therapist

COMMENTARY

The client's core behavior in Figure 5.8 evokes uncertainty in the therapist and, as a behavior, a compliant, avoidant response. This results in a mutual exchange of interpersonal advantages and disadvantages between client and therapist within the therapeutic relationship. The gifted client receives more appreciation and acceptance (advantage) and less criticism (advantage) as a result of the therapist's avoidant response. In return, the therapist receives more appreciation (advantage) from the client. This exchange becomes a vicious circle, perpetuating and reinforcing both the client's and the therapist's behavior. This causes the therapy to stagnate.

TRIGGERING EVENT (CS/Sd)

complex and fascinating situation

CLIENT'S INTRAPSYCHIC EFFECTS (C)

advantages
+C+ kick
+C- self-esteem
+C- satisfaction

EXPERIENCE CLIENT

client's thoughts (COV)
- I am autonomous, quick, clever
- I am different, unusual, exceptional, strange
- I am an outsider, isolated
- others avoid me, find me complicated

disadvantages
+C- incomprehension
+C- stress
+C- frustration
+C- impatience

client's feelings (CER)
intense excitement,
driven, fear of failure

client's behavior (CAR)
quickly and creatively
creating solutions

INTERACTION EFFECTS (C)
CLIENT (CI) ⟷ THERAPIST (T)

disadvantage C
-C+   *esteem & acceptance*
getting less   giving less

giving less   getting less
              esteem   -C+
                        disadvantage T

EXPERIENCE THERAPIST

therapist's thoughts (COV)
- what a headstrong wise guy
- he knows everything better
- this way he will also turn his whole environment against him
- that narcissistic flaunting of his giftedness, I'm going to make him sing a different tune

disadvantage C
+C-   *criticism*
getting more   giving more

giving less   getting less
              esteem   -C+
                        disadvantage T

therapist's feelings (CER)
irritation

therapist's behavior (CAR)
go against it

THERAPIST'S INTRAPSYCHIC EFFECTS (C)

advantages
+C+ sense of control
-C- decrease in irritation

disadvantages
+C- therapy stagnates

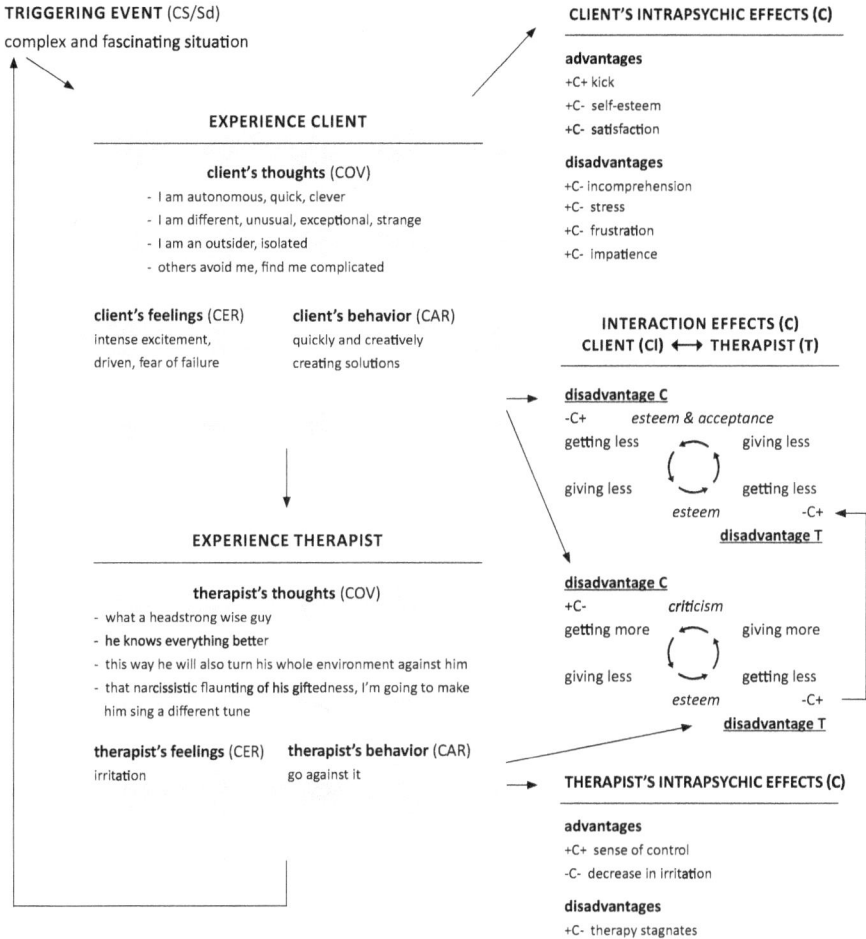

Figure 5.9 Functional analysis of a pitfall in the therapeutic relationship with giftedness: the irritated therapist

COMMENTARY

The client's core behavior in Figure 5.9 causes irritation in the therapist and leads the therapist to oppose the client. This results in a mutual exchange within the therapeutic relationship of interpersonal advantages or disadvantages between client and therapist.

The gifted client receives less appreciation and acceptance (disadvantage) and more criticism (disadvantage) as a result of the therapist's opposition.

In return, the therapist receives less appreciation from the client (disadvantage). This exchange becomes a vicious circle and weakens the behavior of both client and therapist through mutual disadvantage. This causes the therapy to stagnate.

TRIGGERING EVENT (CS/Sd)
complex and fascinating situation

EXPERIENCE CLIENT

client's thoughts (COV)
- I am autonomous, quick, clever
- I am different, unusual, exceptional, strange
- I am an outsider, isolated
- others avoid me, find me complicated

client's feelings (CER)   **client's behavior** (CAR)
intense excitement,   quickly and creatively
driven, fear of failure   creating solutions

EXPERIENCE THERAPIST

therapist's thoughts (COV)
- she is so smart and clever at creating problems
- I'll never beat that

therapist's feelings (CER)   **therapist's behavior** (CAR)
discouraged   get away from it, withdraw

CLIENT'S INTRAPSYCHIC EFFECTS (C)

advantages
+C+ kick
+C+ self-esteem
+C+ satisfaction

disadvantages
+C- incomprehension
+C- stress
+C- frustration
+C- impatience

INTERACTION EFFECTS (C)
CLIENT (CI) ⟷ THERAPIST (T)

disadvantage C
0C+   esteem & acceptance
not to get   not to give

not to give   not to get
           esteem   0C+
           disadvantage T

advantage C
0C-   criticism
not to get   not to give

not to give   not to get
           esteem   0C+
           disadvantage T

THERAPIST'S INTRAPSYCHIC EFFECTS (C)

advantages
+C+ sense of control
-C- decrease in discouragement

disadvantages
+C- therapy stagnates

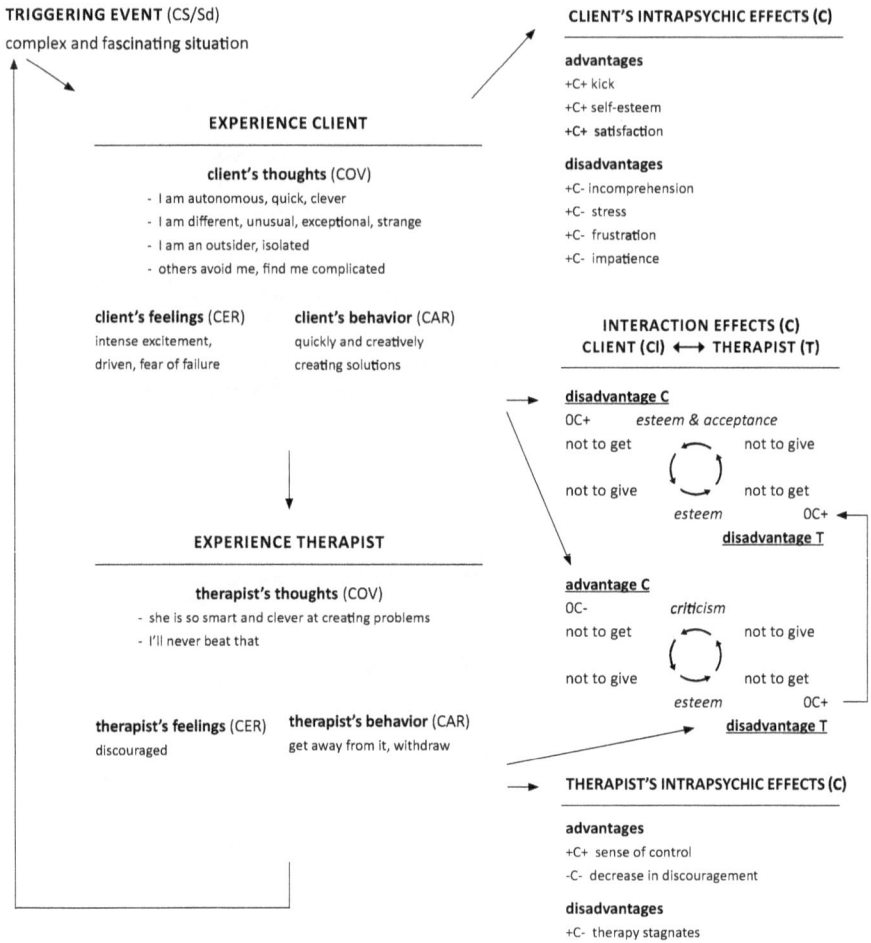

Figure 5.10 Functional analysis of a pitfall in the therapeutic relationship with giftedness: the discouraged therapist

COMMENTARY

The client's core behavior in Figure 5.10 causes the therapist to become discouraged and begin to withdraw and drop out. This results in a mutual exchange of interpersonal advantages or disadvantages between client and therapist within the therapeutic relationship. The gifted client receives neither appreciation and acceptance (disadvantage) nor criticism (advantages) from the therapist's withdrawing response. In return, the therapist receives no appreciation from the client (disadvantage). This exchange becomes a vicious circle and weakens the behavior of both client and therapist through mutual disadvantage. This causes the therapy to stagnate.

TRIGGERING EVENT (CS/Sd)

complex and fascinating situation

CLIENT'S INTRAPSYCHIC EFFECTS (C)

advantages
+C+ kick
+C+ self-esteem
+C+ satisfaction

EXPERIENCE CLIENT

client's thoughts (COV)
- I am autonomous, quick, clever
- I am different, unusual, exceptional, strange
- I am an outsider, isolated
- others avoid me, find me complicated

disadvantages
+C- incomprehension
+C- stress
+C- frustration
+C- impatience

client's feelings (CER)   **client's behavior** (CAR)
intense excitement,   quickly and creatively
driven, stress, fear of failure   creating solutions

INTERACTION EFFECTS (C)
CLIENT (CI) ←→ THERAPIST (T)

advantage C
+C+   esteem & acceptance
getting more   giving more

giving more   getting more
                 esteem   +C+
                        advantage T

EXPERIENCE THERAPIST

therapist's thoughts (COV)
- he resembles my brilliant depressed brother
- what a waste of all his talents
- he could make more progress
- if only I could prevent his depression

advantage C
-C-   criticism
getting less   giving less

giving more   getting more
                 esteem   +C+
                        advantage T

therapist's feelings (CER)   **therapist's behavior** (CAR)
over-involved   go along with it
                                   try even harder and care

THERAPIST'S INTRAPSYCHIC EFFECTS (C)

advantages
+C+ sense of control
+C+ increase in over-involvement

disadvantages
+C- therapy stagnates

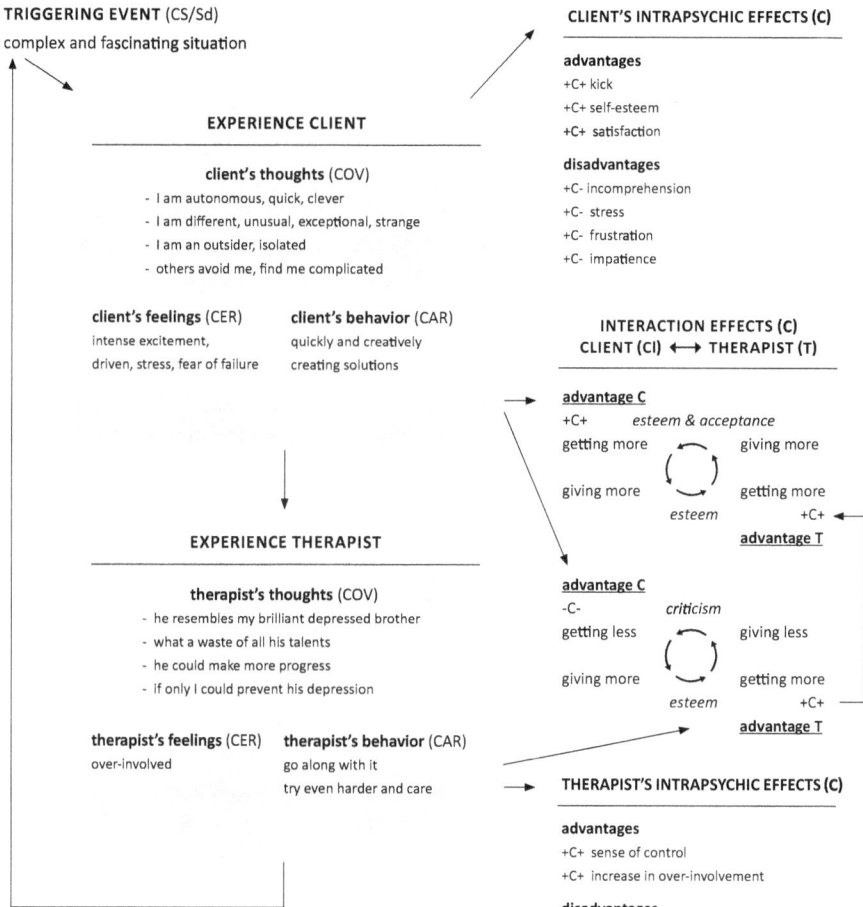

Figure 5.11 Functional analysis of a pitfall in the therapeutic relationship with giftedness: the over-involved therapist

COMMENTARY

The client's core behavior in Figure 5.11 elicits over-involvement in the therapist, who then becomes compliant and does their best. This results in a mutual exchange of interpersonal benefits or disadvantages between client and therapist within the therapeutic relationship. The gifted client receives more appreciation and acceptance (advantage) and less criticism (advantage) as a result of the therapist's avoidance and best efforts. In return, the therapist receives more appreciation (benefit) from the client. This exchange becomes a self-reinforcing vicious circle, perpetuating the client's and therapist's behavior and reinforcing their behavior through mutual reinforcement. This causes the therapy to stagnate.

The therapist, after self-analysis and making a functional analysis of the therapeutic relationship for giftedness, changes his way of responding and allows the stalled therapeutic relationship to develop again. In general, the therapist chooses an autonomous path between going too far with the client's response, going too far opposing it, and going too far away from it. After self-analysis, the therapist is aware of his role as an elicitor and perpetuator of the client's core behavior of giftedness combined with personality traits. He corrects his own response. This includes the response to giftedness in general along with the response to the specific personality traits, which further colors the therapist's response.

The therapeutic alternative for the client with narcissistic personality traits is not to retaliate, nor to take on the role of admirer, but to show appropriate vulnerability. The therapist uses the technique of empathic confrontation to present to the client, in a non-offensive way, the feeling of being hurt and the specific behavior of the client that has caused this feeling. For example, 'I find it very unpleasant that you say that; it hurts me'.

The therapist of the avoidant client does not engage with the client's avoidance, nor does he push the client too hard, but discusses the client's fear of self-disclosure. He explores the client's perception of others as critical and demeaning. The client learns to use behavioral experiments to test whether others are really so critical and demeaning.

Using Socratic dialogue, the therapist engages in awareness raising, testing, questioning, and changing core assumptions, the view of self and of others, including that of the therapist. A relationship-based therapy plan outlines an interaction strategy to reinforce therapy-promoting behaviors in the client. If the therapeutic process becomes stagnant, the functional analysis of the therapeutic relationship is critically evaluated and, if necessary, the functional analysis of the therapeutic relationship and personality traits is revised.

WHAT DOES COGNITIVE BEHAVIORAL THERAPY FOR THE GIFTED REQUIRE OF THE THERAPIST?

The therapist must find giftedness appealing and not threatening, although he does not necessarily have to be gifted himself, only talented with a university degree. Above all, the therapist must be able to counteract intellectually and emotionally without trying to outdo the client, be able to withstand intelligent and sensitive criticism and a high degree of autonomy on the part of the client, and respond to it with empathy and as a fallible example (modeling). The therapist must be aware of his countertransference through self-analysis and use it in an empathic confrontation with his own feelings as they are concretely evoked in the relationship with the client.

5.7   Practice and reflection behavior, dual core behavior, symptom behavior, and therapist behavior: the 'Pentagon Model' for giftedness

After the therapist's self-analysis and functional analysis of the therapeutic relationship, the therapist's behavior appears as a fifth important factor in the 'pentagon'

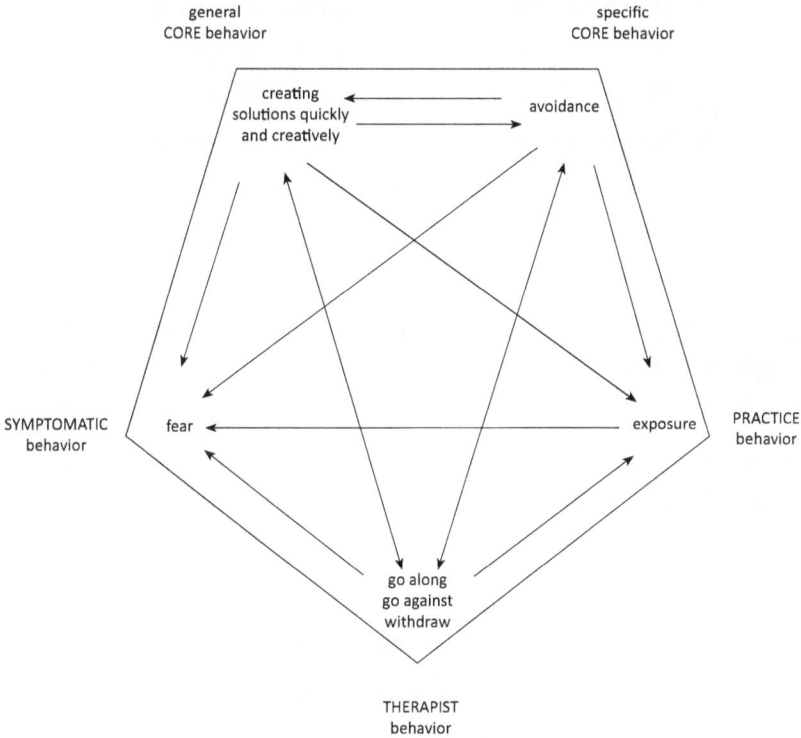

Figure 5.12 Pentagon model for the gifted person with avoidant personality traits

(Figure 5.12). The therapist's behavior is going along with it, going against it, with-drawing, or trying even harder and caring.

The client's symptom behaviors, practice behaviors, and dual core behaviors influence each other, and the therapist's behavior is added as a fifth factor. The pentagon is the 'playing field' of the therapeutic relationship, although most of the client's behavior takes place outside it.

Symptom behavior is the behavioral side of the symptom disorder, for example:

- anxious avoidant behavior
- aggressive attacking behavior
- depressive withdrawal behavior

Protocols for symptom behavior include recommended techniques with empirical evidence of effectiveness, such as exposure for anxiety, self-control for aggression, operant activation and cognitive therapy for depression, and task concentration for social phobia (Keijsers et al., 2011; Barlow et al., 2017).

The *general core behavior* of the gifted person is to create solutions quickly and creatively.

The definition of *core behavior* in *specific* personality traits is trans-situational and trans-temporal behavior. For example, the narcissist devalues, the avoidant avoids, and the obsessive tries excessively, over long periods of time and in many situations.

Practice behavior rarely involves practicing 'by the book'. Clients with personality traits or personality disorders do not practice, do not practice enough, practice randomly, or practice too much. The client with histrionic personality traits makes a charming impression of practicing; the avoidant avoids practice. The narcissist devalues practice as 'vulgar'. The obsessive perfectionist practices excessively. In short, the practice behavior has become the core behavior, and the protocols do not work, either temporarily or in the long term. We enter the realm of interactional dysfunction, including in the therapeutic relationship. These five factors form the pentagon model with arrows illustrating the interrelationships. In the complex therapeutic relationship, all these relationships and behaviors come together.

Reference list

Barlow, D. H., Farchione, T. J., Bullis, J. R., Gallagher, M. W., Murray-Latin, H., Sauer-Zavala, S., Bentley, K. H., Thompson-Hollands, J., Conklin, L. R., Boswell, J. F., Ametaj, A., Carl, J. R., Boettcher, H. T., & Cassiello-Robbins, C. (2017). The unified protocol for transdiagnostic treatment of emotional disorders compared with diagnosis-specific protocols for anxiety disorders: A randomized clinical trial. JAMA Psychiatry, 74(9), 875–884.

Beck, A. T., Freeman, A., Davis, D. D., Arntz, A., Beck, J. S., Butler, A. C., Fleming, B., Fusco, G., Morrison, A. P., Padesky, C. A., Pretzer, J. L., Renton, J., Simon, K. M. (2003). *Cognitive therapy of personality disorders* (2nd ed.). Guilford Press.

Brinkman, W. (1978). Het gedragstherapeutisch proces. In J. W. G. Orlemans, P. Eelen & W. P. Haaijman (Eds.), *Handboek voor gedragstherapie (H. A1 t/m A14)*. Van Loghum Slaterus.

Ellis, A. (1962). *Reason and emotion in psychotherapy*. Lyle Stuart.

Hafkenscheid, A. (2003). Objective countertransference: Do patients' interpersonal impacts generalize across therapists? *Clinical Psychology and Psychotherapy, 10*, 31–40.

Hafkenscheid, A. (2005). The impact message inventory (IMI-C): Generalizability of patients' command and relationship messages across psychiatric nurses. *Journal of Psychiatric and Mental Health Nursing, 12*, 325–332.

Hafkenscheid, A. (2012). Assessing objective countertransference with a computer-delivered impact message inventory (IMI-C). *Clinical Psychology and Psychotherapy, 19*(1), 37–45.

Keijsers, G. P. J., Van Minnen, A., & Hoogduin, C. A. L. (2011). *Protocollaire behandelingen voor volwassenen met psychische klachten, deel 1 en 2*. Boom.

Leary, T. (1957). *Interpersonal diagnosis of personality*. Ronald.

Watzlawick, P., Beavin, J. H., & Jackson, D. D. (1967). *Pragmatics of human communication*. W.W. Norton.

Chapter 6

The narcissistic personality disorder

Summary

This book would not be complete without a survey of the diagnosis, treatment, and therapeutic relationship of narcissistic personality traits or personality disorder.

Giftedness and narcissistic traits overlap in their view of self as being superior and unique. Therefore, the risk of a misdiagnosis is considerable. Too many gifted clients are misdiagnosed as having narcissistic personality disorders. The counter-transference makes this problem even more complex. The therapist reacts in an insecure or irritated manner when the narcissistic client is going to devalue him or her. Moreover there is the problem of distinguishing between pathological and healthy narcissism, especially with giftedness.

Much attention is also given to the disturbances and pitfalls in the therapeutic relationship and how to concretely self-analyze and deal with them. Concrete examples of case histories, test results, and self-analyses are presented, as well as figures from the functional analysis, treatment plan, and functional analysis of the therapeutic relationship. Clear frameworks summarize the clinical and scientific knowledge about narcissistic personality disorder.

6.1 Classification of the narcissistic personality disorder according to DSM-5 categorical model

For the DSM-5 classification, we can consider the five steps from the model.

1 most striking impression
2 screening for DSM-5 criteria
3 screening for core cognitions and core behaviors
4 interaction diagnosis of core behaviors
5 determination of DSM-5 criteria and classification using parts of the SCID-5-PD

6.1.1 Step 1: Most striking impression

The DSM-5 briefly defines the narcissistic personality disorder (APA, 2013) as *a pattern of grandiosity, need for admiration, and lack of empathy.*

DOI: 10.4324/9781003423287-7

The most striking impression of the narcissistic personality disorder is superiority and grandiosity.

Case study Marianne Leery

Marianne Leery is a shy economics student who does not dare to be around people, either at university or in her dormitory. Remarkably, she is able to give presentations. She has pain in her neck, shoulders, and stomach and has difficulty concentrating. She studies hard and does well, but is only satisfied with nines and tens. She often fantasizes about getting a Ph.D. cum laude and working at a top foreign university. When she was 16, she suffered from anorexia nervosa. She seems angry, but also arrogant.

The therapist felt that the anger and criticism were directed at him. He tried to deflect it by complimenting the client. The therapist found her to be vulnerable and very depressed. After the therapist instructed her to approach others more openly and to make social contacts more often, her mood turned around. She saw her peers as jealous of her great talents. She criticized the therapist a lot and devalued him. The therapist became insecure and began to apologize. The client stopped therapy and solved her problem by moving back home and taking anti-depressants. She was disappointed that she was not cured within a few sessions. The therapist realized too late that the client's social phobia was secondary to her narcissistic personality disorder.

We apply to this case the five steps in classification. The most striking impression is superiority and grandiosity. The hypothesis based on this is narcissistic personality disorder. This is the first step in the classification.

6.1.2   Step 2: Screening for DSM-5 criteria

Clinical judgment

The examiner forms an impression of dysfunction in the form of subjective distress and/or objective impairments in the client's personality functioning. The clinician evaluates the DSM-5 criteria (APA, 2013).

According to the criteria, from early adulthood, people with a narcissistic personality disorder exhibit grandiose fantasies and behaviors, an extraordinary need for admiration, and a lack of empathy. They consider themselves enormously important and exaggerate their accomplishments and talents. Many fantasize about unlimited success for themselves, power, genius, beauty, or the 'perfect' romance.

They consider themselves so special and unique that they feel it is appropriate to associate only with similarly special people. They usually also believe that they are entitled to special treatment and that others should naturally live up to their expectations. They are quick to feel and see jealousy in others. They often behave arrogantly and cavalierly, abusing others for their own ends. The full criteria can be found in the DSM-5 (APA, 2013).

Self-assessment

SCID-5-PD

Commentary

On the SCID-5-PD, Marianne scores five criteria on the narcissistic personality disorder questions. The hypothesis based on the most striking impression and based on the results of the SCID-5-PD is a narcissistic personality disorder.

6.1.3   Step 3: Screening for core cognitions and core behaviors

Clinical assessment

For five personality disorders, the five most discriminating items of the PBQ test have been empirically examined (Beck et al., 2003, 2014). These items refer to five automatic thoughts which I refer to as 'the top five' and can be quickly assessed in a clinical interview. The number of possible personality disorders as a hypothesis is thus narrowed or confirmed in a very efficient way. Establishing the presence of many of the discriminating cognitions of the narcissistic personality disorder makes this diagnosis much more likely.

It should be noted, however, that finding many characteristic narcissistic cognitions is not (yet) the same as meeting the required number of DSM-5 criteria using the SCID-5-PD (Step 5). The 'top five' items for the are presented in the box below.

> The Five Most Distinctive Automatic Thoughts of Narcissistic Personality Disorder*
>
> 1   I am not bound by the rules that apply to others.
> 2   I have every reason to look forward to a great future.
> 3   Because I am above others, I am entitled to preferential treatment.
> 4   Others do not deserve the admiration or wealth they receive.
> 5   Because I am so talented, others should adapt to support my career.
>
> *Beck et al. (2003), reproduced with permission

Table 6.1 Core behaviors and core cognitions in narcissistic personality disorder

core behavior	1. devaluate
	2. elevate oneself
core emotion	pride, anger, jealousy, depression
view of self*	unique, special, superior
view of others*	inferior, admiring
core reinforcement	(self-)admiration
core theme	fear of humiliation and being ordinary

(*Beck et al., 2003)

Marianne Leery scores one, half, one, one, one, and one on items 1 through 5, for a total of 4.5 for the most distinctive automatic thoughts of the narcissistic personality disorder.

As a third step, the narcissistic personality disorder hypothesis is also tested using Table 6.1. Marianne's core behavior is to devalue others and to elevate herself. Her core feelings are pride on the one hand and jealousy of her boyfriend on the other. Her image of others is that they are inferior and should admire her. She sees herself as unique and above others.

Core behaviors and core cognitions in narcissistic personality disorder are listed in Table 6.1. The core behavior is the focus of the functional analysis in personality disorders. Core behavior has to be high-frequent, trans-situational, and trans-temporal. The functional analysis is shown and discussed in Figure 6.1. The identification of high-frequency core behaviors – in this case, devaluation and self-aggrandizement – is very important because it leads to the functional analysis and thus directly to a cognitive behavioral (partial) treatment plan. This makes the DSM-5 classification a useful stepping stone to the functional analysis of the core behavior and the treatment plan.

Self-assessment with tests

PBQ (Beck et al., 2003)

6.1.4   Step 4: Interaction diagnosis of the core behavior

Clinical assessment

The clinician also looks at the narcissistic client's core interpersonal behavior, interactional preference position, and attachment mode. The narcissist is detached (rejecting–avoiding) and places himself/herself above/against others. The diagnostician looks at situations and interactional dysfunctions within, but especially *outside*, the therapeutic relationship.

6.1.5   Step 5: DSM-5 classification using parts of the SCID-5-PD

For the DSM-5 classification of narcissistic personality disorder, using the specific part of the SCID-5-PD (First et al., 2015) for the narcissistic personality disorder, Marianne Leery meets criteria 1, 2, 4, 7, and 8. The identified core behavior of

TRIGGERING EVENT
(CS/sd)
(self) admiration
(perceived) hurt

thoughts (COV)
- I am special and unique   **behavior** (CAR)
  and therefore entitled to   devalue
  special treatment   elevate oneself
- I am superior
- others are inferior and
  jealous of me
- others must admire me
- I don't have to follow
  the rules
- being ordinary is a
  disaster

feeling (CER)   **consequences** (C)
anger   *advantages*
pride   +C+ assert superiority and
envy   uniqueness
                                 -C- avoiding hurt

                                 disadvantages
                                 -C+ vulnerable self-esteem
                                 0C+ admiration fails to
                                     materialize
                                 +C- dependent on more and
                                     more (self-)admiration
                                 +C- environment begins to
                                     react negatively with fear or
                                     anger
                                 +C- increase in
                                     compensatory behavior
                                 +C- increase in anger
                                 +C- increase in depression
                                     over time

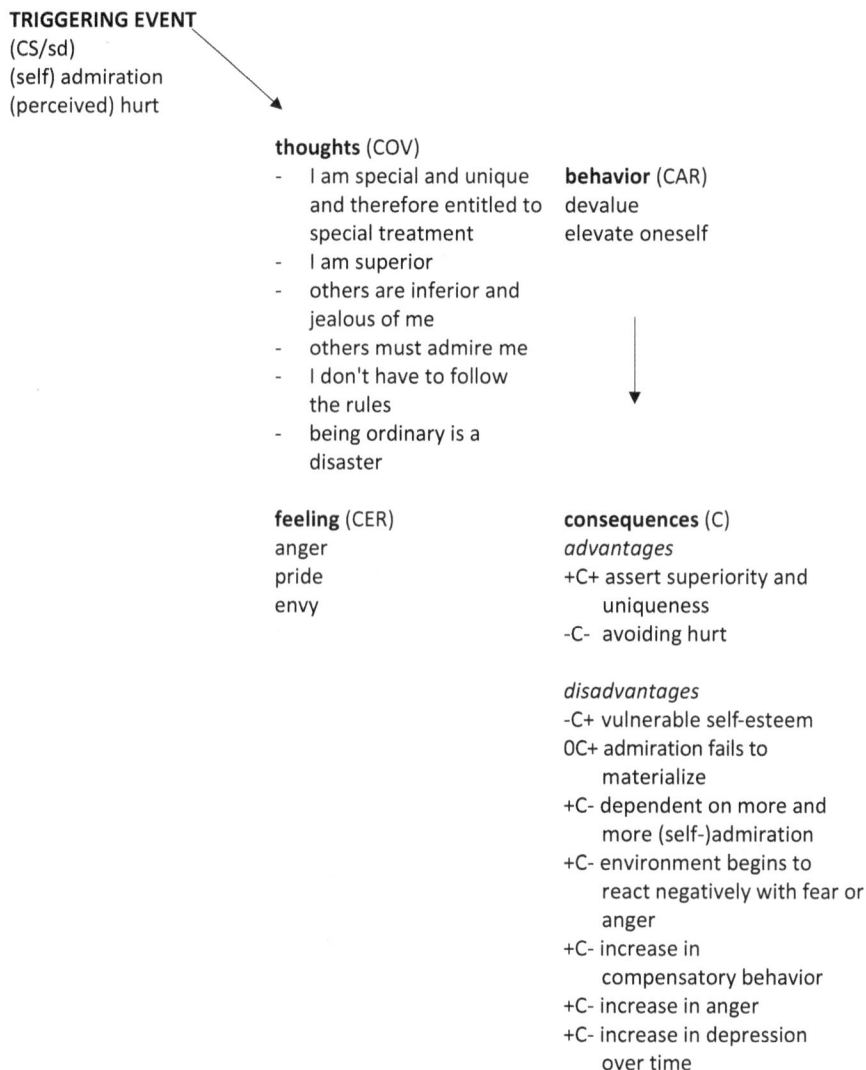

Figure 6.1 Functional analysis of narcissistic personality disorder

devaluation and self-aggrandizement is the focus of functional analysis. The functional analysis leads to the treatment plan for devaluation (Sections 6.3 and 6.4).

6.2   DSM-5 diagnosis, according to dimensional model

6.2.1   The diagnostic phase

After the classification, the dimensional model of DSM-5 offers enriching possibilities for the diagnostic phase. For the diagnostic phase, we go through seven steps (see box below).

Diagnosis of personality dysfunction and pathological traits according to the DSM-5 (APA, 2013) in seven possible steps

1   Most striking impressions and traits
2a Global screening for severity of personality dysfunction
2b Global screening for pathological and general traits
3a Screening for core cognitions and core behaviors
3b Topographical analysis of core behavior through client self-observation
4a Interactional diagnosis of core behavior
4b Self-analysis and functional analysis of the therapeutic relationship
5   (optional) In-depth testing of facet pattern (FFM) and temperament
6a Identification of limitations in personality functioning with the STiP-5.1
6b Identification of pathological traits with the comprehensive PID-5
7   Individualized DSM-5 diagnosis integrated into tested case conceptualization

6.2.2   Step 1: Most striking impression and traits

The most striking impression of narcissistic personality disorder is *superiority and grandiosity* (APA, 2013).

6.2.3   Step 2a: Global screening for limitations in identity, self-directness, empathy, and intimacy

Clinical assessment

The DSM-5 begins with general criterion A, the clinical assessment of personality dysfunction (APA, 2013). An initial global clinical assessment is based in part on the client's current functioning and learning history.

The clinician gives a global score of plus, minus, or average in four areas of the client: 1. identity; 2. self-direction; 3. empathy; and 4. intimacy. An example of this for narcissistic personality disorder is shown in Table 6.2.

For two or more negative scores (2, 3, or 4), the likelihood of a personality disorder is high. If the scores are positive in three or four areas, the likelihood of

Table 6.2 Global self-assessment in narcissistic personality disorder

1 Identity	−/++
2 Self-direction	−
3 Empathy	−
4 Intimacy	−

a personality disorder is low, and we should speak of, for example, narcissistic traits that are important in therapy but not sufficiently maladaptive to speak of a personality disorder. If in doubt, we may also consider going to Step 6a and taking the full STiP5.1.

In narcissistic personality disorder, there are at least moderate personality problems (APA, 2013). This may be expressed in two or more of the following areas:

- identity, for example, exaggerated self-esteem or inferiority feelings
- self-direction, for example, the alignment of goals with gaining the approval of others
- empathy, for example, limited ability to recognize the feelings of others
- intimacy, for example, limited genuine interest in others

For complete definitions, see DSM-5 (APA, 2013).

Clients can be screened by taking the Rosenberg for self-esteem, the SD scale of the TCI for self-direction, the EQ for empathy, and the RQ for attachment. If necessary, another assessment can be obtained from a third party without interests and prejudices with sufficient observational skills and good emotional intelligence.

6.2.4   Step 2b: Global screening for pathological and general traits

DSM-5 and screening for pathological traits

Clinical judgment

Clinical judgment should include two pathological personality traits: grandiosity and attention-seeking (both facets of antagonism) (APA, 2013). These are discussed further in Step 6b.

Self-assessment and assessment by others with tests

A quick screening is possible with the PID-5, short form. The framework lists some items for the antagonism domain.

For differential diagnosis and multiple hypotheses, it is better to use the short form (25 items) (Krueger et al., 2012) or the full version with 220 items (see also Step 6b). If necessary, a second opinion may be obtained using the informant version of the PID-5 (APA, 2013).

The Five-Factor Model and screening for general traits

Clinical judgment

Using the Five-Factor Model as a frame of reference (McCrae & Costa, 2008), a quick and efficient clinical assessment of the client's general characteristics is possible. The clinician generally assesses the client's five factors (N, E, O, A, C) with a high, low, or average score.

Five-factor profile of narcissistic personality disorder (Samuel & Widiger, 2008)
A-

These five factors are neuroticism (low emotional stability), extraversion, openness to new experiences (intellectual autonomy), altruism (kindness), and conscientiousness (orderliness). This gives us a five-factor profile.

Self-assessment and assessment by others with tests

The client's view of the five factors can be assessed using the NEO-PI-3 tests. If necessary, the assessment of others can be obtained from a third party.

6.2.5   Step 3a: Screening for core cognitions and core behaviors

Clinical judgment and self-assessment

The five most discriminating items on the PBQ have been empirically studied in five personality disorders (Beck et al., 2003, 2014). I refer to these five automatic thoughts as the 'top five'. These five items can be quickly assessed in a clinical interview (0 = no recognition, ½ = some recognition, 1 = total recognition).

This form of screening has already been used in the classification phase (Section 6.1.3), and the result can be replicated here in Step 3a. For narcissistic personality disorder, these are the 'top five' items in the box.

The Five Most Distinctive Automatic Thoughts of Narcissistic Personality Disorder*

1   I am not bound by the rules that apply to others.
2   I have every reason to look forward to a great future.
3   Because I am above others, I am entitled to preferential treatment.
4   Others do not deserve the admiration or wealth they receive.
5   Because I am so talented, others should adapt to support my career.

*Beck et al. (2003), reproduced with permission

For confirmation, or if the score is less pronounced, we can use the extended 14 items. In order to rule out other hypotheses (differential diagnosis), we also use the items from other possible personality traits or disorders (see Table 2.5). At a deeper level than the characteristic automatic thoughts are the basic assumptions or core cognitions, such as view of self and of others. These are listed in Table 6.1 in Section 6.1.3.

The core behavior is the focus of functional analysis in personality disorders. It must be high frequency, trans-situational, and trans-temporal. Identifying a high-frequency core behavior, in this case devaluation and self-aggrandizement, is very important because it leads to the functional analysis and thus directly to a cognitive behavioral (partial) treatment plan. The functional analysis of narcissistic personality disorder can be found in Section 6.3 and Figure 6.1.

Self-assessment with tests

PBQ (Beck et al., 2003, 2014)

6.2.6   Step 3b: Topographical analyses of core behaviors through self-observation of the client with a thought record

If the core behaviors of self-deprecation and self-aggrandizement are assessed as high-frequency, this is discussed with the client. The therapist asks the client to note the frequency of the core behavior and the situations in which it occurs or does not occur. This is called topographical analysis. In Greek, 'topographic' means to describe the place.

The method for this is the thought record: Event (situation) > Thoughts > Feelings > Behavior > Consequences (Beck, 1995). It is recommended that this diagram be written down or typed into the smartphone at the end of each half-day session. Self-observation and self-reflection are important skills for the client to learn in therapy. The examples of core behaviors in concrete situations with associated thoughts, feelings, and consequences provide a broad picture of the client's experiences, actions, and frequency of core behaviors.

By zooming in on some specific thought records that occur with strong feelings (the client gives himself a score from 0 to 10 for the strength of his feelings), the client and therapist form a picture of the individual function and meaning of the core behaviors and feelings.

Interaction preference position of narcissistic personality disorder

above/against and detachment (avoidance/rejection of attachment)

6.2.7   Step 4a: Interaction diagnosis of core behavior

Clinical assessment

The researcher also looks at the narcissistic client's core interpersonal behavior, interaction preference, and mode of attachment. This is detached (rejection–avoidance) and over/against. The diagnostician looks at situations and interactional dysfunctions both within and outside the therapeutic relationship.

This form of screening has already been used in Step 4 of the classification phase (Section 6.1.4) and the result can be repeated here in Step 4a.

6.2.8   Step 4b: Self-analysis and functional analysis of the therapeutic relationship

If the therapist feels excessively insecure, irritated, discouraged, or involved in response to the narcissistic client's core behaviors, it is time for self-analysis and a functional analysis of the therapeutic relationship (Section 6.5, Figures 6.2, 6.3, and 6.4).

Assessment with tests

The therapist's response in the therapeutic relationship can be examined using the IMC-CS test (Hafkenscheid, 2005, 2012).

6.2.9   Step 5: In-depth testing of facet pattern (FFM) and temperament

If the therapist has the time and opportunity for in-depth testing, this step provides an additional opportunity to test the hypothesis.

The diagnosis of narcissistic personality disorder is a hypothesis that can be partially shaped, refined, and confirmed or falsified by the profiles of psychological tests as a fifth step. In our example, the client refused to take the recommended tests. Not wanting to be tested may be an indication of a narcissistic personality disorder.

The profiles of psychological tests that are indicative of the diagnosis of a narcissistic personality disorder are listed in Table 6.3.

Table 6.3 Narcissistic personality disorder and psychological tests profiles

Five-Factor Profile*			A–	
NEO Facet Profiles*	N+ 2		A– 2, 5	
			a– 1, 3, 4	
PID-5 domains**			ANT+	
TCI (temperament)***	NS+	HA+	RD+PER–/+	SD– CO– STR–

*Samuel and Widiger (2008)
** Krueger et al. (2012)
*** Cloninger (2000)

6.2.10   Step 6a: Identifying limitations in personality functioning with the STiP5.1

Clinicians can identify no (0), mild (1), moderate (2), severe (3), or extreme (4) limitations in personality functioning by administering the STiP5.1 (Hutsebaut et al., 2015). The cutoff is expressed as characteristic impairments – at least moderate – in two or more areas to establish the presence of a personality disorder and an individual dimensional pattern of severity of dysfunction. This determination, like Step 6b, is a form of descriptive testing.

The hypotheses about dysfunction formed in Step 2a using clinical judgment are thoroughly tested with the STiP5.1 in this step. These four areas are: 1. identity; 2. self-directedness; 3. empathy; and 4. intimacy.

In Part III of the DSM-5 (APA, 2013), these five levels of functioning are generally described in the STiP5.1.

6.2.11   Step 6b: Identifying pathological traits with the short PID-5

In Step 2b, we already screened with the short PID-5 (Krueger et al., 2012), at least the antagonism subscale. This made the narcissistic personality disorder hypothesis more or less likely. For the final test, the comprehensive PID-5 was administered.

Using the comprehensive PID-5, we find a specific and individualized pattern of pathological traits. We then determine whether these fit the *characteristic* profile associated with narcissistic personality disorder or reflect this pattern of traits. If the pattern is correct, then we have established a diagnosis of narcissistic personality disorder. Alternatively, a trait-specific personality disorder may be found if both Step 6a results in a personality disorder and at least one pathological trait is found. It is also possible to find no personality disorder or another of the six 'prototypical' personality disorders.

The narcissistic personality disorder is characterized by two pathological traits (APA, 2013):

- grandiosity, for example, feelings of entitlement to preferential treatment
- attention-seeking, for example, seeking attention from others

For the complete definition, see the DSM-5 (APA, 2013).

6.2.12   Step 7: Individualized DSM-5 diagnosis integrated into the case conceptualization

The diagnostic data from the seven steps are then integrated into a case conceptualization. See Chapter 3.

6.3   Functional analysis of the core behavior

Devaluing and/or using the other person and elevating oneself is the core behavior of a client with a narcissistic personality disorder. In fact, they are two sides of the same coin. When the narcissistic client is 'at rest', he uses the other person for admiration; but when the narcissistic client feels hurt (and this happens disproportionately quickly), he goes on the attack and begins to devalue, compete, and hurt.

Case study Mr. Aláriq

Mr. Aláriq is an asylum seeker from a very difficult background. After the civil war in his country, his parents disappeared and his brothers are untraceable. He has no social contacts or friends. He sees his compatriots in the asylum center as inferior. He feels belittled and disrespected as an asylum seeker. He comes for treatment for obsessive-compulsive disorder and nightmares. He has experienced traumatic situations, imprisonment, and torture. Because of his demanding attitude (above/against position), he is in constant conflict with treatment providers. He has worn many of them out. The client wants special treatment from them and does not like rules and procedures. For example, he does not want to wait in the waiting room, but goes directly to the consultation room at the appointed time. He thinks he does not have to follow the rules because he is so special and unique. He also makes it difficult for the therapist to criticize him. His behavior alternates between devaluing and using. His emotions alternate between anger and pride. When he does not receive the expected and desired admiration, he devalues those around him.

Mr. Aláriq is someone with a particularly wounded narcissistic personality disorder. When he feels humiliated, it makes him angry and jealous. He thinks that he is unique and special and entitled to special treatment, and he sees others as envious of him and as people who should admire him. He does not need to follow any rules, and other people have no right to criticize him. These thoughts and feelings lead to behaviors of devaluation, competition, or rivalry and, when hurt, to retaliation.

As a result, he sees his uniqueness and superiority confirmed, and his hurt is reduced. However, there are many drawbacks to this behavior of devaluation and rivalry, namely, that it leaves him with a vulnerable sense of self that constantly requires more compensation. The environment also begins to react negatively. He is sometimes anxious, sometimes angry. He feels rejected, and admiration is increasingly lacking. As a result, the client's anger increases and, in the long run, depression develops. After prolonged humiliation and constant lack of admiration, a client with a narcissistic personality disorder may become depressed. This particular client is an illustration of the general functional analysis of the narcissistic personality disorder detailed in Figure 6.1.

6.4   Cognitive behavioral therapy, treatment plan, and process

Once we have completed the functional analysis of the narcissistic personality disorder, we can then create a treatment plan with goals and techniques.

In Table 6.4, the five foci of the cognitive behavioral model are presented with specific treatment goals for the client with narcissistic personality disorder. In addition, specific techniques that can be used in the process are listed for each therapy goal. These concrete and specific goals and techniques can be understood as suggestions for creating a treatment plan. An important part of the treatment plan is for the client to learn to just be, to participate with others, and to respond openly to constructive criticism without being overwhelmed by feelings of unworthiness.

The therapist draws a diagram of the preliminary case conceptualization to show how the symptoms (e.g., depressive disorder) and problems at work or in

Table 6.4 The treatment plan for narcissistic personality disorder

Starting point	Therapy goals	Techniques
triggering event (CS/Sd)	insult humiliation	gradual exposure temporary avoidance stop mechanism
thoughts (COV)	• I am good as I am, even when I am ordinary • I am good as I am, even if I am criticized or hurt • being ordinary has advantages • others are equal • when others are critical or jealous, they feel hurt • others are allowed to criticize, maybe I can learn from it	continuum techniques cognitive diary historical test
feeling (CER)	fear of humiliation and being ordinary feeling and reversing anger counter theme: self-acceptance	downward arrow technique COMET relaxation hypnosis EMDR
behavior (CAR)	reciprocal behavior just doing/being reduce retaliation and devaluation being assertive without hurting	behavioral experiments role play self-control techniques self-exposure
consequences (C)	increase disadvantages reduce advantages	awareness and other forms of (self) reinforcement

relationships (e.g., anxiety and annoyance in the environment because of the devaluing behavior) are related to the personality disorder and childhood experiences. He empathically confronts the client with this.

At the end of the diagnostic phase (Section 6.2), the holistic theory is further tested and both core and symptom behaviors can be selected as the problem.

Functional analyses are made of core and symptom behaviors and, based on these, (partial) treatment plans and the planned sequence are established. Guidelines and protocols (Barlow et al., 2017; Keijsers et al., 2011) are used for symptom behaviors. Table 6.4 provides an example of a treatment plan for a narcissistic personality disorder, which is not intended as a mandatory protocol, but as an inspiration for the many possible goals and techniques regarding the five factors.

In the problem selection, a client with narcissistic personality disorder often struggles to choose the benefits of just being and just participating with others as a treatment goal because he feels so easily hurt and so strongly about proving himself to be unique and special.

The cognitive behavioral therapist will need to further motivate the client through the baseline assessment and the analysis of the self-denigration and self-esteem functions, including the advantages and disadvantages of this core behavior. It is then often necessary to select symptomatic behaviors, such as a more peripheral persistent depressive disorder, to work on first, with the narcissistic personality disorder in the background.

6.5   Self-analysis and functional analysis of the therapeutic relationship

After the functional analysis of the individual client with a narcissistic personality disorder, the therapist looks at the functional analysis of the therapeutic relationship and his own reaction as complementary. The therapist's tool is his own feelings: does the client make him feel insecure, angry, or discouraged? Does the therapist feel guilty, worried or, on the contrary, excited and enchanted or jealous? All of the feelings aroused by the client with narcissistic personality disorder and the automatic response with (counter) behavior by the therapist are of diagnostic value and, with the help of self-analysis and reflection, can lead to changes in the therapist's behavior.

The following three cases illustrate the therapist's self-analysis (Ellis, 1962) of the three major pitfalls in the therapeutic relationship: the insecure therapist, the irritated therapist, and the discouraged therapist.

Case study Teddy Rhine

Teddy Rhine is a middle-aged manager. After his vacation, he has been on sick leave for several months because he is a bit tired. He has symptoms of burnout, feels exhausted, and is emotionally unstable. He seems to have always worked extremely hard and set very high standards for himself and his colleagues. His father was traumatized as a professional soldier in a camp in Indonesia in the Second World War and always belittled others. Teddy was never able to compete with his father, even though he is very strong verbally and in his private and professional life easily gains the upper hand. He was never hugged by his mother; their relationship was always distant. The client understands that he works so hard to get compliments and that what he really wants is recognition. He also avoids the feelings of humiliation that have become a core issue. In therapy, the same problem emerges of the client being devaluing towards the therapist.

The therapist feels *insecure* and irritated and decides to do a self-analysis based on the situation that this client often comes late, talks on his cell phone during the session, and takes the therapy completely for granted. The self-analysis is as follows.

Situation (A): The client arrives late and takes a long time to answer his cell phone.
Therapist's thoughts: see Table 6.5.
Therapist's feelings (C): insecurity.
Therapist's behavior (C): apologetically discusses client's cell phone use.
Alternative and balanced thoughts (E) of the therapist (true and helpful)

1 He is walking over me, but this is part of the invalidating behavior of his narcissistic personality disorder.
2 He is not out to abuse me; I need to pretend less and start discussing his pattern with him more.
3 When I discuss his pattern, I am taken seriously.
4 I am a reasonably good therapist with an understanding of personality disorders.

Goal of the therapist (G):

• to feel less insecure and more relaxed
• apply the technique of empathic confrontation

Table 6.5 Assessment of the insecure therapist's thoughts (Ellis, 1962)

	Thoughts of the therapist (B)	Assessment (D)	
1.	He is walking all over me.	true	not helpful
2.	I slave away and he uses me.	not true	not helpful
3.	I am not taken seriously.	true	not helpful
4.	I am not a good therapist.	not true	not helpful

COMMENTARY

Out of insecurity, the therapist did not discuss the client's boundary violations and gave him too much space. He was too late in drawing a boundary that took into account the sensitivity to humiliation that the client had built up as a core theme in his life and that was also expressed in therapy. Once the therapist had developed different feelings and thoughts through this self-analysis, he was able to empathically confront the client. The therapist told the client that he did not feel taken seriously. This surprised the client; he was genuinely surprised. The therapist did not apologize or retort, but chose the third way, that of clarification. He tried to make it clear to the client that his dominant behavior could be an avoidance of past humiliations and that he wanted to be overly dominant and in control in every situation, including therapy. The therapist also showed vulnerability by discussing in a non-blaming way that he did not feel taken seriously. This was something the client had never been told before and was mostly unaware of. At the onset of awareness of this core issue, he shot into dominant behavior. Figure 6.2 shows the pitfall of the insecure therapist.

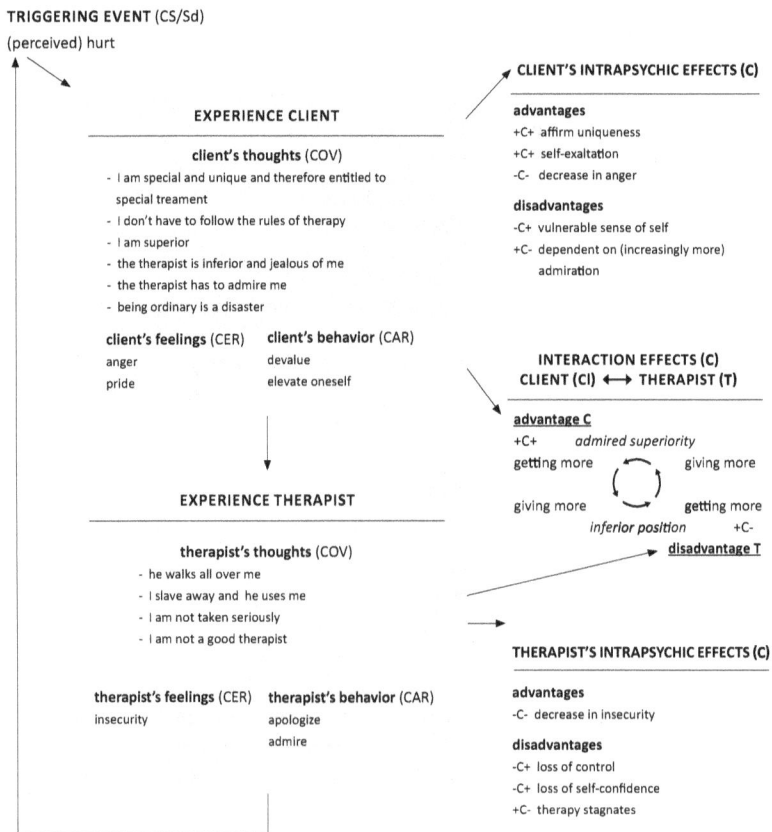

TRIGGERING EVENT (CS/Sd)
(perceived) hurt

EXPERIENCE CLIENT

client's thoughts (COV)
- I am special and unique and therefore entitled to special treatment
- I don't have to follow the rules of therapy
- I am superior
- the therapist is inferior and jealous of me
- the therapist has to admire me
- being ordinary is a disaster

client's feelings (CER)   client's behavior (CAR)
anger   devalue
pride   elevate oneself

EXPERIENCE THERAPIST

therapist's thoughts (COV)
- he walks all over me
- I slave away and he uses me
- I am not taken seriously
- I am not a good therapist

therapist's feelings (CER)   therapist's behavior (CAR)
insecurity   apologize
                              admire

CLIENT'S INTRAPSYCHIC EFFECTS (C)

advantages
+C+ affirm uniqueness
+C+ self-exaltation
-C- decrease in anger

disadvantages
-C+ vulnerable sense of self
+C- dependent on (increasingly more) admiration

INTERACTION EFFECTS (C)
CLIENT (CI) ⟷ THERAPIST (T)

advantage C
+C+   admired superiority
getting more   giving more

giving more   getting more
inferior position   +C-
                    disadvantage T

THERAPIST'S INTRAPSYCHIC EFFECTS (C)

advantages
-C- decrease in insecurity

disadvantages
-C+ loss of control
-C+ loss of self-confidence
+C- therapy stagnates

Figure 6.2 Functional analysis of a pitfall in the therapeutic relationship in relation to a narcissistic personality disorder: the insecure therapist

Case study Antony Fisherman

Antony Fisherman is a person whose job always requires him to do very difficult work and write extensive research papers at the last minute. This makes him feel special and unique, and he eagerly takes on projects that are too difficult for his colleagues. He becomes overworked and develops panic symptoms and a travel phobia. In treatment, the therapist initially focuses too much on his anxiety and burnout symptoms and not enough on his learning history and narcissistic personality disorder. The therapist falls into the trap of blowback and escalation. The client breaks off contact after the therapist fails to respond to his request for an after-hours meeting on short notice. The client attributes his own failure to return to work, which he sees as very humiliating, to the therapist's shortcomings.

The *irritated* therapist then does the following self-analysis.

Situation (A): The client complains to the therapist about his failure to resume work.
Therapist's thoughts: see Table 6.6.
Therapist's feelings (C): irritation.
Behavior of the therapist (C): hurting the client back.
Alternative and balanced thoughts (E) of the therapist (true and helpful):

1 He is too hurt to accept his own part.
2 He has chosen not to return to work himself.
3 The client with a narcissistic personality disorder wants to claim only the successes and certainly not a hurtful failure.

Goal of the therapist (G)

• feel less irritated
• confront empathically

Table 6.6 Assessment of the irritated therapist's thoughts (Ellis, 1962)

	Thoughts of the therapist (B)	Assessment (D)	
1.	He blames me for his failure.	true	not helpful
2.	It was his own choice to return to work.	true	helpful
3.	I didn't do it wrong, he decided for himself after discussing the pros and cons.	true	not helpful

COMMENTARY

The client clearly wants an exception in his request for an out-of-office consultation. The therapist did not pay enough attention to the narcissistic personality disorder and focused too much on work problems and panic. The interaction that was hurtful to the therapist was also an opportunity to discuss the narcissistic personality disorder. Perhaps the therapist could have been more flexible in negotiating a compromise about the appointment, but his anger caused him to jump the gun. Self-analysis after the fact is also particularly instructive and helpful for the next time. Figure 6.3 shows the functional analysis of the therapeutic relationship in the case of the irritated therapist.

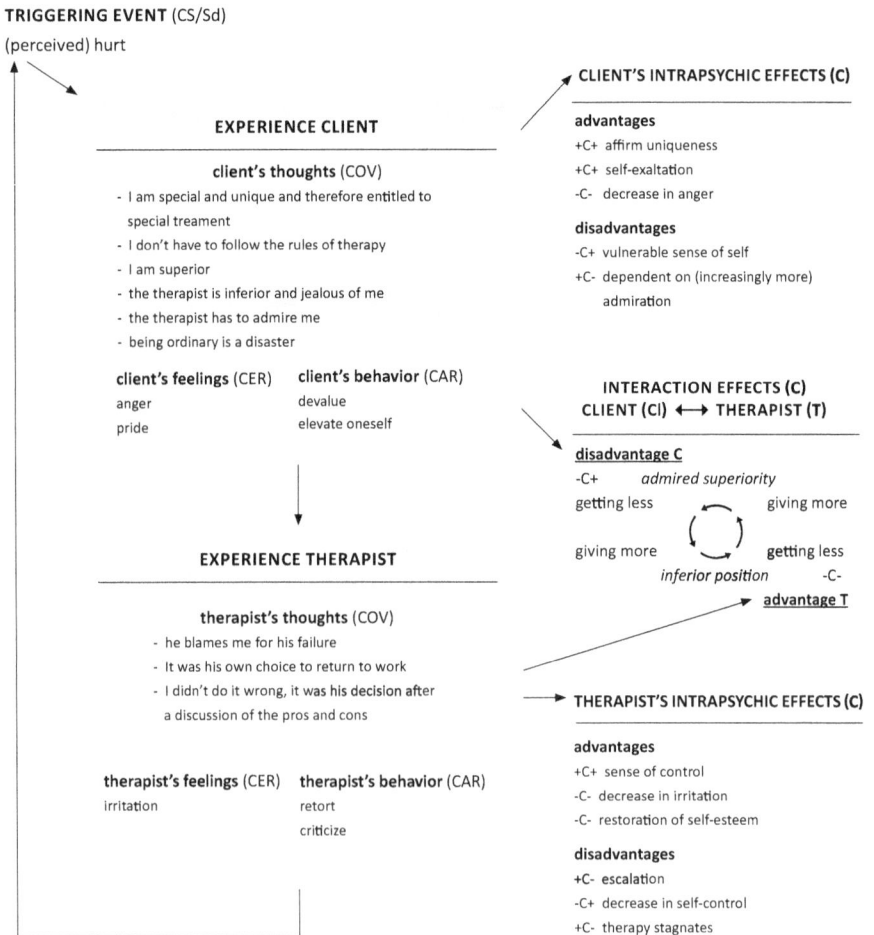

TRIGGERING EVENT (CS/Sd)

(perceived) hurt

CLIENT'S INTRAPSYCHIC EFFECTS (C)

EXPERIENCE CLIENT

client's thoughts (COV)
- I am special and unique and therefore entitled to special treament
- I don't have to follow the rules of therapy
- I am superior
- the therapist is inferior and jealous of me
- the therapist has to admire me
- being ordinary is a disaster

advantages
+C+ affirm uniqueness
+C+ self-exaltation
-C- decrease in anger

disadvantages
-C+ vulnerable sense of self
+C- dependent on (increasingly more) admiration

client's feelings (CER)   **client's behavior** (CAR)
anger   devalue
pride   elevate oneself

INTERACTION EFFECTS (C)
CLIENT (Cl) ⟷ THERAPIST (T)

disadvantage C
-C+   admired superiority
getting less   giving more

giving more   getting less
inferior position   -C-
advantage T

EXPERIENCE THERAPIST

therapist's thoughts (COV)
- he blames me for his failure
- It was his own choice to return to work
- I didn't do it wrong, it was his decision after a discussion of the pros and cons

THERAPIST'S INTRAPSYCHIC EFFECTS (C)

advantages
+C+ sense of control
-C- decrease in irritation
-C- restoration of self-esteem

therapist's feelings (CER)   **therapist's behavior** (CAR)
irritation   retort
                                 criticize

disadvantages
+C- escalation
-C+ decrease in self-control
+C- therapy stagnates

Figure 6.3 Functional analysis of a pitfall in the therapeutic relationship in relation to a narcissistic personality disorder: the irritated therapist

Case study Rose Falcon

Rose Falcon is being treated for bulimia and rages that cause her to hit her young children. She is an articulate, intelligent woman who constantly dominates the therapy sessions and blames others. Her therapist finds it difficult to intervene and becomes increasingly discouraged. He has discussed this behavior several times, but to no avail. Wanting to get rid of her symptoms quickly and achieve lasting healing, Rose goes for a weekend of Gestalt therapy without consultation. She had previously been in psychoanalysis for five years with no effect on her eating disorder. Her friend with the same binge eating and vomiting had improved in 20 sessions of cognitive behavioral therapy, which Rose finds humiliating.

The therapist makes the following self-analysis of his feelings of *discouragement*.

Situation (A): Therapist cannot reach client and is used by client for quick therapy.
Therapist's thoughts: see Table 6.7.
Therapist's feeling (C): discouragement.
Behavior of the therapist (C): withdrawal.
Alternative and balanced thoughts (E) of the therapist (true and helpful):

1   We are now at the heart of their problem.
2   This includes blame and self-justification.
3   Instead of meeting her high expectations, I should make them negotiable.
4   This is a difficult therapy, but I see it as a challenge.
5   If I discuss it, the behavior may change, but this will not happen quickly with a narcissistic personality disorder.
6   I find my work as a therapist difficult but meaningful, despite the frustration.

Table 6.7 Assessment of the discouraged therapist's thoughts (Ellis, 1962)

	Thoughts of the therapist (B)	Assessment (D)	
1.	We won't get there that way.	true	not helpful
2.	I don't want this self-justification.	true	not helpful
3.	I have to live up to these high expectations, I can never do that.	not true	not helpful
4.	I don't achieve anything.	not true	not helpful
5.	When is this superiority thing going to stop? It goes on and on, I'm fed up!	true	not helpful
6.	My work is meaningless	not true	not helpful

Therapist's goal (G):

- feel less discouraged and more confident
- discuss client expectations with empathy

COMMENTARY

By thinking differently, the therapist can become calmer and not be rushed and discouraged by the expectation of quick and effective therapy. The therapist then has the patience and calmness to discuss the client's core problem with a narcissistic personality disorder. As a result, he is able to avoid the pitfall of discouragement. Figure 6.4 illustrates the pitfall of the discouraged therapist.

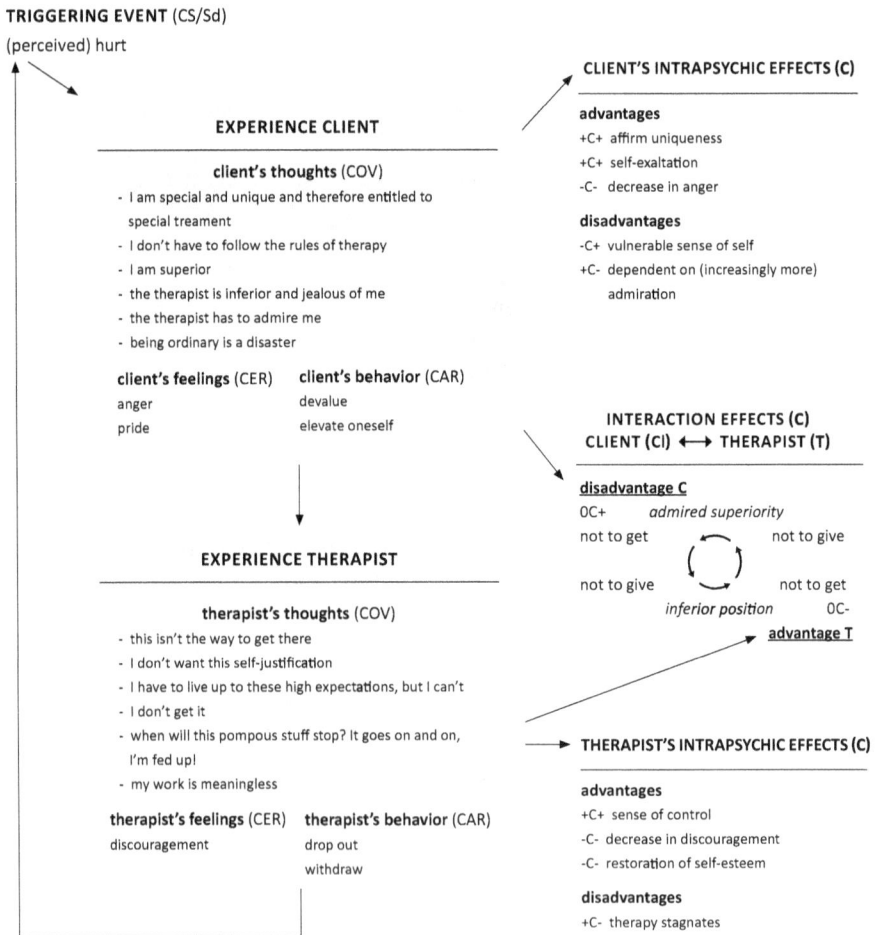

TRIGGERING EVENT (CS/Sd)

(perceived) hurt

EXPERIENCE CLIENT

client's thoughts (COV)
- I am special and unique and therefore entitled to special treatment
- I don't have to follow the rules of therapy
- I am superior
- the therapist is inferior and jealous of me
- the therapist has to admire me
- being ordinary is a disaster

client's feelings (CER)   **client's behavior** (CAR)
anger   devalue
pride   elevate oneself

EXPERIENCE THERAPIST

therapist's thoughts (COV)
- this isn't the way to get there
- I don't want this self-justification
- I have to live up to these high expectations, but I can't
- I don't get it
- when will this pompous stuff stop? It goes on and on, I'm fed up!
- my work is meaningless

therapist's feelings (CER)   **therapist's behavior** (CAR)
discouragement   drop out
                                 withdraw

CLIENT'S INTRAPSYCHIC EFFECTS (C)

advantages
+C+ affirm uniqueness
+C+ self-exaltation
-C- decrease in anger

disadvantages
-C+ vulnerable sense of self
+C- dependent on (increasingly more) admiration

INTERACTION EFFECTS (C)
CLIENT (Cl) ⟷ THERAPIST (T)

disadvantage C
0C+   admired superiority
not to get   not to give

not to give   not to get
        inferior position   0C-
                    advantage T

THERAPIST'S INTRAPSYCHIC EFFECTS (C)

advantages
+C+ sense of control
-C- decrease in discouragement
-C- restoration of self-esteem

disadvantages
+C- therapy stagnates

Figure 6.4 Functional analysis of a pitfall in the therapeutic relationship in relation to a narcissistic personality disorder: the discouraged therapist

In summary, the invalidating behavior of a client with a narcissistic personality disorder has the function of asserting superiority and avoiding humiliation, as explained above. And the client's behavior and sensitivity to the validation of (self-)admiration elicit specific responses from the therapist. If the therapist often falls into all three traps simultaneously, even within a single session, he or she will inadvertently reinforce the devaluation and the therapy will run aground. It is then time for self-analysis, peer evaluation, or supervision.

A summary of the pitfalls for the therapist in working with a narcissistic personality disorder is shown in the box.

Pitfalls for the therapist of the narcissistic personality disorder

1   apologizing, admiring
2   hurting back, criticizing
3   withdrawing, ignoring

Reference list

APA, American Psychiatric Association. (2013). *Diagnostic and statistical manual of mental disorders* (5th ed.). American Psychiatric Press.

Barlow, D. H., Farchione, T. J., Bullis, J. R., Gallagher, M. W., Murray-Latin, H., Sauer-Zavala, S., Bentley, K. H., Thompson-Hollands, J., Conklin, L. R., Boswell, J. F., Ametaj, A., Carl, J. R., Boettcher, H. T., & Cassiello-Robbins, C. (2017). The unified protocol for transdiagnostic treatment of emotional disorders compared with diagnosis-specific protocols for anxiety disorders: A randomized clinical trial. *JAMA Psychiatry, 74*(9), 875–884.

Beck, A. T., Davis, D. D., Freeman, A., Arntz, A., Beck, J. S., Behary, W. T., Brauer, L., David, A. C., Daniel, O. D., DiTomasso, R. A., Fournier, J. C., Fusco, G. M., Gündüz, A., Hilchey, C. A., Mankiewicz, P. D., Mitchel, D., Padeksy, C. A., Rebeta, J. L., Reinecke, M. A., (…), Treadway, M. T. (2014). *Cognitive therapy of personality disorders* (3rd ed.). Guilford Press.

Beck, A. T., Freeman, A., Davis, D. D., Arntz, A., Beck, J. S., Butler, A. C., Fleming, B., Fusco, G., Morrison, A. P., Padesky, C. A., Pretzer, J. L., Renton, J., Simon, K. M. (2003). *Cognitive therapy of personality disorders* (2nd ed.). Guilford Press.

Beck, J. S. (1995). *Cognitive therapy: Basics and beyond.* Guilford Press.

Ellis, A. (1962). *Reason and emotion in psychotherapy.* Lyle Stuart.

First, M. B., Williams, J. B. W., Benjamin, L. S., & Spitzer, R. L. (2015). *Structured clinical interview for DSM-5 personality disorders SCID-5-PD.* American Psychiatric Association Publishing.

Hafkenscheid, A. (2005). The impact message inventory (IMI-C): Generalizability of patients' command and relationship messages across psychiatric nurses. *Journal of Psychiatric and Mental Health Nursing, 12,* 325–332.

Hafkenscheid, A. (2012). Assessing objective countertransference with a computer-delivered impact message inventory (IMI-C). *Clinical Psychology and Psychotherapy, 19*(1), 37–45.

Hutsebaut, J., Berghuis, H., Kaasenbrood, A., De Saeger, H., & Ingenhoven, T. (2015). *Semi-gestructureerd interview voor persoonlijkheidsfunctioneren DSM–5.* Kenniscentrum Persoonlijkheidsstoornissen. StiP5.1. Retrieved August 26, 2024, from www.kenniscentrumps.nl/wp-content/uploads/2023/03/STIP-5.1a_A4_spreadsNW.pdf

Keijsers, G. P. J., Van Minnen, A., & Hoogduin, C. A. L. (2011). *Protocollaire behandelingen voor volwassenen met psychische klachten, deel 1 en 2*. Boom.

Krueger, R. F., Derringer, J., Markon, K. E., Watson, D., & Skodol, A. E. (2012). Initial construction of a maladaptive personality trait model and inventory for DSM−5. *Psychological Medicine*, *42*(9), 1879–1890.

McCrae, R., & Costa Jr., P. T. (2008). Empirical and theoretical status of the five-factor model of personality traits. In G. J. Boyle et al. (Eds.), *The SAGE handbook of personality theory and assessment volume 1 personality theories and models*. SAGE Publications Ltd.

Samuel, D. B., & Widiger, T. A. (2008). Meta-analytic review of the relationships between the five-factor model and DSM-IV-TR personality disorders: A facet level analysis. *Clinical Psychology Review*, *28*, 1326–1342.

Screening definition

A gifted person is highly intelligent and has at least five of the other nine personality characteristics:

1a Most gifted persons are either highly intelligent or
1b exceptionally competent and belonging to the best 10% of their reference group in creativity, arts or leadership;
2 High sensitivity, an intense emotional world or easily over-stimulated;
3 Fast, complex, diverse and divergent thinking;
4 Idealistic and with a strong sense of right and wrong;
5 Asynchronous personal development (motor, social and intellectual development);
6 Curious, with an intense, wide-ranging and/or unusual pattern of interests;
7 Fast and creative in coming up with solutions;
8 Autonomous thinking;
9 Autonomous acting;
10 Perfectionistic.

This definition for screening is derived from Webb et al. (2016) for characteristics 1 through 7 (reproduced with permission).

Appendix B

Screening for giftedness with balance of advantages and disadvantages

giftedness characteristic	strength 0–10 self-assessment/ assessment by other	advantages	disadvantages
highly intelligent			
IQ ≥ 130			
• highly sensible			
• highly sensitive			
• overexcitability (OE)			
• quick thinking			
• complex thinking			
• divergent			
idealistic and with a strong sense of justice			
asynchronous development (learning history) motor, social, intellectual			
curious with an intense, broad or unusual pattern of interest			
quick and creative in finding solutions			
autonomous thinking			
acting autonomously			
perfectionistic			

This screening definition is based on Webb et al. (2016) for characteristics 1 through 7, reproduced with permission, Kuipers and Van Kempen (2007) for characteristics 8 and 9, and Rogers and Silverman (1997) for characteristic 10.

Rate from 0 (not at all true) to 10 (totally true) using self-, other-, and therapist judgment. Also ask the client to write down his or her own balance of advantages and disadvantages. Look at the correlation between the two and correct for overestimation or underestimation by the client.

Elaboration

Six or more characteristics with a score equal to or above 7.5 indicate giftedness. When in doubt, or when the client has little self-awareness, you can supplement this with an assessment by a 'healthy', disinterested person from the client's immediate environment and a clinical assessment. If necessary, check with tests.

Case conceptualization for giftedness

	S	O	R (CER/CAR)	C
EARLY		Learning history		
0–10 jr **10–20** **20–30** **30–40** **40–50**				
MIDDLE	Stress or support, expected or actual	Coping, traits, core cognitions, etc.	Core behavior	Balance of costs (−) and benefits (+)
	Stress	Coping style Pathological traits DSM-5*		
	Support	General DSM-5-traits Five factors Core cognitions/ Schemas Core theme		
LATE	Specific symptom triggers	Interaction diagnosis Temperament	Symptomatic behavior	Balance of costs (-) and benefits (+)
	Specific symptom triggers	Dysfunctional personality* Somatics		
	Background stress	Intelligence		

Functional analysis (general) for giftedness

TRIGGERING EVENT
(CS/sd)
complex and
engaging situation

thinking process
fast, complex, highly
associative, divergent,
creative, and autonomous

behavior (CAR)
thinking up quick and creative
solutions

thoughts (COV)
- I am autonomous, quick thinking, and creative
- I am different from others
- I am curious and have many and intense interests
- I am responsible
- I need to be competent
- everything has to be perfect and fair
- I want to make things (the world) better
- I want to be fair and just (or am disillusioned)
- I am clever but lack social, sporting, or artistic skills
- different rules apply to me
- others are different, smarter or less smart, jealous or admiring, more social or sporty
- it is not possible for me to just be normal and participate
- I am an exception and I am not one of them
- others exclude me
- others don't like me
- others find me strange

consequences (C)
advantages
+C+ pride, self-esteem
+C+ appreciation, acceptance, admiration from others
+C+ satisfaction, flow, kick
+C+ creativity
-C+ dullness diminishes

disadvantages
-C+ less sense of belonging
-C+ others drop out
+C- negative reactions from others, insecurity, jealousy, irritation
0C+ no resistance
+C- social isolation
+C- lack of understanding
+C- haste, impatience
+C- stress, tiredness
+C- frustration, dissatisfaction

emotional process
intense, usually overexcitable,
and highly sensitive

feeling (CER)
driven, intense excitement,
stress, fear of failure

Treatment plan for giftedness

Starting point FA	Therapy goals	Techniques
triggering event (CS/Sd)	decrease the number of complex and engaging situations and the number and breadth of interests	temporary avoidance stop mechanism self-control response prevention
thought process	simplify complexity slow down the fast, highly associative thinking from diverging to converging from autonomous to empathic	task concentration training cognitive diary convergence training
thoughts (COV) content of specific features	improve view of self thoughts on specific traits	positive journaling, COMET cognitive therapy
feeling process	intense usually overexcitable and highly sensitive	de-intensifying desensitization recovery time
feeling (CER) generally	reduce the feeling of being driven and of intense arousal stress ▼ fear of failure ▼ impatience ▼	relaxation self-hypnosis EMDR mindfulness heart coherence
feeling (CER) related to specific traits	improve feelings related to specific traits	COMET relaxation hypnosis imaginary rescripting role play EMDR
behavior (CAR) create solutions quickly and creatively	improve creative stagnation create fewer problems but solve more	self-registration role-play slow, attentive slowing down mindfulness self-exposure cognitive therapy
consequences (C)	reduce disadvantages increase advantages > see Functional Analysis	awareness and other forms of (self) validation to improve the balance of advantages and disadvantages

Functional analysis of the therapeutic relationship

Functional analysis of a pitfall in the therapeutic relationship with giftedness: the insecure therapist

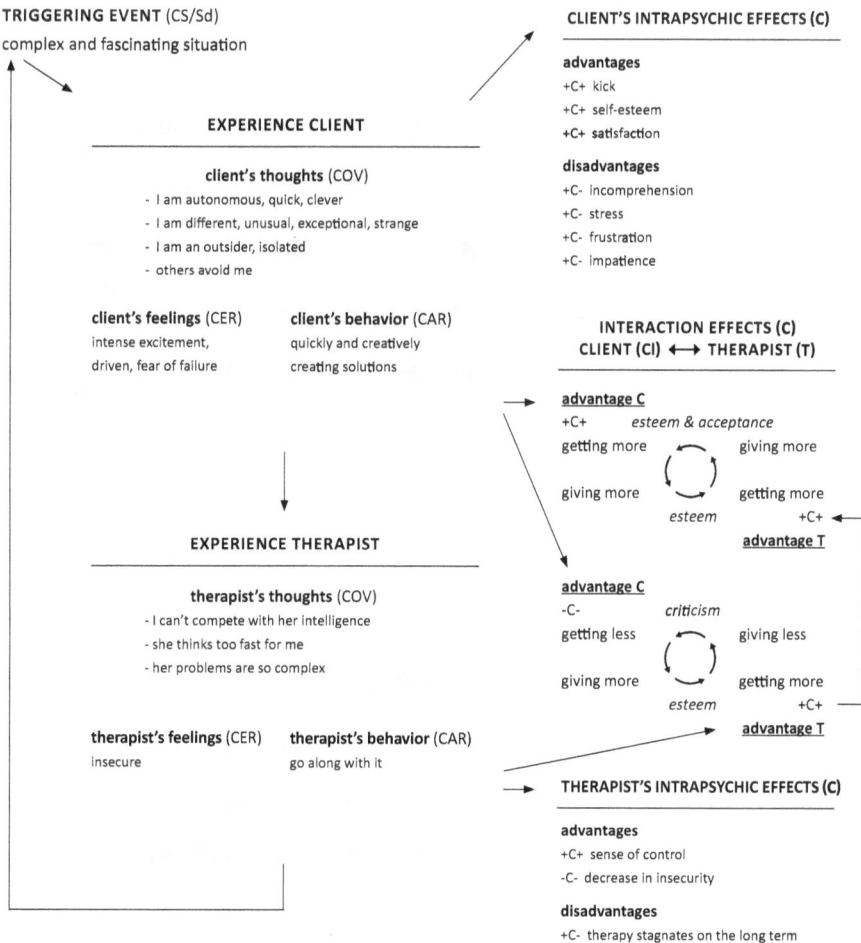

TRIGGERING EVENT (CS/Sd)

complex and fascinating situation

EXPERIENCE CLIENT

client's thoughts (COV)
- I am autonomous, quick, clever
- I am different, unusual, exceptional, strange
- I am an outsider, isolated
- others avoid me

client's feelings (CER)
intense excitement, driven, fear of failure

client's behavior (CAR)
quickly and creatively creating solutions

EXPERIENCE THERAPIST

therapist's thoughts (COV)
- I can't compete with her intelligence
- she thinks too fast for me
- her problems are so complex

therapist's feelings (CER)
insecure

therapist's behavior (CAR)
go along with it

CLIENT'S INTRAPSYCHIC EFFECTS (C)

advantages
+C+ kick
+C+ self-esteem
+C+ satisfaction

disadvantages
+C- incomprehension
+C- stress
+C- frustration
+C- impatience

INTERACTION EFFECTS (C)
CLIENT (CI) ⟷ THERAPIST (T)

advantage C
+C+   esteem & acceptance
getting more   giving more

giving more   getting more
            esteem   +C+
                    advantage T

advantage C
-C-   criticism
getting less   giving less

giving more   getting more
            esteem   +C+
                    advantage T

THERAPIST'S INTRAPSYCHIC EFFECTS (C)

advantages
+C+ sense of control
-C- decrease in insecurity

disadvantages
+C- therapy stagnates on the long term

Functional analysis of a pitfall in the therapeutic relationship in giftedness: the irritated therapist

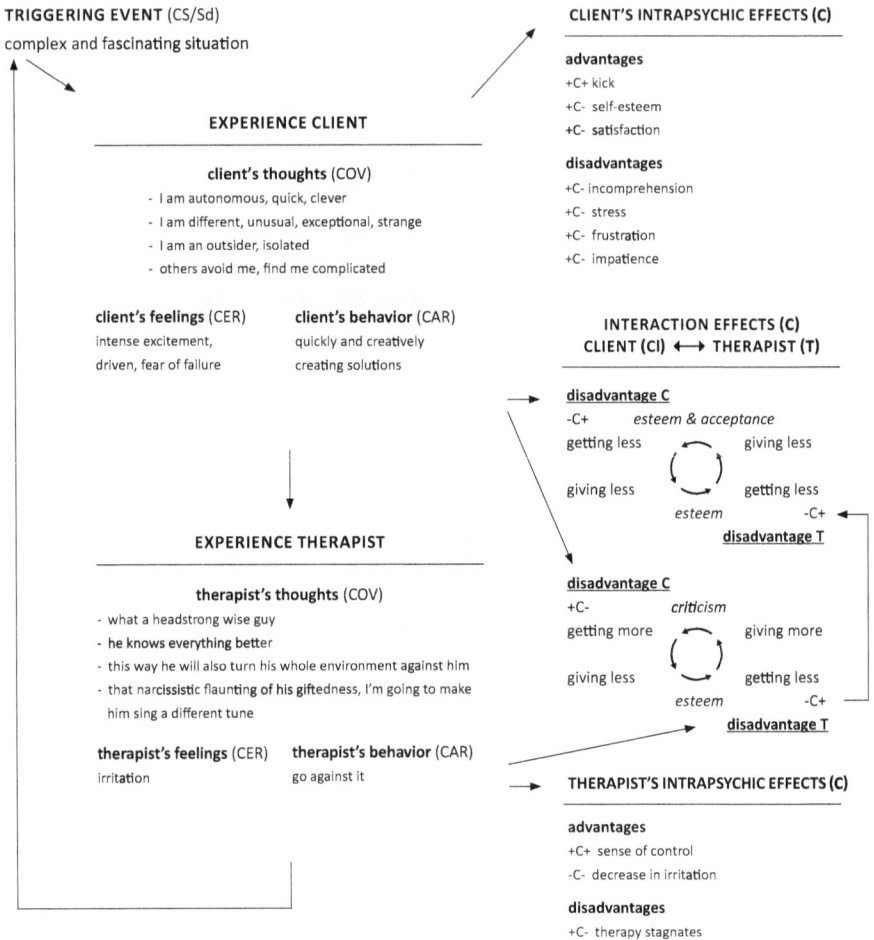

TRIGGERING EVENT (CS/Sd)

complex and fascinating situation

EXPERIENCE CLIENT

client's thoughts (COV)
- I am autonomous, quick, clever
- I am different, unusual, exceptional, strange
- I am an outsider, isolated
- others avoid me, find me complicated

client's feelings (CER)   **client's behavior** (CAR)

intense excitement,   quickly and creatively
driven, fear of failure   creating solutions

EXPERIENCE THERAPIST

therapist's thoughts (COV)
- what a headstrong wise guy
- he knows everything better
- this way he will also turn his whole environment against him
- that narcissistic flaunting of his giftedness, I'm going to make him sing a different tune

therapist's feelings (CER)   **therapist's behavior** (CAR)

irritation   go against it

CLIENT'S INTRAPSYCHIC EFFECTS (C)

advantages
+C+ kick
+C- self-esteem
+C- satisfaction

disadvantages
+C- incomprehension
+C- stress
+C- frustration
+C- impatience

INTERACTION EFFECTS (C)
CLIENT (Cl) ⟷ THERAPIST (T)

disadvantage C
-C+   esteem & acceptance
getting less   giving less

giving less   getting less
           esteem   -C+
           disadvantage T

disadvantage C
+C-   criticism
getting more   giving more

giving less   getting less
           esteem   -C+
           disadvantage T

THERAPIST'S INTRAPSYCHIC EFFECTS (C)

advantages
+C+ sense of control
-C- decrease in irritation

disadvantages
+C- therapy stagnates

Functional analysis of a pitfall in the therapeutic relationship with giftedness: the discouraged therapist

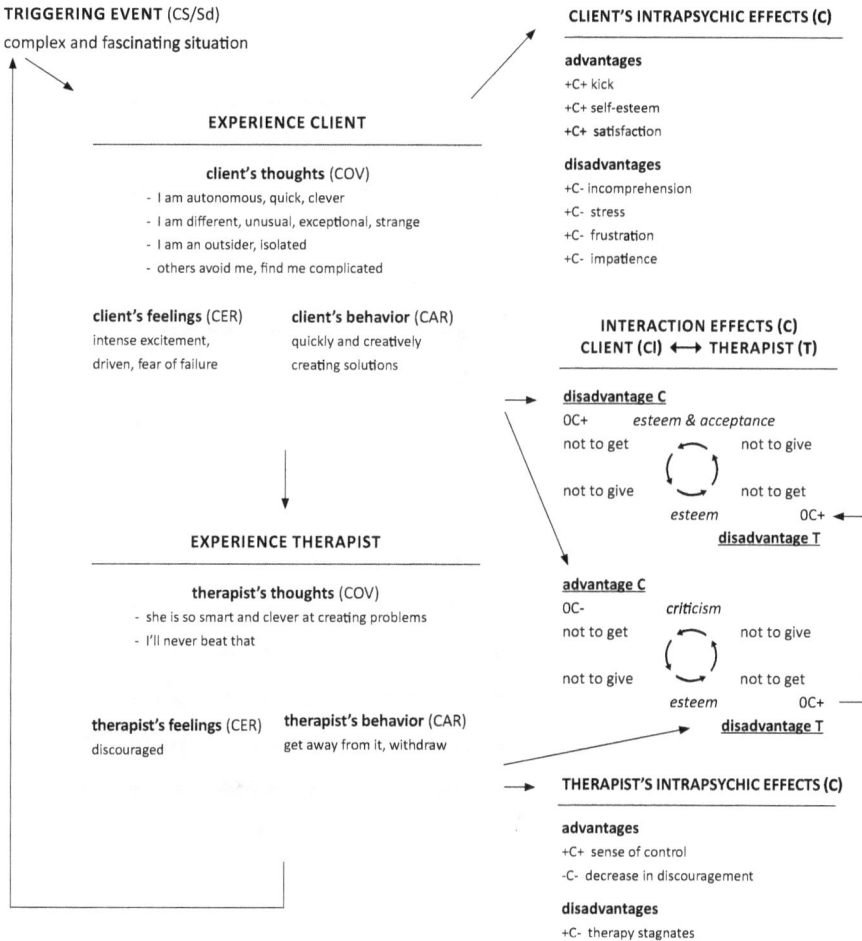

TRIGGERING EVENT (CS/Sd)

complex and fascinating situation

EXPERIENCE CLIENT

client's thoughts (COV)
- I am autonomous, quick, clever
- I am different, unusual, exceptional, strange
- I am an outsider, isolated
- others avoid me, find me complicated

client's feelings (CER)
intense excitement, driven, fear of failure

client's behavior (CAR)
quickly and creatively creating solutions

EXPERIENCE THERAPIST

therapist's thoughts (COV)
- she is so smart and clever at creating problems
- I'll never beat that

therapist's feelings (CER)
discouraged

therapist's behavior (CAR)
get away from it, withdraw

CLIENT'S INTRAPSYCHIC EFFECTS (C)

advantages
+C+ kick
+C+ self-esteem
+C+ satisfaction

disadvantages
+C- incomprehension
+C- stress
+C- frustration
+C- impatience

INTERACTION EFFECTS (C)
CLIENT (Cl) ⟷ THERAPIST (T)

disadvantage C
0C+   esteem & acceptance
not to get   not to give

not to give   not to get
                esteem   0C+
                        disadvantage T

advantage C
0C-   criticism
not to get   not to give

not to give   not to get
                esteem   0C+
                        disadvantage T

THERAPIST'S INTRAPSYCHIC EFFECTS (C)

advantages
+C+ sense of control
-C- decrease in discouragement

disadvantages
+C- therapy stagnates

Functional analysis of a pitfall in the therapeutic relationship with giftedness: the over-involved therapist

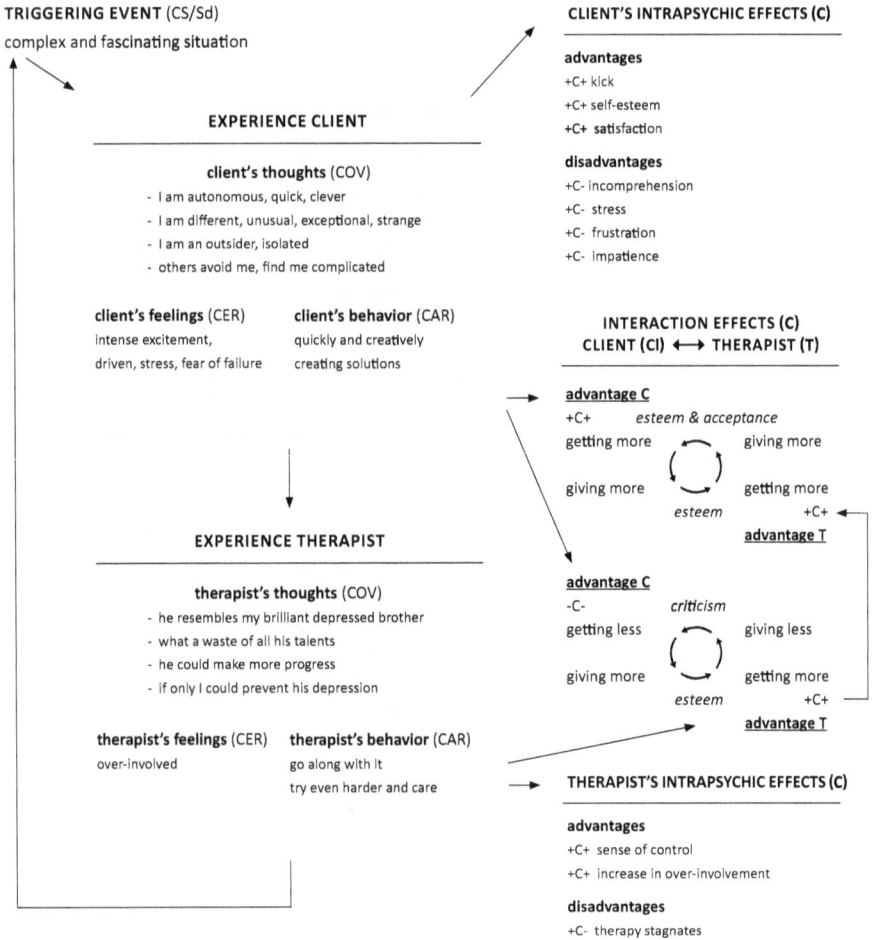

TRIGGERING EVENT (CS/Sd)

complex and fascinating situation

EXPERIENCE CLIENT

client's thoughts (COV)
- I am autonomous, quick, clever
- I am different, unusual, exceptional, strange
- I am an outsider, isolated
- others avoid me, find me complicated

client's feelings (CER)   **client's behavior (CAR)**
intense excitement,   quickly and creatively
driven, stress, fear of failure   creating solutions

EXPERIENCE THERAPIST

therapist's thoughts (COV)
- he resembles my brilliant depressed brother
- what a waste of all his talents
- he could make more progress
- if only I could prevent his depression

therapist's feelings (CER)   **therapist's behavior (CAR)**
over-involved   go along with it
                                     try even harder and care

CLIENT'S INTRAPSYCHIC EFFECTS (C)

advantages
+C+ kick
+C+ self-esteem
+C+ satisfaction

disadvantages
+C- incomprehension
+C- stress
+C- frustration
+C- impatience

INTERACTION EFFECTS (C)
CLIENT (Cl) ⟷ THERAPIST (T)

advantage C
+C+   esteem & acceptance
getting more   giving more

giving more   getting more
              esteem   +C+
              advantage T

advantage C
-C-   criticism
getting less   giving less

giving more   getting more
              esteem   +C+
              advantage T

THERAPIST'S INTRAPSYCHIC EFFECTS (C)

advantages
+C+ sense of control
+C+ increase in over-involvement

disadvantages
+C- therapy stagnates

Index

For Product Safety Concerns and Information please contact our EU
representative GPSR@taylorandfrancis.com
Taylor & Francis Verlag GmbH, Kaufingerstraße 24, 80331 München, Germany

www.ingramcontent.com/pod-product-compliance
Lightning Source LLC
Chambersburg PA
CBHW052009270326

41929CB00015B/2855

9 781032 707556